Old Testament Women in Western Literature

OLD TESTAMENT

WOMEN

in Western Literature

edited by

*Raymond-Jean Frontain
and Jan Wojcik*

UCA Press
1991

Library of Congress Cataloging-in-Publication Data

Old Testament women in Western literature / edited by Raymond-
    Jean Frontain and Jan Wojcik.
                            p.   cm.
            Includes bibliographical references and index.
            ISBN 0-944436-12-9 (lib. bdg.) : $28.95
            1. Women in literature. 2. Women in the Bible. 3. Bible
    in literature. I. Frontain, Raymond-Jean. II. Wojcik, Jan, 1944-
    PN56.5.W64044   1991
    809' .93352042--dc20   91-25299 CIP

Contents

Oh, where shall I find a virtuous woman,
for her price is above rubies. . . .
—Proverbs 31:8

For Jill Gambino
and Patricia McTavey Frontain;
in memoriam Mary Kearns McTavey

Preface

For William Blake, as for much of the Western literary tradition, the Bible contains "the Great Code of Art." But as Northrop Frye frankly puts it, even though the Bible is a major element in our imaginative tradition, "it insistently raises the question: Why does this huge, sprawling, tactless book sit there inscrutably in the middle of our cultural heritage like the 'great Boyg' or sphinx in *Peer Gynt*, frustrating all our efforts to walk around it?"[1] So many cultural issues first raised by the Bible are still largely informed by the Bible.

This is the third collection of essays that we have collaborated upon whose purpose is to map specific biblically-inspired literary traditions. *The David Myth in Western Literature* (1980) traced some of the literary transformations made upon the character and the narrative events in the life of Israel's greatest king as Western writers have explored the issues of government, piety, friendship, sexuality, heroism, and even of how to tell a story. Likewise, *Poetic Prophecy in Western Literature* (1984) attempted to show how one form of biblical poetry has both shaped numerous Western concepts of writing and speaking, and served as a primary justification of the function of the imaginative, inspired artist. In turning to the Old Testament women,[2] we confront the texts and exempla which have been central to the formulation and reformulation of the social status of women for the past 2,000 years.

"In my perspective as literary critic," writes Frye, "the 'real meaning' of a myth emerges slowly from a prolonged literary life, and then its meaning includes everything it has effectively been made to mean during that life."[3] The women who appear in Hebrew biblical narratives have had just such prolonged literary lives, their stories being retold countless times through the centuries. As one of the essays that follows illustrates, sometimes the meanings that a biblical woman's story has accumulated can be so deep and so rich that one level gradually supersedes a former even while contradicting it, leaving the literary historian to carefully excavate and date the different strata of meanings in order to make sense of a writer's allusion. At other times alchemical changes can occur so swiftly that only the literary historian's slowing the motion of change can catch it for the student's eye; in less than a hundred years, another of our essays shows, Ruth ran the gamut from idealized pastoral figure to archetypal fallen woman. A biblical heroine may even change focus across the span of a single writer's imaginative life, as a third essay demonstrates regarding the change in the signification of the Levite concubine of Judges in Milton's poetry and prose. The first witness to their mythic and literary value is the simple fact that biblical women are capable of bearing the weight of such continuing accretion of meaning which makes such an excavation process necessary.

More importantly, in studying the ways in which biblical stories about women have been used as "pre-texts" (that is, both as earlier texts and as the occasion for moralistic views for women in later literature), we propose a search for more accurate definitions of femaleness (and, by extension, maleness) in a given culture. Many of the essays that follow seek to show that both biblical literature and the writers/artists of a later era who used biblical themes were guided by a more complex and subtle understanding of female identity and reality than the partriarchal traditions that formed the cultural context in which the biblical texts were first compiled and read.

In selecting essays for this volume, we have tried to cover as much ground in as compact an effort as possible. We have, thus, organized the essays so that each treats a work, or works, from a separate major literary period as well as a separate biblical woman.

Thus, while the essays extend from patristic and medieval times down to the twentieth century, they also cover as many different biblical women as possible: Eve, Job's wife, Rachel and Leah, Jephthah's daughter, Judith, the Levite concubine of Judges, Dinah, Ruth and Hagar. The only significant overlapping in this regard occurs in Mary De Jong's essay which, surveying popular Victorian American attitudes towards a number of women, inevitably touches upon motifs treated in other essays; her perspective is so different, however, as to make a dramatic contrast with them, proving again the extraordinary vitality of these narratives. Space simply does not permit consideration of such fascinating and culturally influential figures as Deborah, Hannah, Gomer, Miriam, Susannah or the Shulemite Maiden, much less the personification of Jerusalem as a woman in the prophetic oracles.

The editors are grateful to Professors Mieke Bal, Jonathan Glenn, Jeff Henderson, Joseph B. Trahern, Allison Ensor, Dottie Hebel and Joan Hartwig for advice along the way. The Division of Research at Clarkson University orginally prepared a uniform type-script; Charlene Bland and Barbara Whisnant prepared the final typescript with unrelentingly cheerful efficiency. The John C. Hodges Fund of the University of Tennessee generously offered a subvention which made printing of the illustrations possible, while the Art Institute of Chicago graciously permitted reproduction of prints in its collection. The editors regret that delay in collecting these essays prevented the volume's appearing in time to honor Professor Hugo M. Reichard on the occasion of his retirement from the Purdue University English faculty, as one essay was written specifically to do.

"It is for Adam to interpret the voices which Eve hears," Jacques Maritain ruminated (in words which Caroline Gordon had carved on her tombstone). In both this and our two previous volumes we have been moved to interpret the voices first heard by such colleagues and friends as Florence Michels, Ruth Gillah Rothenberg, Rita Easterwood, Eunice Barbera, Verna Emery, Penny Tschantz, Joyce Ward, and Nancy Stricklin. Their contributions of service and example have made them worth far more than their respective weights in rubies. Three very particular women, however, have provided the light that animates our thought herein. Conscious that no matter how well cut a stone, it is dead without the light's animation, we most gratefully acknowledge our indebtedness, and dedicate our efforts, to Jill Gambino, Patricia McTavey Frontain and, *in memoriam*, Mary Kearns McTavey.

Notes

[1]Northrop Frye, *The Great Code: The Bible and Literature* (New York: Harcourt, Brace, Jovanovich, 1982), xviii-xix.

[2]The terms Old Testament and New Testament are now usually considered archaic, and sometimes even prejudicial, if New implies some improvement upon the Old. Today scholars use the nomenclature Hebrew Bible, Apocrypha, and Christian scriptures to refer, respectively, to the older scriptures written in Masoretic Hebrew, the older scriptures written in Septuagint Greek, and the newer scriptures written in Koine Greek. Without prejudice we use the traditional term Old Testament to refer to the Hebrew Bible and Apocrypha, and New Testament to refer to the Christian scriptures. (We recognize, of course, that the Masoretic text which forms the basis of rabbinic Judaism differs in both form and substance from the Hebrew Bible, but it is the Texts transmitted in the order established by the latter which have been most influential in the traditions we survey.) The authors in the Western tradition sampled here used these terms this way; Jan Wojcik's essay has a discussion of the literary relations of these three canons to each other.

[3]Northrop Frye, *Creation and Recreation* (Toronto: U of Toronto P, 1980), 28.

Introduction:

The Price of Rubies: The Weight of Old Testament Women in Western Literature

Raymond-Jean Frontain

Hanging in the great hall of the Marcia Blaine School for Girls at the opening of Muriel Sparks' *The Prime of Miss Jean Brodie* is the "manly" portrait of the school's founder, beneath which on a table is a Bible opened to Ps. 31: 8, its text underlined in red: "Oh where shall I find a virtuous woman, for her price is above rubies."[1] Sparks' novel is an ironic meditation upon the source and meaning of true womanliness, but more significantly upon the price that a young woman may have to pay in pursuing her own idea rather than imitate the ideal proposed by social authorities. The girls who attend the school are exposed to and must evaluate the relative weights of the conflicting models of female behavior represented by Miss Brodie and the other members of the teaching staff. In addition, they must sort among the attractions offered by the romantic and dramatic models that Miss Brodie holds up for them—Anna Pavlova, Sybil Thorndike, Cleopatra, Helen of Troy, Mary Queen of Scots—and the more pedestrian women whom they meet in the course of their daily routine, such as a Girl Guides leader and an investigatory policewoman. Each exerts a hold over their imaginations. Curiously, although no biblical heroine is cited as a model for the girls, the single verse from Psalms quoted at the outset of the novel frames the larger questions which the story raises: what exactly is the source of a woman's virtue? And, does her fulfillment lie finally in her virtue, or is "virtue" a shibboleth the myth of whose power she must overcome before she can obtain actual fulfillment?

Sparks' novel dramatizes a problem addressed either implicitly or explicitly by each of the essays in this volume. A supposed biblical standard for women's behavior fades like the Cheshire Cat when one gets close enough to examine its particulars. "Woman in life and woman in art are not the same person," observes Stevie Davies.[2] Yet the problem concerning many Western attitudes about women's roles is that too many social and religious leaders have presumed that they should be. This is patently impossible for, in the first place, as Carol Meyers has pointed out, "The emotional justification for the existence and continuation of [many] present unacceptable gender roles is embedded in religious texts that shape the psyche of western humanity," yet "the women we glimpse in the Hebrew Bible are, almost to a woman, exceptional. They are women who rose to positions of prominence," and who were not intended by their authors to serve as models of quotidian behavior.[3]

A second necessary qualification stems from the very nature of the narrative that makes women like Ruth, Esther, Deborah, Susannah, and Judith such powerful and memorable figures. Perhaps it may best be illustrated by the exchange that took place between Ben Jonson and John Donne over the latter's representation of Elizabeth Drury in his *Anniversaries*. Jonson reports that, after he had protested that Donne's funeral elegy for a fourteen year old girl praised her so excessively that it was actually "profane and full of blasphemies"— that "if it had been written of the Virgin Mary it had been something" — Donne justified his procedure by claiming "that he described the Idea of a Woman, and not as she was."[4] Clearly this division between Elizabeth Drury (or a woman "as she was") and some neoplatonic "Idea of a Woman" is what has allowed readers to assume that the "shee" of the poem has allegorical significance, whether morally and intellectually as Wisdom, or politically as Queen Elizabeth I. The problem of narrative art, however, is that in order for it to succeed, the "Idea of a Woman" must be incarnated in a flesh-and-blood female character; yet the rounder and more successful the character, the less possible that she can be allegorically reduced to a single idea or value. Thus, the only consistent biblical description of a virtuous woman—that found in the Wisdom writings[5] —simply cannot accommodate women as diverse as Deborah and Esther, as Judith and Ruth. Nor can it explain the power of their narratives to hold a reader's—much less an entire civilization's—imagination.

Perhaps more significantly, any attempt to extrapolate some code of behavior from the narratives themselves has only shocked and dismayed the pious, for careful reading of the details of these stories reveals behavior and values more often than not at variance with cultural expectations. Thus, as Mieke Bal has shown, centuries of readers have been troubled both by the sexual suggestiveness of the scene of Jael's assassination of enemy leader Sisera and by the fact that a woman should succeed where the Jewish male leaders have failed, thus seeming to put the male hierarchy to shame. In order to "idealize" the scene, such readers have been forced to reject Jael's behavior on the grounds that it violates the hospitality code dramatized elsewhere in scriptures. Here, the "Idea of a Woman" can be preserved only by the sacrifice of the protagonist herself![6] Likewise, as we shall shortly see, readers offended by the possibility that Judith beheaded Holofernes while he enjoyed a post-coital snooze have defended the matriarch's "honor" through the following catch-22 reasoning: if Judith engaged in intercourse with Holofernes, she would not deserve the praise that Scripture accords her; yet her very appearance in the Bible ensures that she was not an adulteress; therefore, anyone concluding that her engagement with the enemy leader was sexual can only be falling victim to some satanic temptation to "misread" the divinely inspired words. (Louise Simons' essay shows how Milton first had to free himself of traditional thinking that the Levite concubine's fate must have been merited by prior adultery. By this line of reasoning, her ordeal was in some way "a morally edifying illustration of trespass punished." Instead, he read the episode recorded in Judges 19-21 as a biblical "indictment of all kinds of social, religious, and political injustice.") Such insistence that a biblical woman's actions either satisfy some para-narrative ideal or, conversely, not violate some para-narrative convention inevitably leads the reader away from the text and not more deeply into it.

Finally, it is impossible to extrapolate some consistent "Idea of a Woman" from the Hebrew narratives that have women as their central character because it is precisely their successful functioning as narrative creations that prevents them from being allegorized. The great Hebrew heroines, in short, are simply too real to be ideal. This is in part due to the general nature of Hebrew literary narrative. "The Old Testament is full of people . . . heroes and black-guards," William Faulkner once remarked, "and I like to read the Old Testament because it's full of people, not ideas."[7] One feature of Hebrew narrative that allows for this peculiar kind of realism, Erich Auerbach has argued, is that it is governed by the "suggestive influence of the unexpressed" whereby the narrator permits

> the externalization of only so much of the phenomena as is necessary for the purpose of the narrative, all else [is] left in obscurity; the decisive points of the narrative alone are emphasized, what lies between is nonexistent; time and place are undefined and call for interpretation; thoughts and feeling remain unexpressed, are only suggested by the silence and the fragmentary speeches; the whole, permeated with the most unrelieved suspense and directed toward a single goal, . . . remains mysterious and "fraught with background."[8]

Because the narrator never invades the interior life of his characters, their motivation is never explained. The resulting ambivalence leaves wide room for interpretation. Thus, it is never clear, for example, what transpires between Dinah and Shechem in Genesis 34. Does "defiled" mean that she was raped by the local squire or that she was rendered impure by willingly entering into a sexual liaison with a man who had not been circumcised? (As Raymond Frontain argues in his essay below, it is the distance between these two possibilities that allows for the comic irony that governs Sterne's portrait of Aunt Dinah in *Tristram Shandy*.) More troubling is the exact nature of the relationship between Bathsheba and David in 2 Samuel 11. Is a resisting Bathsheba taken by David, or does she reluctantly submit to her king out of fear? Either instance would be rape. On the other hand, is she a willing partner in adultery, or a seductress, even, who deliberately bathes where she knows she can be seen by the king, who is known to walk on the roof of the palace at a certain time each day? Like Keats' urn, Hebrew narrative refuses to answer the questions it provocatively raises. In their complexity lies the reality of these women, and ultimately they are too real to be reduced to a single idea or value. As Hamlet might put it, the heart of their mystery is simply not for the plucking.

Biblical woman's lack of monolithic stature could be visually suggested several years ago by the presence in nearly adjoining rooms of the Chicago Art Institute of two radically different representations of Judith. Jan van Hemessen's "Judith" (Plate I) is the portrait of determined and powerful innocence. The nude torso of the woman, with its thick belly and heavy buttocks, is in dramatic contrast with the sweet, even delicate beauty of her face; her aureole of red-gold hair separates her from the darkness that threatens to envelop her. Her long, powerfully muscled arm seems to raise a heavy sword effortlessly, and she gazes upon the instrument of justice with calm resolve as she prepares to strike off the head of the sleeping Holofernes. It is ultimately a frightening scene, the darkness that bathes the room broken only by some invisible source of light off the field of the canvas but into whose beams Judith half turns as she gathers the energy to strike. This play of light and dark helps also to mediate between her innocence and her ferocious determination, as does the tableau's most striking visual disjunction: Judith's body is much too heavy and large for her young girl's head and its sweetness of expression. It is as though van Hemessen himself could barely reconcile the ferocity of her act with the virginal sweetness that must belong to a woman of the Lord, or perhaps he was determined to show that some part of the avenger remains pure despite the sordidness of the scene and the brutality of her act. The final effect on the viewer of van Hemessen's Judith is of the bold yet troubling self-confidence of righteousness.

The "Judith" of Felice Ficherelli (Plate II), on the other hand, is far more restrained. A young cavalier mistress in a flounced blue dress with full sleeves, wearing a beaded choker, her hair fashionably curled, half turns to an older maidservant as though to impart some confidence. The portrait might easily be called "The Secret," suggesting some domestic conspiracy as the girl prepares to meet her lover with the help of her scheming duenna, except for two almost unobtrusive details: the ornate object that the girl holds daintily in her right hand, even as with her left she gracefully gathers her skirts

Plate I

Jan Sanders van Hemessen, *Judith*, c.1560, oil on panel, 99.8 x 77.2 cm, Wirt D. Walker Fund, 1956.1109, courtesy of The Art Institute of Chicago.

Plate II

Felice Ficherelli (called Il Riposo), *Judith*, c.1650, oil on canvas, 98.5 x 75.6 cm, Charles H. and Mary F.S. Worcester Collection, 1939.2240, courtesy of The Art Institute of Chicago.

as though in preparation for a stroll, is not a walking stick but a sword; and, in the lower right hand corner of the canvas, hidden in the shadows and further obscured by the flounce of Judith's sleeve, is the severed head of Holofernes, presumably clutched by the maid-servant. Ficherelli casually presents the assassination as a *fait accompli*, devoid of all drama except the women's presumable need to escape the enemy camp. But even here the lack of identifiable setting, and the focussing of the viewer's attention upon the faces of the conspiring women, alleviates the tension that their situation ought to arouse. They might just as easily be on their way home, or even safely home already, as well as in the midst of Holofernes' still-oblivious defenders. Ficherelli's image lacks that ferocious energy provided in van Hemessen's painting by the woman's twisting torso, her upraised sword, and her straining muscles. Political assassination seems no more an exertion to Ficherelli's Judith than dressing herself handsomely for a ball.

Such ambivalence—or ambiguity, even—is sustained among other representations of Judith who, with the New Testament's Mary and the Old Testament's Eve, is among the most commonly figured biblical women in Western art. Most consistently, as Marina Warner demonstrates, Judith the tyrannicide is, like the allegorical Justice, depicted standing calmly with sword in hand. In such guise she represents "the subversive power of the armed maiden . . . harnessed to work magic on the side of the good against the bad."[9] The biblical tradition of the Lord's manifesting his power by choosing to work through the seemingly least considerable of human vessels—as when he defeats the giant Goliath through the boy David, or chooses mama's boy Jacob over manly Esau as the father of his nation—is being extended here as it is the seemingly helpless and piously retired widow who outwits the overwhelming enemy force that threatens to destroy her people. As Warner explains, "the victory of a girl redounds all the more blazingly to her cause's justice because she is weak; that is the underlying premise of the triumph of good over evil when it is represented as a battle between feminine virtue and brute vice."[10] Thus, Donatello's bronze Judith of 1457 presents a wimpled matron who is clearly iconographically related to such emblematizations of Justice as Breughel's engraving of the penalties meted out in virtue's name, and W.H. Thornycroft's Victorian sculpture for the Gladstone monument in London (see Warner, plates 53-54).

Likewise emphasizing her modesty, but endowing the biblical scene with more dramatic particularity and less allegorical generality, are the frescoes of Michelangelo and of Andrea Mantegna. In the "Judith and Holofernes" spandrel of the ceiling of the Sistine Chapel (1508-12), Judith is depicted as preparing to leave the Assyrian camp. Her maid bows under the weight of an enormous salver that she balances on her head; Judith reaches up to adjust the linen cloth that covers but cannot disguise the tray's contents. The visual center of the scene is Holofernes' enormous head, which is at least twice the size of either woman's and is made more mysterious by being covered. Both women avert their gaze from it, as though from a thing profane, the maid bowing her eyes modestly and Judith turning her face to the wall and away from the viewer in a gesture of self-effacement, perhaps. In Mantegna's wood panel (c. 1495) Judith is likewise impassive, her face saddened as though with thought of the gravity of what she has just done, but somehow she is almost casual in her acceptance of its inevitability.[11] Emphasis in the Mantegna panel, as in the Michelangelo spandrel and the Donatello sculpture, is on the heroic Judith—whether upon what Sir Walter Scott would call the "bow-wow" sort of historical bravura or upon a spiritual greatness that comes from Judith's resignation and resolve. The modesty of the woman in all three representations absolves her of any blame, as well as releases the viewer from any fear or revulsion; it reflects clear interpretive choices made by the artists as they confront the biblical text.

More disturbing, however, are the representations by Lucas Cranach the Elder (1472-1553) and Artemesia Gentileschi (1598-1651), which clearly aim at depicting the psychological horror of Judith's action. In Cranach's panel, a woman in a richly colored velvet and brocade grown stands at a table on which she has placed the severed head of Holofernes, his eyes still half open and his mouth agape in the surprise of death. One of her gloved, beringed hands clutches the general's head by his hair; the other holds upright the sword of Truth and Justice. A broad red hat is cocked stylishly atop her long auburn braids, her shoulders are still seductively bared, and her delicate neck is adorned with expensive gold necklaces. The fashionable luxuriance of her dress, however, is betrayed by the seriousness of her expression: her lips are still pursed in calm resolve even though the deed is done, and her eyes are slightly narrowed as she gazes in melancholy at some point off the canvas. Gruesomely, the pallor of the dead Holofernes contrasts starkly with the warm flesh tones of the woman; the severed muscles and veins exposed in the stump of his neck grotesquely mirror the pattern in the raised velvet of her gown and in the long strands of her hair. Cranach's is the portrait of a court beauty who is tired of posing. The viewer is startled by this sudden revelation of what cool resolve and even what physical power may be concealed beneath such a soft, seemingly imperturbable surface.

The psychological drama of Gentileschi's representations of the story is even more powerful and disturbing. Her "Judith and Holofernes," for example, expresses a strong sexual tension as Judith's maid struggles to hold the dazed general down while Judith, her sleeves rolled up and her bracelets pushed high on her forearm, gingerly but decisively begins to sever his head from his body. In the confusion of the bedclothes, Hans Kleinschmidt points out, "the powerful, heavy arms of Holofernes resemble thighs, and his head, partly covered by hair and foreshortened, could well be mistaken for his genital area at first glance," giving the impression that "this is a scene depicting castration."[12] The panic of Holofernes, the dramatic postures of the two women, and the chaos of the tangled bedsheets lend a ferocious energy to the scene; the viewer is the terrified witness to a Freudian nightmare in which the male's fear of experiencing castration in coitus is vividly if symbolically enacted. An additional psychological drama is inherent in Gentileschi's seeming obsession with the Judith story: she painted it several times, reputedly painting herself as Judith, thus using her art to revenge herself against Agostino Tassi who was charged with raping her repeatedly when she was only nineteen.[13] Sexual violence—divorced from the scene as depicted by Donatello, Michelangelo, and Mantegna—is brutally depicted here, and simmers suggestively beneath the surface in Cranach.

Clearly no single "idea" of Judith dominates her multiple representations. Such ambivalence is possible only because of the interpretive questions that the biblical text seems deliberately to beg answering. Was Judith's murder of Holofernes an act in which she was fully engaged emotionally, or did she behave in a controlled, dispassionate way? At the crucial moment did she give in to sudden, unbridled physical ferocity, or was she governed by a cold, steady calculation? Was her modesty never offended by the foreigner's venery or might she actually have enjoyed the momentary release from a straight-jacketing decorum that her play-acting allowed her? The narrative in each case admits of both possibilities, the ambivalence sustained by three shrewd maneuvers. First, there is the narrator's decision to focus largely upon the sensuous surface of the woman Judith, seeming to take delight in reporting both the pains that Judith takes to enhance her beauty (10: 1-5) and the response made to it by her own people (10: 7), by the enemy soldiers who listen to her story while thinking only of her face (10: 14), and by the great Holofernes himself (10: 23). Once Judith dolls herself up, no one in the narrative seems capable of seeing past her surface appearance, nor does the narrator himself try to do so. It is as if he attends to Judith's warning to the village elders that one "cannot plumb the depths of the human heart or understand the way a man's mind works" (8: 14, NEB).

Second, there is Judith's own strategy of secrecy. "Do not try to find out my plan," she cautions the elders before setting out for the Assyrian camp; "I will not tell you until I have accomplished what I mean to do" (8: 34). The warning extends to the reader as well, who must endure the suspense of watching Judith seem to prostitute herself and betray her people, uncertain of just how far she is willing to go to accomplish her secret design.

Finally, there is the maneuver in which Judith and the narrator conspire—in the irony of her replies to the general. When Holofernes worries that Judith has brought so little kosher food with her yet refuses to eat from the Assyrian tables, she replies, "As sure as you live, my lord, I shall not finish what I have brought with me before the Lord accomplishes through me what he has planned" (12: 4). The joke, of course, is on Holofernes, who does not know that he has not long to live. And when the enemy leader invites the beautiful defector to his tent as part of his seduction plan, she coyly submits saying, "Who am I to refuse my master?" although refraining from naming what master she serves. "I am eager to do whatever pleases him; and it will be something to boast of till my dying day" (12: 14). The full weight of this irony is not felt until Judith's plan is revealed in its accomplishment, nor that of the enemy's exclamation after first seeing and hearing Judith: "Who can despise a nation which has such women as these? We had better not leave a man of them alive, for if they get away they will be able to outwit the whole world" (10: 19). It is the Jewish women they need take heed of, not the men; and it is precisely through their wit, not their beauty, that these women will triumph. How deeply set in her cheek does Judith hold her tongue when, upon first meeting Holofernes, she exclaims: "We have heard how wise and clever you are. You are known throughout the world as the man of ability unrivalled in the whole empire, of powerful intelligence and amazing skill in the art of war" (11: 8). He may be the wisest and the cleverest man that the Assyrians have to boast of, but in seducing him with such praise she shows just what a fool he really is, and who of the two of them is wiser, cleverer, and more adept in the art of war.

Under such circumstances, it is impossible for the reader to be certain of Judith's character. In its sensuous descriptions of Judith's beauty or of the appointments of Holofernes' tent, the narrative seems to delight in arousing the reader's sexual expectations. Is it possible that Judith enjoys her teasing too? Is the irony of her speeches to the general comic or serious? Does she enjoy the cat and mouse game she plays, or does she speak in deadly earnest? Is she a woman who knows the full value of the beauty she's renounced as a widow by living in sackcloth and, therefore, takes pleasure in momentarily resuming the sensuous life? Or does she despise the vanity of physical charms, as well as those who are foolish enough to

be seduced by them? Judith cautions the village elders against trying to guess the secrets of another person's heart, but is she entirely
informed of the contents of her own? When she donates to the
Temple the trappings of Holofernes' tent that she'd been given by
the grateful townspeople as her share of the spoils of war, is it because, modest and pious, she's indifferent to such vanities? Or is it
in penance for some shocking discovery her adventure allowed her
to make—discovery of the force of sexual feelings she thought to
have conquered long ago? or of the savagery with which she was
stunned to find herself capable of acting? The text does not say. Like
a well-cut gem only so many faces of which can be seen at any given
time, Judith's character reflects different depths of light at every
turn.[14]

"The function of that particular class of legends known as
myth," explains Georges Dumezil, "is to express dramatically the
ideology under which a society lives; not only to hold out to its conscience the values it recognizes and the ideals it pursues from generation to generation, but above all to express its very being and
structure, the elements, the connections, the balances, the tensions
that contribute to it; to justify the rules and traditional practices
without which everything within a society would disintegrate."[15]
The Old Testament stories that have women as their protagonists
clearly function in this way, Ruth's story being among the five
Megilloth or Scrolls read in public at the Feast of Weeks, and
Esther's at Purim. But myth, as we argue in the introduction to an
earlier collaboration,[16] is more than this; its most important characteristic is that its story can stretch to meet the expanding needs
of a community. It is precisely because the values at the heart of the
myth are so important that it is necessary for each age to rediscover
their significance, retelling the story in its own words and in the
light of its own immediate concerns. The moment that a story's
values cease to be a vibrant concern for a community, the story is
fossilized, remaining "myth" only in the pejorative sense of beliefs
held by ancestors that are dismissed or disparaged by a later generation. But as a story whose concerns continue vital, myth is the very
texture of the dialogue of generations, the way in which parts of a

civilization talk among themselves and thus constitute a whole.
Writers are required to return to them again and again as to an un-
derground storehouse of deep meaning that is never really exhausted. Myths consequently accumulate such resonance and carry
such enormous weights of meaning that they become part of the
cultural lexicon—an easy way of telegraphing meaning through allusion.

Like the double helix of a DNA code that possesses the information allowing for inconceivable numbers of genetic recombina-
tions, the stories of Eve, Ruth, Esther and Judith; of Hagar, Rachel,
and Leah; of Jephthah's daughter and the Levite's concubine of
Judges; and even of Job's wife, carry such elusive meaning and possess such mysterious power that they provoke constant retelling.
These women are not important culturally because they represent
some model of behavior that women are socially obliged to emulate, but because their stories are multifaceted and never exhausted,
their meaning never fully revealed. They are at the font of some
ongoing process of disclosure, at the source of a dialogue that continues to engage us.

The essays that follow attempt to join in that dialogue. Jan
Wojcik's essay assumes that the Jewish Apocrypha and the New
Testament were the first literary works to retell or interpret the stories of Old Testament women. The Gnostic works were the next
generation of interpretations and retellings; as Pheme Perkins demonstrates, exegetical and literary gnostic works about Eve can be
referred to without distinction because both were self-conscious
revisions of the texts already handed down. Perhaps there is never
a clear distinction in literary history between interpretation and
midrash, between new readings and new tellings. Whatever the distinction, it was blurred in the early years, including those years during which the Old Testament canon was shaped. As Jan Wojcik
concludes, the Old Testament was itself "typical" literature, referring to itself and retelling its own stories continuously.

Thus, as Jayne Blankenship's essay on the appearance of
Rachel and Leah in Dante's *Purgatorio* illustrates, sometimes the
meanings that a biblical woman's story has accumulated can be so

deep and so rich that one level gradually supersedes another even while contradicting it, leaving the literary historian to carefully excavate and date the different strata of meanings in order to make sense of a writer's allusion. At other times, alchemical changes can occur so swiftly that only the literary historian's slowing the motion of change can catch it for the student's eye. In less than a hundred years, Eve Stoddard shows, Ruth ran the gamut from idealized pastoral figure to archetypal fallen woman. A biblical heroine may even change focus across the span of a single writer's imaginative life, as Louise Simons shows was the case of the Levite's concubine in Judges in Milton's poetry and prose. Even a seemingly minor character like Job's Wife may take on a highly consequential life outside the Bible in later periods, as Ann Astell demonstrates. Hagar lives as fully on the nineteenth century Canadian prairie and in the imagination of a novelist in the Somaliland desert as in ancient Israel, Rosalie Baum shows. And, concludes Nona Fienberg, Jephthahs continue to sacrifice their daughters in Hamlet's Elsinore and Shakespeare's London. In sum, biblical women bear the weight of such continuing accretion of meaning that makes the excavation processes conducted in these essays fruitful.

Notes

¹ Muriel Sparks, *Prime of Miss Jean Brodie*, Laurel ed. (New York: Dell, 1966), 8-9.

² Stevie Davies, *The Idea of Woman in Renaissance Literature: The Feminine Reclaimed* (Brighton: Harvester P, 1986), 1.

³ Carol Meyers, *Discovering Eve: Ancient Israelite Women in Context* (New York: Oxford UP, 1988), 7, 5.

⁴ Ben Jonson, *Conversations with Drummond of Hawthornden*, quoted in A.J. Smith, ed., *John Donne: The Complete English Poems*, corrected ed. (Harmondsworth: Penguin Books, 1973), 594.

⁵ See, for example, the distinctions made between the virtuous and the evil woman in Proverbs 5: 15-20; 6: 20-35; 7: 1-27; 9: 13-18; 11: 16; 12: 4; 18: 22; 19: 13-14; 21: 9, 19; 27: 15; 31: 2-3 and esp. 10-31 (NEB).

[6] Mieke Bal, *Murder and Difference: Gender, Genre, and Scholarship on Sisera's Death*, trans. Matthew Gumpert (Bloomington: Indiana UP, 1988), esp. chap. 6.

[7] Quoted in David Minter, *William Faulkner: His Life and Work* (Baltimore: Johns Hopkins UP, 1980), 228.

[8] Erich Auerbach, *Mimesis: The Representation of Reality in Western Literature*, trans. Willard R. Trask (Princeton: Princeton UP, 1953), 23, 11.

[9] Marina Warner, *Monuments and Maidens: The Allegory of the Female Form* (London: Weidenfeld and Nicolson, 1985), 147.

[10] Warner, *Momuments and Maidens*, 149.

[11] John Walker both reproduces the panel and discusses this feature in his *National Gallery of Art* (New York: Harry N. Abrams, n.d.), 114-15: "the actors, in spite of the gruesomeness of the event, are as impersonal as the sculptured figures of the Parthenon. Judith turns away from her bloody prize with a look of calm detachment; she accepts impassively her predestined triumph. The stone-colored panel seems chiseled rather than painted, like an enlarged cameo which has survived from the ancient world."

[12] Hans J. Kleinschmidt, "Discussing Laurie Schneider's Paper [on castration symbolism in Donatello and Carravaggio]," *American Imago* 33 (1976): 92-97; 95.

[13] See Mary D. Garrard, *Artemisia Gentileschi: The Image of the Female Hero in Italian Baroque Art* (Princeton: Princeton UP, 1988), and Anna Banti's 1947 novel, *Artemisia*, trans. Shirley D'Ardia Caracciolo, recently reprinted (Lincoln: U of Nebraska P, 1988).

[14] Because painting must telegraph an interpretation of Judith's story in a single image, focus has been on visual interpretation for efficiency's sake. But the range of interpretive possibilities offered by the biblical narrative has been just as fully explored in literature as it has been in art. Seeking to unveil the inner typological meaning in Old and New Testament scenes by setting them side by side, the medieval *Speculum Humanae Salvationis* paralleled Judith's triumph over Holofernes with the all-conquering Virgin Mary's transfixing Satan with a Vexillum thrust deep in his gullet. (See Marina Warner's discussion in *Alone of All Her Sex: The Myth and Cult of the Virgin Mary* [New York: Alfred A. Knopf, 1976], 55, 370n.12.) The Old English *Judith* celebrates her wisdom and chastity; likewise, in medieval drama Judith's defeat of Holofernes so easily fits the traditional dramatic triumph of Virtue over Vice that the sexual

nature of their encounter is usually all but ignored. Not so on the modern stage, however, where Adah Menken's *Judith*, for example, anticipated and possibly inspired her friend Oscar Wilde's disturbingly sensual treatment of the better known *Salome*. Likewise, Thomas Sturge Moore's play, *Judith*, caused a controversy in London in 1916 by suggesting that Judith was the mistress of Holofernes before she killed him, while Arnold Bennett's *Judith* (1919) scandalously allowed its heroine to appear on stage in a revealing costume. Jean Giraudoux's psychological comedy (*Judith*, 1931) perversely presented Judith as an opportunistic courtesan and Holofernes as not unlikable.

The sexual issue has not been the only one explored in later retellings. Significantly, the biblical story could be used as successfully by Frederico della Valle (*Judith*, 1628) to tune baroque religious sensibilities as by Marko Marulic (*Judita*, 1501) to arouse Croatian national feeling against the Turkish oppressor. Likewise, the Italian Jews of Pesaro daringly staged a play about Judith and Holofernes at the wedding festivities of the tyrant Giovanni Sforza (1489). It is the plastic quality born of the biblical refusal to specify thought or motivation even while successfully recording the details of the external drama that makes of Judith as much the woman of a hundred faces as the frame on which to hang any number of authors' concerns.

[15] Georges Dumezil, *The Destiny of the Warrior* (Chicago: U of Chicago P, 1970), 3.

[16] See our Introduction to *The David Myth in Western Literature* (Lafayette, IN.: Purdue UP, 1980), esp. 1, 10.

One:

Angel Narrators and Biblical Women: The Fluid Voices of Uncanonical Readings

Jan Wojcik

> What feelings
> Welled up from beings no longer here.
>
> Rainer Maria Rilke, "The Third Elegy"

So much has been made of the Bible for so long that it can be a surprise to discover it is a collection of old stories. Individually they stand up well. But reading them still raises pertinent questions. And many of them, especially the stories featuring female characters, raise troubling questions.

What, for example, are we to think when Abraham twice passes Sarah off as his sister lest a strong leader, through whose territory he is passing, kill Abraham and appropriate the beautiful Sarah for his own (Genesis 12:9-20; 20:1-18)? Isaac tries the same ploy with Rebekah (Genesis 26: 1-11). Lot offers his two daughters to a rapacious mob of Sodomites to do with as they please, as long as they leave his angelic guests alone (Genesis 19:1-11). In Judges we find a similar episode in which a Levite, to save his host from harm, hands over his concubine to a mob which rapes and kills her (Judges 19:16-30). Laban manipulates Jacob's great desire for Rachel into indenturing him for fourteen years (Genesis 29: 15-35). Dinah's affair with Schechem becomes the occasion for her brothers to slaughter him, his family, and his tribe (Genesis 39: 1-31).

Sometimes the sacrifice of a woman is politically tactical. King Saul says explicitly that he uses his daughter Michal as "bait" to lure David into making a fatal mistake (1 Samuel 18: 17-30). David himself seduces Bathsheba, the wife of Uriah, one of his soldiers, then tries to cover the pregnancy that results from his adultery by arousing Uriah's desire to sleep with his wife (2 Samuel 11: 1-12:14). Amnon, David's son, forcibly seduces his sister Tamar; Absalom, his brother, uses the incident as an excuse to forment a rebellion against David his father (2 Samuel 13-18). Women seem but tokens in a man's game.

If we read these stories as reflections of history, as is commonly done, we can shudder that times past have been harsh to women.

It is Gerda Lerner's recent and highly influential thesis that this literary phenomenon in the Judaic scriptures directly reflects certain highly regrettable historical circumstances. A patriarchal social structure among the archaic Hebrews becomes incorporated as a value in the literature.

> The combined pressure of the need for agricultural labor in settling a desert environment and the concurrent loss of population due to wars and epidemics crisis [sic] in the very period when the rudimentary principles of Jewish religious thought came into being may explain the Biblical emphasis on the family and on woman's procreative role. In such a demographic crisis women would most likely have agreed to a division of labor which gave their maternal role primacy.[1]

In a patriarchal system, the mother is not far from the prostitute or rape victim, if only in the sense that her sexuality is available primarily for the purposes of men. Lerner expresses particular dismay over the story of Lot's daughters being offered up to a rapacious mob: "If we analyze this Biblical story, we notice that Lot's right to dispose of his daughters, even so as to offer them to be raped, is taken for granted. It does not need to be explained; hence we can assume it reflected a historic social condition" (173).

Using what she calls a strictly historical method, Lerner dismisses the efforts of Phyllis Trible who wants to read the stories about women selectively, even serenely, by gathering together a smaller canon than Lerner's more inclusive one. Trible's is a "counter-culture" of stories which opposes the "patriarchal culture of Israel."[2] In this counter culture, reflected in stories such as Deborah the Judge and Judith the savior of Bethulia, women are sometimes shown to be more than the equal of their men. According to Lerner, Phyllis Bird states correctly that women are legally and economically deemed inferior to men in the biblical narrative and that this reflected actual conditions in Hebrew society. Yet when Bird asserts that man in the Old Testament sometimes recognizes woman "as his opposite and equal,"[3] Lerner dismissively labels this an assertion for which she faults Bird for offering precious little evidence.

She says the same thing of John Otwell's assertion that "the status of women in the Old Testament was high and that they fully participated in the life of the community."[4]

Lerner rejects the notion, central to each of these studies, that occasional radiant exceptions disprove the general rule of patriarchy in the biblical narratives. She herself points out the exceptional story featuring a female prophet, Deborah, in which an unassuming female Jael manages to kill Sisera, an enemy of the people of Israel, by driving a phallic tent peg into his head.[5] There are no retiring women here. But rather than puzzle over the exception, Lerner instead wonders why the Bible's mostly male interpreters have failed to consider the questions it seems to raise about the otherwise apparently natural male superiority throughout the biblical narratives. She leaves the matter there.

But there are many ways to read even the harshest of these stories about women, and to receive impressions different from those that Lerner insists upon. Although these impressions do not cancel her complaint, they indicate there is more to these biblical stories—and all biblical stories—than things to complain about. In this essay I would like to focus upon the impressions left by the voices of the narrative angels, the intimates of close biblical readers.

Take perhaps the darkest episode about women in the Bible, which Lerner features. This is the scene in Genesis in which Lot offers his two daughters to a mob to rape. The mob is demanding that he throw out to them two angel visitors whom they have followed to his door. Certainly it is possible to read the episode as approving of Lot's response—if one already considers women to be the disposable property of men. But the reader is equally free to interpret the episode as a cautionary tale. The narrator is saying that there are men who consider women this way, that this sort of thing does happen, but that there are alternatives to Lot's spontaneous and miserable (and let us say "historical") effort to handle the situation.

On one level, the lesson here is that if women are to be treated well, it is better to think and act like the angel guests than to think and act like the father Lot. In this episode, angels save the day by blinding the members of the mob, and they enlighten the reader.

They have more wit than either the mob or Lot or, sadly, even the helpless daughters are allowed to have. They are fluid thinkers in desperate straits.

Other angelic voices appear in the biblical stories with brighter thoughts than the male characters have about the roles of female characters. Oftentimes they appear as characters sympathetic to women. They tell the women that their story is about to take a fortuitous turn and that their sadness will yield to gladness. As such, these character angels find a desperate Hagar in the wilderness, and a wild Hannah before the altar; they visit Sarai in her tent. Like narrators who know the way the story is going to go, they alert privileged characters to future fortuity. They tell their female characters that the desperate present is preamble to better times: the biblical story is bigger than they think.

Yet another kind of angel appears in the narratives as narrators. They are everywhere in the Bible, of course, because the Bible's stories are narratives. Even the lyric psalms usually manage to suggest a terse story of hope lost and regained. Let's call them "angelic narrators" because they bear messages, the message of the story. (The Greek root of *angel* means "messenger.") But primarlily they are messengers with powerful voices who do not moralize about earthly, historical happenings. They attend to the higher meaning of events and provoke fluid thoughts.

This last attribute is their most remarkable one. Angelic biblical narrative voices rarely signal an attitude about how the story unfolds. Never once does the biblical narrator indicate that he shares any derogatory views which male characters might have of any female characters in these stories. The closest a narrator comes to making an editorial comment on any of these male attitudes occurs in the Dinah story (Genesis 34), and there the narrator is distinctly ambivalent. The narrator reports that her lover Schechem did a "dishonorable thing," but also that he remained true to her. The narrator seems to share the perspective of the brothers when he reports that they call the affair "an intolerable thing," but then the same narrator calls the murderous ruse they perpetuate against Shechem's family "dishonest." The ambivalence resolves into the intriguing irony of the story's conclusion: "Jacob said to Simeon and Levi, 'You have brought trouble on me, you have made my name stink among the people of the country, the Canaanites and the Perizzites.' They answered, 'Is our sister to be treated as a common whore?'" (30-31). Significantly, the narrator neither passes any judgment on what Dinah did, nor even tells whether she was a willing lover. We cannot take the lack of narrator's judgment to mean that Dinah lacked judgment. The narrator is simply silent about what she thought, while her brothers are rigidly explicit.

We can say that this narrator, like every biblical narrator, has an angelic voice. To elaborate further: such narrators are invisible. Their voices come from nowhere, but they flow in and around every word in the scriptures. And of course, they borrow their breath for each reading from the reader peering down onto the page, reviving again their angelic speech. Of course these angels are going to imbibe thereby some of the reader's spirit.

Can we read the Bible wrongly if we are attending to the nuances of these fluid angelic narrative voices? They tell us harsh stories, but as in the stories of Lot's daughters and of Dinah's lover they do not insist that the reader come only to harsh conclusions—conclusions without hope about the continuing history of the male oppression of the female aspirations for freedom. I think many authorities do not want to trust their readings only to these angelic voices precisely because they tell their stories one at a time, to one reader at a time, the structure of the exchange suggesting there is a freedom to what biblical stories can come to mean—even the stories about women.

The Problem of Canonical Reading

When Lerner wants to read even the story of Deborah against the whole context of biblical stories about women, she wants to suppress the image of an exception and thus rob the angelic narrative of its nuance. Not, of course, because she accepts the patriarchal view of women. She wants to identify the view without sentiment as without any modern currency, so that religious prac-

tice can advance beyond it. But while I certainly accept her reading of patriarchal history, and applaud her conclusions about our
own times, I think that reading the Old Testament canon
monolithically, as she does, silences many angelic voices she and
others like her would find consoling.

One has to be very careful in critizing her method. This kind
of canonical reading has become widely fashionable in our time,
often under the guise of reading the Bible "as literature." One must
read each story in its context, authoritative voices tell us, and we
must be scrupulous about what the context must be. These readers
feel comfortable within the confines of canon—especially if it is the
"right" or the orthodox canon.

Robert Alter is one of the more recent biblical scholars to warn
us not to make the mistake the Church Fathers did in receiving the
Judaic and Christian scriptures as a unified canon. They assumed
that a holy spirit presided over the authorship behind the biblical
scriptures. This spirit was intent upon foreshadowing Jesus's story
through every episode of the venerable Judaic scriptural narrative,
even when the original writers might have been blissfully unaware
whither the providential plot tended. This is an assumption with
the force of a prejudice, with which it is all too easy to disregard the
religious convictions of Jewish writers who knew their own minds
very well. Instead, Alter would have readers respect the canonical
circumscriptions of those who established the Judaic scriptures as
an independent family of texts. By and large, the Jewish Fathers did
not receive the non-semitic, so-called apocryphal texts as canonical; and they certainly did not wish to add the Christian scriptures
to their canon. Apparently, Alter would also have readers respect
the canonical circumscriptions of other traditions as well. Christians
initially received the entire Septuagint Greek translation of the
Bible as canonical, including the apocryphal stories that had been
passed down only through Greek texts. Protestants in the sixteenth
century downgraded all but the originally Hebrew Judaic texts to
the apocryphal. Catholics, after the Council of Trent in 1546, confirmed that the Hebrew Judaic texts were canoncial, the Greek
apocryphal texts deuterocanonical.[6]

When Alter reads the story of Lot's daughters he calls it a cautionary tale: "a grim parody of the primeval command to be fruitful and multiply." He finds it thereby a more readable, and bearable, tale than Lerner's reading would allow. But like Lerner, he still embeds the story in a Judaic canonical context, recalling in this instance the opening chapter of Genesis. He goes on to say that the Lot story sets the "checkerboard" scene of moral ambiguity onto which the biblical patriarchs such as Isaac, Jacob, and Joseph will move—and occasionally sacrifice a token female in the game.[7] The metaphor suggests that the moves these patriarchal men can make are rigidly restricted ahead of time.

More recently, however, other scholars such as Gerald L. Burns and Elaine H. Pagels have criticized canonization precisely for its efforts to limit the reader's range of reading. Canonization does this two ways: first by excluding certain stories from the canon; then by insisting that all those that remain be read together.

Burns and Pagels focus on the first principle. Burns sees the process of canonizing the Judaic scriptures as an effort of priests, or at least those dedicated to writing, to absorb the terrifically free energy of prophetic oral pronouncement into their own political agendas. The priests had often been opposed by prophets, especially in the tumultuous centuries before exile and deportation. With the restoration of the Second Temple, the priestly Ezra constituted a decorous, bookish Judaism. The prophets still have a voice, but only as boxed within written texts that the priests and later the rabbis transmit and interpret. This means that "canon is not a literary category, but a category of power."[8]

Some scholars in fact think that one of the official reasons certain stories featuring heroic women such as Susanna and Judith have been excluded from the Judaic canon is that male authorities making the decision what narratives to canonize, themselves share conventional prejudices either about women or about male perogatives. Solomon Zeitlin argues that the Jewish Fathers did not accept Susanna as canonical "because in its present form the story clearly contradicts a Pharisee *Halakhah* in the Mishananh, namely, when witnesses had contradicted one another and were discredited, those witnesses could not be punished unless two other individuals who had not been at the scene of the crime testified that at the time of the alleged crime the accusing witnesses were actually with them, thereby proving that the accusing witnesses had deliberately offered false testimony and had not simply made an honest mistake (Sanhedrin V 1)."[9] David M. Kay puts the matter more succinctly: "The story would not be popular with elders; and it was elders who fixed the canon."[10]

And, according to Burns, the canonization of the Judaic scriptures took place when one group of elders became fearful of another. It occured "only very late, in the first and second centuries of the common era, as part of the development of rabbinic Judaism, and in the context of conflicting scriptural traditions—that it was thought necessary to cast the Scriptures into something like a canonical form of single, fixed, authoritative versions (as in the Masoretic texts, which give us the modern Hebrew Bible)" (66). Thus we can look upon the Judaic canon as a response to other canons, including what would eventually be declared to be the Christian canon. At the same time we can certainly see the Christian canon as a simultaneous effort to confront and correct the Judaic canon, with authorities in both traditions having differing views about the canonicity of the Septuagint Greek Apocrypha. Both Jewish and Christian authorities, for different reasons, and at different times, found the canonical ambitions of Gnosticism to be obnoxious.

If these theories of canon are correct, then certain readers have had an extraordinary power to limit the readings of others when they canonize scriptures. Obviously, removing a story from the canon altogether effectively and drastically limits the number of readings a story will have. But now the secondary practice of boxing all the stories within the canon as Lerner and Alter do is almost as bad. This practice deadens the reader's sensitivity to what a single story says. Its meaning is always and largely what it contributes to the common denominator of meanings.

The reason certain Judaic stories in particular were canonized might have been that, as Lerner says, they "seemed to decree that by the will of God women were included in His covenant only through the mediation of men" (198). But when Lerner recognizes what the original canonizers did and forgives them their history, her only response is to come to a different conclusion about what the role of religious women should be in our very different religious history. It is very different to insist, as Phyllis Trible does, that some of the original stories, read one at a time, dissent from this over-arching and oppressive canon of bad ideas. I submit that discounting canon as Burns and Pagals suggest, and reading selectively as Trible does, we can still pay our respects to the linguistic and stylistic sublties of these stories, as Robert Alter would have us do, even while remaining grateful that the age of the patriarchs which Lerner describes so well has passed.

Uncanonical Reading

But now, what if we read one story at a time, remaining deaf to the reverberating echoes of stories within one canon, and willy nilly, we find other stories from other canons filtering into our minds while we read? We love the Bible. We read it again and again— sometimes even in Hebrew and Greek. Sometimes we cannot help remembering an Old Testament story while reading a New Testament story, or an Apocryphal story, or even, sometimes, biblical stories in *any* order.

This, of course, Alter expressly forbids us to do, especially if we are reading back against the flow of history. He is justifiably afraid of the excesses of the Fathers who compounded the Judaic scriptures into the Christian Bible with the Gospels as their culminating narrative. Yet, what if the nuance of the angelic voice bids us to remember? Should we repress the call? The biblical stories are stories, after all, ignorant of, or irreverent to the canons of the book binders.

Perhaps there are few other idiosyncratic readers beside myself who will read the story of Mary Magdala while remembering the stories of prostitutes and seducers in the Judaic scriptures. Granted the evidence is slim that the angelic narrator is remembering this way. Here the reading itself remembers the ways of readings that the

Fathers used, so unfashionable these days, especially among feminist critics of the Bible such as Mieke Bal. But surely the results do
not have to be similar to theirs. The stories can flow into each other,
rather than closing around a dogma. If the stories of Magdala are
perhaps the oldest and most primitive of the New Testament stories which re-read the stories of oppressed women in the Old Testament with a glimmer of hope for oppression's end, can not the
result of the reading justify the method?

Mary Magdala has become a vivid popular biblical character
in many non-canonical re-readings of the Gospel story such as *Jesus
Christ, Superstar* and *The Last Temptation of Christ.* Yet she is more
elusive when seen in her original stories in the Gospels. Matthew
(26: 6-13) and Mark (14: 3-9) record episodes in which a woman
anoints Jesus with costly oil (*murou barutimou* in Matthew; *murou
nardou pistikaes polutelous* in Mark) before his passion. Luke places
a similar episode earlier in the Jesus story and identifies an anonymous woman with a jar of, simply, oil (*murou*) as one "who was living an immoral life in the town." He does not specify what the
nature of her immorality was (7:36-50). Like Matthew and Mark,
John puts his version of the episode immediately before the passion
narrative. He uses the same, more elaborate name for the oil as
Mark. Yet he is the only one who says nothing about any immoral
life (12: 1-8). In another context Luke identifies Mary Magdala as
a woman "from whom seven devils had come out" (8: 1-3), as does
Mark (16:9). This appears to be a reference to exorcism, that might
have something to do only with devil possession and nothing intentionally immoral in the woman at all. Joseph Fitzmyer in his
commentary on Luke argues for a common oral tradition behind
these various retellings.[11] Yet when Fitzmyer emphasizes the significant differences between each retelling he makes it possible to consider each version as a separate story, with a distinct character,
whether or not the original model for the story was a single episode.

This is especially so when we hearken to the angel narrator
telling the story. The voice tells us that there were seven devils cast
out of Mary Magdala. The number recalls, perhaps, the number of
previous suitors that Sarah's demon had killed on her wedding

nights with Tobias. With details such as these, the angel narrator appears to be remembering stories regardless of where the canonical boundaries have been made to fall.

To compound the identification, all four evangelists name Mary Magdala as one of the women who visit Jesus' burial site. Two of them, Mark (16:3) and Luke (24:1), mention that she brings aromatic oils (*aromata*) to anoint his body. The word for the liquid is not the same. And the anointing after burial is never done.

Consistently she is a woman generous with precious liquids who occupies a space on the edge of propriety. There is a suggestion of unrestrained sexuality in the free pouring out of liquids with a heady scent, especially when she dries Jesus' anointed feet with her hair. She is not a prostitute in any literal sense. There is never a statement that she made money with her sexuality. In fact, it is just the opposite: in every episode in which she anoints Jesus with oil, disedifed onlookers complain precisely about her wasting money. Furthermore, she does not appear to act in her own selfish interest when she continues to manifest her devotion to Jesus after he has died. And certainly in none of the scenes of their encounters is there any suggestion that she comes to seduce Jesus.

To sum it up, this woman, with whom we associate the name Mary Magdala, is a sexually active, free thinking woman in the Bible. She gives of her self in her own way, notwithstanding any notion of propriety. She is a free lover. Perhaps the ambiguity about who she is and what she represents indicates that even the evangelists (in addition to the characters in the story) had a difficult time sorting out what her presence meant in Jesus' story.

We read, and we remember—we cannot help ourselves—the unconventional seductresses in the Hebrew scriptures. In Genesis we read of Tamar adopting the pose of a temple prostitute to seduce Judah. She thereby successfully forces him to meet his obligation to her to produce a male through her from his family line (Genesis 38: 1-30). [12] In Joshua we read of the good prostitute Rahab who decides to cast her lot with Joshua's scouts, the vanguard of the newcomers to her ancestral land. In Judges we read of Jael whom Sisera seeks out to protect him. He is a Canaanite general sent on a punitive raid against the Israelites when they were becoming restless under Canaanite rule. He comes to Jael's tent because he knows Jael's husband is an ally of Jabin the Canaanite king. He does not know that Jael herself sympathizes with the Israelites, at this time ruled by Deborah, a rare female judge in Israel. He asks Jael for a drink of water; she provides him warm blankets and a soothing drink of warm milk. Yet, when he falls to sleep, she drives a tent peg through his head.

When we recall Jael, we pause, as even Lerner did. Like Mary Magdala's, Jael's story contains the trappings of sexual imagery in the blankets, warm liquid milk, and tent peg, suggesting that Jael can manipulate male expectations about passive women to her own special advantage. As Lerner herself sensed, Jael does not quite fit her general model of the oppressed biblical female. Is the impression her story makes strong enough to be remembered while an angelic narrator tells another, or while the reader reads another? Certainly the latter is more probable than the former. But let us apply another test. Does reading this way distort either story? Does it celebrate male hegemony? or suggest that repressed women have no resources? If the answers are no, then let us call the reading justified—Lerner's justifiable complaint and Alter's justifiable warning notwithstanding.

But perhaps another reader would be more comfortable if a character in a story in one canon remembered a character in a story in another canon. Then it would seem that the angelic narrator would have overheard, and remembered too. Fluid memory recalls another famous story featuring a man, a woman, and a liquid.[13]

Jesus asks a woman for a drink of water in one of John's Gospel's most intriguing scenes. Without our being able to detect whether she is truly incredulous, flirtatious, or ironic, she responds "What! You a Jew, ask a drink of me, a Samaritan woman?" The narrator intrudes with a helpful aside: "Jews and Samaritans, it should be noted, do not use vessels in common" (4:9). Jesus does what he frequently does in John. He starts using metaphors that he suspects his listener will take literally. Again, we are unable to detect whether he is being pompous, playful, or earnest: "If only you knew what God gives, and who it is that is asking you for a drink, you would have asked him and he would have given you living water" (11). Her response is complex. She chooses to understand Jesus literally, and to ask where is the bucket he is going to use to draw up some water. But she also appends a lesson on religious history. The well before which the two of them stand belonged to the same Jacob whom Rebekah counseled and Rachel married. When she calls him "our father Jacob" (*tou patros haemon Iakob*), she might be implying that Jacob is the common ancestor of both the Jews *and* the Samaritans. That means that the rivalry and suspicion between the two groups is of recent origin and does not have deep roots. Jesus responds again with poetry. She again asks him to give her water but this time with the suggestion that she understands what Jesus promises as magic: a special water jar, like the oil jar that Elijah gave the poor widow, that will never fail.

This time Jesus, apparently frustrated with his inability to get the upper hand over this verbally clever woman, counters with a sexist, *ad feminam* retort. "Bring your husband here," he says, as if to suggest that a man could understand the higher level of discourse that he is trying to maintain. He manages to throw her off stride, it seems, for she admits that she has no husband. He counters again, harshly it seems, that she has had five, and that currently she is living with a man out of wedlock. (One has to use the word "seems" here because no narrative indication is given any place in the scene of the tone the two characters use. The reader supplies the counterpoint.) The exchange does seem to go beyond humor or irony when the woman proves equal to Jesus's challenge. She ignores his obviously irrelevant and biased observation. She brings up a point of doctrine about which Samaritans and Jews contend: "Sir," she replied, "I can see that you are a prophet. Our fathers worshipped on this mountain, but you Jews say that the temple where God should be worshipped is in Jerusalem." The loaded question implied in her statement appears to anger Jesus. In any case, it catches Jesus in a prejudice. He forgets his lofty tone, and for a moment descends to accusing this woman, and Samaritans in general, of "not knowing what you worship, while we worship what we know. It is from the Jews that salvation comes" (22). Then he catches himself, and returns to a lofty tone in speaking of the new God of spirit that anyone can worship in truth.

Thus it appears, when Jesus has a chance to reflect, that he finds that he actually shares this woman's belief that the true spiritual life resides beyond the reach of rigid, dogmatic dissections and outside canonical boundaries. John's narrator has him win the encounter only by absorbing her heartfelt position to his own poetic style. There are several other rhetorical maneuvers in the scene, as it widens to include Jesus' provincial Jewish disciples and the woman's provincial Samaritan townspeople. But its climax matches that of the scene between Rebekah and same Jacob of which the Samaritan woman speaks. Both scenes prove a woman to be the equal of a man by denying him the upper hand through a clever use of language.

Rebekah had changed the course of patriarchal history by two timely observations and three brief remarks. After observing Isaac talking to Esau and planning a ritual blessing that will pass on to his elder son the birthright to his inheritence, she instructs Jacob to prepare disguised venison and disguised skin to fool his father (Genesis 27). Later, when she receives a report that Esau is planning to kill Jacob for stealing his birthright, she instructs Jacob to leave for another country. She gains Isaac's approval for Jacob's journey by suggesting it is time Jacob return to the land of their ancestors to find a proper wife (27; 28: 1-4). It is still Isaac who gives the blessing and orders Jacob to leave, yet at rare moments this female character saves the day with the eloquence of a Moses.

Indeed, when her words remind us of Rebekah's, we could call this ostensibly heretical Samaritan woman the guardian angel of an uncanonical reading. In her encounter with Jesus, she meets and bests a male who makes a dogmatic pronouncement about religious distinctions. He wants to narrow the definition of orthodoxy; she, on the other hand, looks back into sacred literary history for a common religious ancestor the male and female share. At the moment she does she regains the eloquence of a Moses who finally finds sufficient words to confront a narrow-minded Pharoah. She even does

Moses one better by convincing her man of the rightness of her bid for spiritual freedom.

The studies that follow this one recount the literary history of the re-readings of Old Testament women that the stories of Magdala and the Samaritan Woman begin. Those written after the biblical canons were closed are uncanonical stories by anyone's reckoning. But here they come together within the bindings of yet another book beguiled by the fluid voices of angels.

Notes

[1]Gerda Lerner, *The Creation of Patriarchy* (New York: Oxford UP, 1986), 164.

[2]Phyllis Trible, "Depatriarchalizing in Biblical Interpretation," *The Interpreter's Dictionary of the Bible, Supplementary Volume*, ed. K.R. Crim (Nashville: Abingdon P, 1976), 963-66. (First published in *Journal of the American Academy of Religions* 41: 31-34).

[3]Phyllis Bird, "Images of Women in the Old Testament," *Religion and Sexism*, ed. Rosemary Ruether (New York: Macmillan, 1974), 41-88; 48.

[4]John Otwell, *And Sarah Laughed: The Status of Women in the Old Testament* (Philadelphia: Fortress P, 1977), 101.

[5]On the phrase "Deborah was a prophetess," Robert G. Boling comments: "Offered as both a statement of fact and the narrator's own value judgement, the latter being indicated by the exclamatory syntax. A variety of female prophets having political involvements at Mari is well known." Boling, however, draws attention away from the dramatic hints in the narrative that females could assume and exercise considerable military skill. He says that the point of the narrative is "that neither Deborah nor Baraq subdued Sisera on that day—But God did!" Robert G. Boling, *Judges: A New Translation with Introduction and Commentary*, Anchor Bible (Garden City, NY: Doubleday, 1974), 123. This overlooks the realistic encouragement Deborah gives Baraq, his effective humility in recognizing the valid advice of a female, and the resolution of the woman Jael. She apparently was a member of the single family among the rival Qeuite clan who remained loyal to the Yahwists when they were threatened by an invasion of powerful Sea People.

⁶Robert Alter, *The Art of Biblical Narrative* (New York: Basic Books, 1981).

⁷Robert Alter, "Sodom as Nexus," in *The Book and the Text: The Bible and Literary Theory*, ed. Regina Schwartz (London: Basil Blackwell, 1990), 157.

⁸Gerald L. Burns, "Canon and Power in the Hebrew Scriptures," in *Canons*, ed. Robert von Hallbert (Chicago: U of Chicago P, 1985), 81.

⁹Solomon Zeitlin, "Apocryphal Women," *Jewish Quarterly Review* 40 (1950): 230-242; 236.

¹⁰David M. Kay, *Susanna in The Apocrypha and Pseudepigrapha of the Old Testament*, ed. R. H. Charles, 2 Vols. (Oxford: Clarendon P, 1913), 642.

¹¹Joseph Fitzmyer, *The Gospel According to Luke*, Anchor Bible (Garden City, NY: Doubleday, 1979), 684-688.

¹² As Donald A. Seybold has shown, what Tamar does in seducing her father-in-law Judah reiterates the central theme of the Joseph narrative and many other typical biblical stories. Any strategy that preserves the family and propagation of the tribe is "acceptable. . . .[Even] incest is paradoxically natural under such a compelling natural law." Likewise, Judith understands how men tend to mistake the seductions of women for their own masculine sexual attractiveness. She manipulates Holophernes' mistake into the salvation of her small town of Bethulia. This small town, in turn, seals off the access of the militant foreigners to the land of Israel. Rahab the prostitute of Jericho trades at the margins of respectability. It is from this margin that she can see that the power in this city and land is about to pass to a new people, to whom she offers vital protection. Similarly, the immoral woman of the Gospels understands profoundly the shift of focus in Jesus' new social message. One can be spiritually generous whatever one's profession. Like the fisherman Peter, the tax collector Matthew, or the rich official Zacchaeus in other episodes whom Jesus exhorts to be good precisely as they are, she has an unconventional style of thinking. Donald A. Seybold, "Paradox and Symmetry in the Joseph Narrative," in *Literary Interpretations of Biblical Narratives*, ed. Kenneth R. R. Gros Louis et al. (Nashville: Abingdon P, 1974), 67.

¹³ The word "character" is being used here to denote a realistic human being who has some effect on the action in a biblical scene or story. Since Henry James' oft-cited dictum: "What is character but the determination of incident? What is incident but the illustration of character?" it has been fashionable to treat narrative characters only as threads among

the narrative weave. See, for example, Wallace Martin, *Recent Theories of Narrative* (Ithaca: Cornell UP, 1984), 43. According to Hans Frei and others, this caution also holds for biblical narratives. We tear away essential tissue when we tease characters from the narrative to consider them in isolation. But with biblical characters we do not tear away much. That is not because they are less implicated in their incidents but because the incident is usually almost entirely a description of what a character says and does. There is little description of physiognomy beyond an occasional, vague reference to the character's beauty. There is virtually no description of background details. The scene is most often riveted on one or two characters intensely in the foreground, as if the Bible observed the ancient theatrical prescriptions against having more than two characters on stage at the same time. And the stage was usually bare. What gives a biblical character depth is not the narrative shadowing or perspective in a single scene. It is diffusing the character's characteristics over many scenes in many different settings. Strong biblical characters are always realistic *and* typical. See Hans Frei, *The Eclipse of Biblical Narrative* (New Haven: Yale UP, 1974).

Two:

The Gnostic Eve

Pheme Perkins

The Faces of Eve

As debates over creationism and evolution divide churches, parents, and school boards in the United States, the stories of Gen. 1-3 even figure in news reports and legal briefs. Students are often surprised to learn that "Adam and Eve" do not figure in the religious imagery of the rest of the Hebrew Bible. Only in the exegetical and story-telling traditions which begin with apocryphal Jewish works from the third century B.C.E. and continue into Christian and Rabbinic materials do we find "Adam and Eve" as the archetypes of human destiny.[1] Fundamentalist literalism often ignores the tensions within the biblical stories themselves. Yet, it is these very tensions which gave rise to divergent and even contradictory renderings of the story of Adam and Eve in the early centuries of the Common Era. [2] The descriptions of human origins in Gen. 1 and Gen. 2-3 stand in tension with each other. According to Gen. 1:26-27, God creates humankind, male and female, in the divine image to have dominion over the earth. The creation of humans takes place on the final day as the capstone of God's creative activity. God gives them all the plants of the earth for food. But according to Gen. 2:7, God shapes a man (Heb. *adam*) from the earth (Heb. *adamah*) before creating the plants of the garden. There is no reference to a divine image. Rather, God endows *Adam* with life by breathing in his face. God, placing *Adam* in the garden, tells him that he can eat of all the plants except the tree of knowledge of good and evil (Gen. 2:16-17). Only then does God decide that *Adam* needs a "helper" of his own kind. Creating the animals and asking *Adam* to name them reveals that they are not the necessary partner for *Adam* (Gen. 2:18-20). Only then does God create the woman from the side of *Adam*, who recognizes her as his true counterpart (2:21-23).

Schooled by a theological tradition that reduced the story of "Adam and Eve" to one of "original sin,"[3] contemporary interpreters pass over the divergent accounts of human creation and its relationship to the divine image. They presume that what is primarily of interest appears in the story of human disobedience to the divine command. J. P. Fokkelman's essay on Genesis in *The Literary Guide to the Bible* argues that the poetic lines in the narrative account can be harmonized in a single whole:

> It is no coincidence that the first lines of poetry in the Bible occur at 1:27 and 2:23. Together they show that man's essence is defined by two dialogical dimensions, his relation to his partner and his relation to God.... [H]umankind is only in its twofoldness the image of God, which in its turn incorporates the fundamental equality of man and woman. . . . The sin of man in chapter 3 evokes the fearful question, "Will the image of God be preserved in us?" It receives a positive answer through the thread of poetry in 5:1-2 (in 5:3 man, now called Adam, transmits the image of God to his offspring) and in 9:6.[4]

While this reading challenges the traditional assumptions that Gen. 1-3 asserts the patriarchal domination of male over female and explains the corruption of human nature by sinfulness, it is still much less probing than the interpretations of the early centuries C.E.

Philo of Alexandria applies the philosophical insights of first century C.E. Platonism to the Genesis stories.[5] Creation involves a double process. First, the perfect image of creation's order is present in the divine mind. The genus "human," which includes both male and female, is the crown of creation. The divine image of Gen. 1:27 is to be found in the reasoning faculties of the human soul (*De Opificio Mundi* 16, 35, 69-77).[6] Second, the heavenly and material worlds are molded. The molded Adam of Gen. 2:7 is a mortal being unlike its heavenly image. Without the divine inbreathing, it would have only the corruptible soul characteristic of animal creation (*Legum Allegoria* I. 31-32). Without this divine gift of reason, humans could not be held responsible for the virtue or vice of their actions.[7] Commanding humanity to till the garden of Eden, God showed that the role of the higher human was to cultivate virtues. The "molded human" was merely placed in the garden, where it fails to keep in mind or practice virtue and is cast out (*Leg. All.* I. 53-55).[8]

The dual creation of *Adam* will find a fruitful home in gnostic texts[9] as well as in speculative mythologies from the "underworld" of Middle Platonism.[10] But what of Eve? We have seen that the "image" of Gen. 1:27 is prior to any division into gender. It is "noetic, incorporeal, neither male nor female, incorruptible by nature" (*Opific.* 134). The "molded" human beings are mortal, divided into male and female. The female becomes the occasion for human sinfulness by awakening passions in the soul and turning it from the noetic world to the sensible.[11] Philo psychologizes the story of Adam and Eve. Adam represents the mind; Eve, sense-perception or the irrational soul (*Leg. All.* II. 24; *Cherubim* 58-60). Admittedly, material human beings require both. However, only the rational soul is directly created by God. Philo takes the "let us" of Gen. 1:26 to indicate that God turned over the creation of the fallible parts of the human being, both soul and body, to angelic or demiurgic powers. God cannot be held directly responsible for anything that departs from what is good (*Opific.* 75).[12] Elsewhere Philo appears to expound a doctrine of "two souls." The lower, the "life principle" of Gen. 2:7, has been created by angelic powers and is mortal (*Fuga* 67). Although it might appear that the rational soul of every human being is immortal while the lower soul perishes along with the material body, Philo appears to concur with Platonist tradition that only the soul of the wise or virtuous person attains immortality (*Questions on Genesis* III. 11).[13]

According to this exegetical tradition, Gen. 1-3 reveals the truth about the structure of God's creation. Gen. 2-3 are not about events among primordial anthropoids.[14] The story concerns the structure of human beings as such, particularly those intellectual capabilities and psychological attributes which govern their behavior. This interpretation is developed by Philo. When he refers to the allegorical meaning of a biblical text, the interpretation concerns the soul's progress in virtue.[15] Eve disappears as a character in a narrative and now represents the mortal soul or the faculty of sense perception through which passions are awakened that must be disciplined in order for the soul to make progress.[16]

We also find a mixture of interpretations in gnostic readings of Genesis. Like their Jewish counterparts, gnostic exegetes will focus upon small details, words or contradictions in the narrative as the evidence that a naive literal reading is impossible and interpretation is required. Gnostics characteristically invert the apparent values attached to persons or episodes by the narrative. To Jewish and Christian readers, their interpretations appear to foster revolt, especially against the god who created and governs the universe.[17] The exegetical traditions represented in gnostic works include both the hellenistic philosophical readings typified by Philo and narrative twists and word plays more typical of Palestinian haggadic traditions.[18] Scholars have begun to ask whether this tradition of exegesis simply represents the revolt of heretical sectarians, as both Jewish rabbis and Christian heresiologists would assert, or might have developed within Jewish circles at the turn of the millenium.[19] The process of "de-construction" in gnostic exegesis might in fact have been internal to Jewish hermeneutics. For example, rather than presume that the orthdox evaluation of rabbinic legends about Eve's daughter Norea as "naughty girl,"[20] and the gnostic treatments of Norea as "revolt," scholars might compare Norea to Jewish heroines like Aseneth in the romance, *Joseph and Aseneth.*[21]

Gnostic traditions typically treat Eve as a higher spiritual principle rather than a lower psychic function. Her role as "helper" lies in awakening Adam to his true nature as a creature of the spiritual world of light, not the material realm of darkness. Pagels asserts that a psychological understanding of the role of Eve is the key to all gnostic readings.[22] Because she treats gnostic writers as "true Christians,"[23] she downplays the Jewish exegetical origins of these traditions in favor of their attachment to slogans found in the Pauline letters which refer to the two Adams (1 Cor. 15; Rom. 5) and the incompatibility of spiritual and psychic or material perspectives (1 Cor. 2).[24] She comments:

Above all, what interests gnostic exegetes is psychodynamics (or maybe we should say "pneumato-psychodynamics"). They take as their primary theme the religious conviction that the capacity for spiritual insight is hidden, ordinarily unseen, within psychic and bodily experience. For gnostic interpreters, the story of Eve often becomes the story of that spiritual intelligence. Such interpreters love to tell, with many variations, how she emerges and separates from the psyche; how she encounters resistance, is attacked, and mistaken for what she is not. Finally, she attains the proper recognition from the psyche, she unites with him and becomes spiritually powerful and fruitful.[25]

Pagels castigates orthodox Christians for failing to acknowledge the spiritual Eve, or rather, the principle she represents, which is that the potential for spiritual consciousness is innate in human nature. Instead, they fix on Genesis as an historical tale about the first human couple involved in an act of moral choice.[26]

Presuming that the true meaning of Eve in gnostic texts is always a variant of psychological allegory simplifies the complexities of gnostic myth-making. The psychodynamic approach appears to emerge at a stage later than the initial formation of a narrative tradition in which Genesis stories are retold, expanded, commented upon and the like.[27] Walter Burkert notes that both ancient and modern interpreters tend to short circuit the problems of mythic speech by substituting some form of direct reference for the elements of the myth. It may be said to refer to phenomena of nature, to events of history, or to meta-empirical realities like psychodynamic processes.[28] Where Pagels gratuitously identifies as a story about Eve the gnostic tale in *Exegesis of the Soul* of the soul's departure from her heavenly home, her wanderings in subjection to male aggression and prostitution in the world, and her eventual rescue, repentance, and return,[29] a structuralist approach would look to the mythic variations on the tale of the young girl's tragedy. In its Greek variants this tale is often the prelude to the emergence of the hero.[30] Elements of this tale of separation, idyllic seclusion, rape or attempted rape by divine beings, danger of death, and rescue by the divine offspring do emerge in gnostic tales about Eve.

Taken as mythic tales which also comment upon inherited stories of Genesis, gnostic versions show the same divergent pluralism that one finds in Philo's accounts. The psycho-allegorical rendering does not even negate the inspired character of the other interpretations of the story.[31] Could there be a Jewish exegetical tradition which generated the understanding of Eve as a higher spiritual principle? The "image of God" in Adam was an "image" of the divine Logos. Associated with the Logos, we find in Philo traditions about the feminine principle of divine creativity, Wisdom. She can be described as the mother of all creation (*On the Drunkenness of Noah* 30). The Logos is sometimes described as proceeding from Wisdom and God (*Fuga* 109). Since this feminine principle is not consistently integrated into Philo's thought, he would appear to depend upon prior traditions.[32] Speculation in Wisdom literature itself held that the union of the soul and Wisdom was necessary for immortality (Wisd. 8:2, 9, 16-18). She is the basis for all true human knowledge or understanding. She calls out to humanity in the town square to learn understanding, truth, and righteousness from her, since she was present with God from before the creation (Prov. 8:1-31). She also has her antitype in the foolish, ignorant woman who calls out to the ignorant. If they follow her, they will wind up in Sheol (Prov. 9:13-18). Wisdom's antitype is the woman as seductive prostitute (4 Q184).[33]

The tradition has played out the wickedness of women as repeating Eve's seduction of Adam (eg. Sir. 25:13-26). [34] However, Eve can also serve as the beginning of wisdom and the archetype of all the wise women in Hebrew history. Meyers argues that this possibility is already established in the dynamics of the Genesis narrative[35]:

> the Eden tale sets forth a primal relationship between woman and the acquisition of whatever it is that the tree of knowledge provides. It portrays the female rather than the male as the first human being to utter language, which is the quintessential mark of human life. And it has the female respond to the overtures of an animal described as the "shrewdest of all the wild animals that Yahweh God had made" (3:1). The serpent at this point is not a

cursed creature. Hence the woman's dialogue with the prudent reptile should be considered not a blot on her character but a comment on her intellect. [36]

Gnostic writers identify the spiritual Eve with heavenly Wisdom. She is given the epithet *epinoia* (Gk. for "thought, purpose, inventiveness").

Gen. 2:24 follows Eve's emergence with an affirmation of the unity of man and wife in marriage. When spiritualized, this text becomes evidence for the oneness of the soul and Wisdom.[37] The image of a spiritual marriage between the rational soul and Wisdom as it appears in Philo attributes both feminine and masculine roles to Wisdom[38]:

> Let us then pay no heed to the discrepancy in the gender of the words, and say that the daughter of God, even Sophia, is not only masculine but father, sowing and begetting in souls aptness to learn, education, knowledge, wisdom, good and laudable actions. (*Fuga* 52)[39]

Since Philo takes Eve to represent the lower activities of the mortal soul associated with sense perception, he does not identify her with Wisdom. For him, spiritual marriage requires that the rational soul become a stranger to the body and all its cravings (*Leg. All.* I. 103; cf. Wisd. 9:15). If the soul makes the mistake of becoming one flesh with sense perception, the "wife" of Gen. 2:24, it has abandoned God. Instead, the soul should seek spiritual marriage with the Logos (*Special Laws* II. 30). The soul is transformed from being a "woman" into its true virginal state:

> when the souls become divinely inspired, from (being) woman they become virgins, throwing off the womanly corruptions which are (found) in sense perception and passion. Moreover, they follow after and pursue the genuine and unmated virgin, the veritable Sophia of God. And so rightly do such minds become widows and are orphaned of mortal things and acquire for themselves and have as husbands the Orthos Logos of Nature, with whom they live. (*Questions on Exodus* II. 3)[40]

Though Philo avoids associating Eve with Wisdom, the Wisdom traditions which he used need not have done so. Indeed, equating Eve with Wisdom and interpreting Gen. 2:24 as a reference to spiritual marriage fits as well with the text as Philo's claim that the soul must return to her virginal state from the corruption of its marriage with sense perception.[41] Thus, there is nothing peculiarly "gnostic" in an exegetical tradition which understands Eve to be a principle of Wisdom and spiritual enlightenment for humanity. This view may go back to the origins of the Genesis material itself. It certainly fits into the speculation about divine Wisdom which characterized hellenistic Judaism in the Greco-Roman period.[42]

Challenging Moses

Philo's negative appraisal of Eve in Gen. 2:24 presumes that "one flesh" refers to identification with the corruptible material body or its animating principles. We have seen that Philo dissociated God from the creation of the lower human being by turning the process over to lesser powers. An alternative solution would deny that "flesh" means the human body. The rendering of Gen. 2:21-24 in the gnostic *Apocryphon of John* reflects this option:

> And he [= the Creator] brought a part of his power out of him. And he made another creature in the form of a woman according to the likeness of the *Epinoia* which appeared to him. And he brought the part which he had taken from the power of the man into the female creature, and not as Moses said, 'his rib bone.' And he [= Adam] saw the woman beside him. And in that moment the luminous *Epinoia* appeared, and she lifted the veil which lay over his mind. And he became sober from the drunkenness of darkness. And he recognized his counter-image, and he said, 'This is indeed bone of my bones and flesh of my flesh.' Therefore the man will leave his father and mother and he will cleave to his wife and they will both become one flesh. (CG II. 22,34-23,14)[43]

Scholars often take the expression "not as Moses said" to be evidence for the spirit of revolt in gnostic hermeneutics. The author of *Apocry. Jn.* certainly understands the phrase as one of opposition. A hostile Pharisee challenges John, the son of Zebedee, to defend following a teacher who turned his disciples away from ancestral tradition (CG. II 1,11-17). However, the traditional material in Philo's Genesis interpretation provides evidence of another possibility, anti-anthropomorphic exegesis. Eve is a spiritual principle, not a "rib-bone."

Tobin finds a common pattern in the passages which are derived from this tradition:

1) Reference to the scriptural text.
2) Rejection of the apparent anthropomorphism.
3) Non-anthropomorphic interpretation using philosophical concepts.[44]

The claim that *Adam* is in the image of God (*Opif.* 69) and the story of Adam naming the animals (*Opif.* 149-50) require reinterpretation. In Philo's examples, the reinterpretation involves assertions about what is fitting or suitable to God. They do not engage in detailed exegesis of the wording of the text. Rather, philosophical concepts are brought forward to provide an acceptable context for understanding the passage in question.[45] This tradition of interpretation reflects the earliest type exegetical material found in Philo.[46] Educated Jews in the hellenistic milieu of Alexandria might hold out against cultural absorption if they could show that their heritage contained the deeper truths of philosophy even where it appeared most vulnerable. The hellenistic Jewish exegetes responsible for this tradition as we find it in Aristobulus and Philo drew on the techniques used by Stoic allegorizing of Homer. However, they avoid speaking of their interpretation as allegory and may have drawn their Platonic material from circles opposed to Stoic philosophy.[47]

Tobin postulates a philosophical school tradition linked to Alexandrian synagogues in which written interpretations of Scripture were formulated and preserved. He does not think that the anti-anthropomorphic collections developed as a response to hostile challenges from outsiders.[48] Our two best gnostic examples suggest otherwise. *Apocry. Jn.* contains a series of four "not as Moses said" sections which have been used by the author as part of the frame- work of revelation dialogue.[49] Each involves a possible anthropo- morphism resulting from failure to recognize that Genesis is referring to the activity of Wisdom or her offspring, *Epinoia*, the spiritual Eve:

> 1) "moving to and fro" (Gen. 1:2) does not refer to moving over waters but to Wisdom's repentance when her offspring, the creator of the material world, arrogantly claims to be the only, true god (CG II. 13,17-23);
>
> 2) it was not the serpent (Gen. 3:1-5) who taught Adam and Eve to eat of the tree of knowledge but the luminous *Epinoia* (CG II. 22,10-18);
>
> 3) "forgetfulness" is not God putting *Adam* to sleep (Gen. 2:21) but a lack of perception as is proved by Isa. 6:10, which is corrected by *Epinoia*, who hides inside *Adam* (CG II 22,22- 29);
>
> 4) and Adam's co-image, Eve, is not made from a rib but from the spiritual power of the Mother formed in the image of *Epinoia* (CG II. 22,29-23,4).

Another fragment of this tradition appears in the discussion of the Tree of Knowledge (Gk. *gnosis*) in *On the Origin of the World* (CG II. 110,29-111,1). Eating from the tree causes Adam to love his true co-image as well as condemn alien likenesses. The author claims this interpretation is found in the *Sacred Book*. Its point appears to be that Adam falls in love with the spiritual Eve rather than the carnal or material woman. Becoming aware of his "nakedness" im- plies recognition of the spiritual condition in which he had existed prior to that moment.[50] The union of Adam and Eve is not repre- sented in the sexual intercourse of men and women.[51]

Though not a direct attack on Genesis as such, this tradition presumes that the revelation offered by Genesis requires external correction. Use of anthropomorphisms as a direct attack upon the arrogant claims of the creator appears in a polemical work, *Testimony of Truth*. Its author attacks both orthodox Christians and other gnostic sects.[52] However, the section on the paradise story includes a midrash on the serpent as wiser than all other animals which has been derived from Jewish aggadah.[53] After recounting the story of Adam and Eve eating from the tree (CG IX. 45,23-47,14), the author attacks the credibility of the god depicted in the narrative (47,14-50,7).[54] The biblical statement that Adam is cast out of paradise is a resolution taken by the creator (47,10-11).[55] The objections are punctuated with the question, "What sort is this god?" A god who:

1) envies Adam and tries to keep him from eating the tree of knowledge (47,15-17) [56] or gaining immortality (47,24-30);
2) demonstrates his ignorance by having to ask where Adam is (47,18-23);[57]
3) brings the sins of the parents on the children (Exod. 20:5; 47,4-8);
4) and hardens peoples' hearts and blinds their mind (48:8-13).

What is worse, these sayings are directed by this god to persons who are his followers. They should be able to see that such a one is not worthy of worship, but instead they read the Old Testament blindly (48,2-4, 13-14). Returning to the theme of the serpent, the author apparently seeks to show that elsewhere in the same scripture the serpent is a sign of salvation. Aaron's rod is stronger than that of the Egyptian magicians (Exod. 7:8-12; CG II. 48,21-26). Like Christ, the bronze serpent raised up by Moses in the wilderness saved those who gazed upon it (Num. 21). Philo, by contrast, distinguishes the serpent of Eden from the sign of salvation in Numbers. For him, the serpent in the Eden story represents pleasure, while that of Numbers represents moderation or self-control (Gk. *sophrosune*). Combination of the two serpent passages was probably an exegetical commonplace. *Testim. Truth* draws on a tradition which has been shaped to turn the biblical witness against itself. As such, it serves the author's polemical goal, to demonstrate the absurdity of an orthodox Christianity which remains as subservient to the creator as those who blindly follow Moses.[58]

The Victim Conquers

Although traditional readings of Gen. 1-3 identify Eve with weaker, unstable powers which must be subordinated to the authority of a superior lest they become harmful rather than helpful, we have seen that some exegetes developed a counterpoint to this depiction. The idea that god would keep knowledge and immortality from the *Adam* created in the divine image was intolerable. Only malice and envy, both unworthy of a divine being, could account for such behavior. Philosophical reflection showed humans to be an uneasy mixture of imperfect mortality, grounded in the material nature they share with animals, and the rational soul which is capable of apprehending what is divine and eternal. The instability of rational insight and moral purpose is a function of this unhappy union. An unpredictable cosmos or fate might overwhelm human action as in the tragic poets. An irrational passion may bring down the best human beings.[59] For Jews, the biblical accounts seemed to implicate God in this sorry state of affairs, at once commanding obedience and ordering creation so that compliance was obedience to the will of a superior power, not reasoned choice of the good.[60] Philo attempts to reconcile the conflict by attributing those characteristics of God which are expressions of divine power and will— mercy, zeal, vengeance, imperiousness—to lesser powers which assist God in the creation and governing of the material world.[61]

Evidence of a dual creation of Adam, spiritual and psychic/ material, was found in Gen. 1-2. Anti-anthropomorphic exegesis sought to mitigate offending characterizations of God in biblical narrative. Some interpreters point to the Tree of Knowledge as a source of enlightenment. Perhaps activating a dormant link to archaic myths of the wise goddess, Eve likewise has a dual identity. The spiritual Eve manifests the power of Sophia. In that capacity, she is Adam's helper and co-image. Those who mistake the fleshly images of Adam and Eve for reality and think that the divine commandments to marry and propogate refer to physical intercourse and birth rather than the production of virtue through union with wisdom will perish. As myths about Satan and evil angels entered Jewish tradition in the post-exilic period, responsibility for destroying God's creation was attributed to demonic powers. *Vit. Ad. Eve*, which depicts Eve as weaker and more easily subject to deceit that Adam, insists that Satan is the villain. He is thrown out of heaven for refusal to obey God's command to worship *Adam*, the divine image (*Vit. Ad. Eve* 13-14). Satan claimed that rather than obey he would set himself up on a throne like God's (*Vit. Ad. Eve* 15). This self-exaltation is characteristic of Wisdom's offspring, the lower creator god in gnostic myths. The banished angel attacks Eve, first through the serpent (*Apocalypse of Moses* 15-21) and then disguised as an angel of light when she and Adam seek to do penance (*Vit. Ad. Eve* 9-10).

In such apocalyptic traditions, the promise of a return to Paradise is held out to humanity after Satan's eventual defeat. The obedient, righteous ones will attain the glory they had lost and eat from the tree of Immortality (*Vit. Ad. Eve* 29; *Apoc. Moses* 28). The sword guarding the tree will be taken away and the faithful will trample on the evil spirits (*Testament of Levi* 18,2). Gnostic interpreters, who have endowed the creator of the material world with the envy and hostility of Satan, frequently invoke this tradition. A fragmentary version of the Gen. 3 story associates the trampling of demons and removal of the sword with the enlightenment attained by the true Adam and Eve upon eating the tree, which is associated with the spiritual Eve (*Melchizedek* 9,24-10,28).[62] Fragmentary sentences in the context suggest that the treatise contrasted the true Adam and Eve with those called males and females in nature (CG IX. 9,26-10,1). The latter are creatures who have been led astray by angels who dwell on earth, so that they are subject to imprisonment and death (15,22-25).[63]

A pervasive anthropological dualism is the price of salvation. This phenomenon is nowhere more evident than in the gnostic remythologizing of Jewish legends about the fallen angels and the daughters of men (Gen. 6:1-4). This story attracted even more attention from Jewish apocalyptic writers than the sin of Adam and Eve.[64] Gnostic mythology brings the two mythemes together. When the evil creator or his powers see Eve, they attempt to rape her. The luminous *Epinoia* escapes by hiding in a Tree, which happens to be the Tree of Knowledge, leaving behind a carnal image of herself:

> Then the authorities came to their Adam. And when they saw his female counterpart speaking with him, they became agitated with great agitation; and they became enamoured of her. They said to one another, "Come, let us sow our seed in her," and they pursued her. And she laughed at them for their witlessness and their blindness; and in their clutches, she became a tree, and left before them her shadowy reflection resembling herself; and they defiled [it] foully. — They defiled the stamp of her voice, so that by the form they had modelled, together with [their] (own) image, they made themselves liable to condemnation. Then the female spiritual principle came in the snake, the instructor; and taught [them] saying, "What did he [say to] you (pl.)? Was it, 'From every tree in the garden shall you (sg.) eat; — yet from [the tree] of knowing evil and good do not eat'?" (*Hyp. Arch.* CG II. 89,17-90,2)[65]

The point of the ruse in gnostic mythology is to ensure that the seed born by the spiritual Eve is not contaminated by the lustful archons. In a version which Epiphanius attributes to the Archontic sect, the devil unites with Eve begetting Cain and Abel. Seth, the ancestor of the gnostics, derives from the union of Adam and Eve in which the seed was provided by angels. Consequently, Seth never served the creator god (*Panarion* 40.5,3-4; 40.7,1-3).[66]

An early version (ca. 2nd cent. B.C.E.) of the Jewish legend about the Watchers and the daughters of men is found in *1 Enoch* 6-8. Additional Aramaic fragments of this legend were found at Qumran, leading some scholars to conclude that Gen. 6:1-4 is actually an allusion to a fuller version of the myth like that found in these sources.[67] Genesis omits a fundamental element in the myth, that the Watchers taught the women various arts necessary to salvation, since its author is only interested in providing another example of sin as a prelude to the flood. The real focus of the myth was on the divine gift of knowledge to humanity.[68] The ambiguity of such knowledge was expressed in Greek myths about Prometheus and Pandora, which have also colored some of the gnostic versions of this story where Pandora is connected with the earthly Eve.[69] Genesis notes that city-building and the arts of music and metallurgy, working bronze and iron (necessary for tools and weapons) were taught by offspring of Cain (Gen. 4:17-22).

The sequence of mythemes in *1 Enoch* is followed almost exactly in the gnostic account of the archons and the daughters of men in *Apocry. Jn.* (CG II. 29,16- 30,10):[70]

> 1) attracted by the beauty of the women, the fallen angels desire offspring (*1 Enoch* 6,1-2; *Apocry. Jn.* CG II. 29,19-20);
> 2) the chief angel binds the others in a solemn oath to carry out the crime against the women (*1 Enoch* 6,3-8; *Apocry. Jn.* CG II. 29,16, 21-23);
> 3) mating with human women, the fallen angels are responsible for the evils experienced by humanity: (a) promiscuous sex (*1 Enoch* 7,1; *Apocry. Jn.* CG II. 29,23-29; 30,7-9);[71] (b) the evils of violence, bloodshed and war; and (c) dubious arts like magic and astrology as well as those which generate other evils like make-up (seduction), use of gold and silver (wealth), and metallurgy (war) (*1 Enoch* 7,2-8,4; *Apocry. Jn.* CG II. 29,30-30,3).

Not surprisingly the anti-anthropomorphic tradition influenced some variants of this myth. Spiritual beings like angels, even fallen ones, could not really have had intercourse with human women. Since popular tradition had it that an adulteress who thought of her lover while having sex with her husband would produce children who looked like the lover, the explanation was easy. The women, who had seen the beauty of the angels, lusted for them while actually sleeping with their own mates. This version appears in *Testament of Reuben* 5:6-7. It shifts the guilt of lust back onto the women,[72] a change which the misogynist warning about all the evils that befall a man who becomes subject to a woman in *Test. Reuben* intensifies. Palestinian rabbinic tradition blames the women, said to be descendents of Cain, for painting themselves like prostitutes and exposing their genitals in order to seduce the angels (*Pirke Rabbi*

Eliezer 22).[73] Philo, who notes that the giants might also be associated with Greek mythology, seeks to avoid any mythological overtones to the tradition (*Giants* II. 7, 58; *Questions on Genesis* 92). He proposes that the "angels" are really demonic spirits or souls that inhabit the air and sometimes find their way into human bodies. The bodies taken on by the souls are the "daughters" referred to in the text. His view is repeated by Origen (*Contra Celsum* 152).[74]

Apocry. Jn. had the angels change into the likeness of the women's husbands, though the reason is unclear. The author may have known a version that included this anti-anthropomorphic detail. But since the author also holds that the beastly shape of the archons makes them less exalted than humankind, the transformation would seem to be a necessary ruse on their part. After the creator attacks Eve in order to beget Cain and Abel, he gives them the theophoric names Elohim and Yahweh in order to conceal their formless nature. Elohim has a bear face, Yahweh that of a cat (*Apocry. Jn.* CG II. 24,8-25).[75] In a somewhat puzzling twist, the creator then implants the sexual desire in Eve which leads to the emergence of a generation endowed with the creator's counterfeit Spirit (*Apocry. Jn.* CG II. 24,28-31). But Adam then catches sight of his real partner, the spiritual Eve. Through her agency he begets an image of the heavenly Man, Seth (CG II. 24,35-25,7). According to *Apocry. Jn.* the ideal human being, he who is possessed of the divine Spirit and not the counterfeit, has abandoned passions as far as possible for one living in the flesh. The gnostic epithet "immovable race" (*Apocry. Jn.* CG II. 25,20-23) refers to this state:[76]

> Those upon whom the Spirit of life will descend and exist with the power in them will be saved and they will become perfect and be worthy of the greatnesses and be purified in that place from all wickedness and attention to evil. Then they attend to nothing except incorruptibility alone, since from here on they are concerned with it, without anger or envy or jealousy or desire and greed for everything. They are held by none of these things, except only the substance (Gk. *hypostasis*) of the flesh, which they carry around while they wait for the time when they will be visited by the Receivers. Now persons of this sort are worthy of incorruptible,

eternal life and the calling, since they endure everything and bear everything, so that they might complete the good and inherit eternal life. (*Apocry. Jn.* CG II. 25,23-26,7)[77]

The idea that passionlessness is a sign that the soul has attained wisdom and with it immortality was common in philosophical circles. It is the consequence of the soul's marriage with Wisdom or the Logos in Philo. The mythic structure of *Apocry. Jn.* assigns the fundamental passions (pleasure, desire, grief, and fear) to the four principal demons engaged in shaping the material Adam (CG II. 18,14-31).[78]

The version of the archons' attack on the spiritual Eve in *Orig. World* (CG II. 116,13-19) involves recognition that Adam and Eve possess "life," the divine Spirit. By defiling Eve with their seed they hope to make it impossible for her to ascend to her light. Her offspring will be forced to serve the archons. Escaping into the Tree, she leaves behind a shadowy likeness (117,1-4). The "sons" born of this image constitute a "mixed seed" subject to the Fate which governs the world (117,18-23). "Eve" had already given birth to the seven planetary demons responsible for Fate (101,24-25). Sliding back and forth between the spiritual and carnal Eve, *Orig. World* presents an image of Eve who is both raped by the archons and escapes their clutches by deceiving them.[79] This paradoxical overlap of the defiled and heavenly Eve is played out in the "knowledge" appropriate to each. The virginal Eve is full of knowledge; the defiled, of guile. She incorporates the ambiguities of goddess figures like Aphrodite as well as the several faces of Eve in Jewish and gnostic Genesis exegesis.[80] Eros moves the lower Providence associated with the creator to spill her "light"—that is, blood—on the earth (*Orig. World* 108,2-31). Elaborate word-plays on *Adam* involve both semitic etymologies (*'adam, 'adama* = "earth", *dam* = "blood") and Greek (*'adamas* = "strong iron, steel").[81] Unable to unite with the angelic being, who despises her darkness, this Providence gives birth to the Primordial Adam by casting her blood (= an aborted fetus) on the earth. A similar process is responsible for the birth of the first Eve. Wisdom casts a drop of light on the waters where it fashions itself into the female shape, "Eve of life, i.e. the instructor of life" (CG II 113,22-34). When the archons spill their seed in the navel of the earth, the seven archons produce a material Adam corresponding to the image of the heavenly one (CG II 114,27-32).[82] Stroumsa suggests that the mythologizing of "lust" and the necessity of seduction evident in this reformulation of the gnostic traditions about the origins of Adam and Eve is a step in the direction of Manichaean myths where the archons must be seduced to spill their seed so that the light it contains can be restored to the heavenly world. All living creatures on the earth arise from the semen/blood spilled by the powers when they become enamoured of the heavenly messenger, who appears as a male to females and a female to males.[83]

Manichaean traditions resolve the ambiguity attached to the Eve figure by enlisting her on the side of the demonic powers. According to the Turfan fragments, she seduces Adam because the demonic creator, Saklon, has inspired lust in her. But she is unwilling to nurse the new born child (= Seth?), and Saklon seeks to kill him. In another tradition, the demon, Ashaqlun (= Sakla), son of the King of darkness, united with his consort Namrael (= Nabroel),[84] to give birth to Adam and Eve. Eve is said to commit incest with both her father and her son Cain. She joins the chief archon in plotting against Adam's son who is a stranger (Gk. *allogenes*) to the evil powers by not nursing him. When the demon destroys the cows and fruit that Adam proposed to use as a substitute, Adam draws magical circles around the child and prays for divine assistance. A milk-producing lotus tree springs up. Eventually, the son, a Manichaean equivalent of Seth, persuades his father to break the bonds of lust, leave Eve and go east to paradise, where Adam dies. Not surprisingly, Eve, Cain, and the latter's wife, "Daughter-of-Corruption," perish in Hades.[85] Unlike its gnostic predecessors, Manichaean mythologizing retains no exegetical links to the Hebrew Bible. Eve is not a divine creation, a bearer of knowledge or Adam's co-image and helper. Instead, she is the complete embodiment of the demonic lust which separates men from the divine and traps them in the material world. Instead of conquering the demons through a combination of spiritual Wisdom, which they cannot grasp, and deceit, which turns their lust against them, the Manichaean Eve has joined the enemy!

No Male and Female

The demonic Eve of Manichaean mythology has developed from Jewish and gnostic speculation about the carnal Eve. This Eve has no spiritual counterpart in the divine world. Adam must abandon her if he is to return to the divine world. Rejection of the feminine is a common gnostic exhortation.[86] The "feminine" implies sexuality and birth, which stand as a code for humanity's subjection to death. The Savior instructs the disciples to "pray in the place where there is no woman" (*Dialogue of the Savior* CG III. 144, 15-23). Mary cannot enter the Kingdom unless she becomes like Jesus' male disciples (*Gospel of Thomas* Log. 114).[87] In this tradition, masculinity implies being a "living Spirit." Sexual desire, birth, and death are all the result of the division of the primordial Adam into male and female. This division is subsequent to the creation of the heavenly Adam in Gen. 1:27. At the purely narrative level of Jewish haggadah, Eve's separation from Adam or from her angelic guardians left her vulnerable to the assaults of Satan (*Vit. Ad. Eve* 33; and *Apoc. Moses* 15, where the male and female creatures were separated in Paradise). In the tradition of a dual creation of Adam, the heavenly image of the Logos is not gendered. Rather the earthly, mortal human is gendered as well as divided into soul and body, composite beings who are subject to dissolution and death. Thus, the tradition employed in Philo's psychological allegory understands the "male and female" of Gen. 1:27 to mean "neither male nor female." This reading is the most common understanding of the passage.[88]

We have seen that the tradition of a spiritual marriage of the soul with Wisdom or with the Logos restored its proper masculinity by wiping out the corruption which comes with desire. Valentinian tradition included a ritual celebration of the "marriage chamber" which restored the soul to unity with its heavenly counterpart. Unlike the unity between Adam and Eve which was broken, this new state is permanent (*Gospel of Philip* CG II. 68,22-26; 70,5-12).[89] Some scholars presume that the unity of the bridal chamber is a return to a primordial androgynous state in which Adam and Eve, a spirit-endowed soul, are reunited.[90] However, the unique and indissoluble syzygy is that of Christ and the Holy Spirit (*Gos. Phil.* CG II. 69,1-10).[91] *Gos. Phil.* takes the tradition that Eve begot Cain through intercourse with the serpent to show that intercourse between beings unlike one another is adultery (CG II. 61,4-12). Unless the believer becomes Spirit, thought or light, he or she cannot participate in the spiritual world (*Gos. Phil.* CG II. 78,25-79,13). The Spirit, not Eve, is Adam's true companion.[92]

Since *Gos. Phil.* is familiar with the gnosticized Jewish traditions about Eve,[93] the distinction that it makes between the earlier union of Adam and Eve, which did not involve the "bridal chamber," and the union of the perfect with their heavenly counterparts, suggests a correction of that tradition. There is no "spiritual Eve" because Eve only emerges with the division of the human that is required for begetting and coming into being in the material world. The *Apocalypse of Adam* describes Adam and Eve as going about in the glory which Eve had seen:

> When God created me out of the earth along with Eve your mother, I went about with her in a glory which she had seen in the aeon from which we had come forth. She taught me a word of knowledge of the eternal God. And we resembled the great angels, for we were higher than the god who had created us and the powers with him, whom we did not know. (CG V. 64,5-19)[94]

The ruler of the powers divides Adam and Eve into two aeons, their glory and knowledge enters the seed of the gnostic race, and they become acquainted with "dead things," slaves to the creator god. Heavenly angels reveal the existence of this seed to Adam in a dream. To counter that revelation, the creator claims to be the one who breathed life into Adam and Eve. After begetting a son with Eve, the creator awakens sexual desire in the couple and they are subject to death (CG V. 64,20- 67,14). Although contemporary scholars have often spoken of this text as evidence that Gen. 1:27 was understood as an androgynous Adam-Eve,[95] the text only emphasizes Eve's Wisdom-like role as the revealer of heavenly knowledge.

The unity envisaged by most gnostic texts is not some form of psychological or social male/female equality but an androgyny that is primarily "male." We have seen Philo refer to Wisdom's father-like role in her union with the soul. According to Hipplytus, the Naasenes saw Attis as the perfect male-female (Gk. *'arsenothelus*) but held that the elect were to become perfectly male (*Refutation* 5.7.15; 5.8.44). In *Nat. Arch.* the vain, boastful archons appear as androgynous males, who are opposed at every turn by the voice of the virginal Spirit from above. Norea, Seth's sister, who is the mother of the gnostic race, has two epithets: (a) virgin, begotten for the assistance of many generations; and (b) virgin whom the forces did not defile. In this text, the virgin Wisdom figure unmasks the pretensions of the archons. As McGuire points out, the sexual symbolism does not refer to human male and female devotees, but fuctions as part of the logic of revolt which asks the reader to identify with the undefiled Norea and her offspring by opposing the claims of the powers.[96]

Though gnostic readings of Genesis point to a much richer tradition of depicting Eve than can be found in the Hebrew Bible, they only intensify the ambiguity of her status. Most ancient readers would be perplexed by Fokkelman's affirmation that "humankind is only in its twofoldness the image of God" as well as the claim that Genesis presents a fundamental equality of man and woman. Nor will appeals to use of the androgyne myth as the key to Gen. 1:27 provide support for such modern doctrines. As we have seen, "no male and female" means renouncing the works of femininity. As MacDonald rightly concludes, "Contrary to the opinion of many interpreters, the androgyne myth is not antiquity's answer to androcentrism; it is but one manifestation of it."[97] What we can learn from this quest for the gnostic Eve is that the text belongs to the material/psychic world in which no meanings are permanently

fixed. Whether as Wisdom begetting virtues or as the "violated seductress," like Eve, she is "Mother of the Living."

Notes

Following editorial practise for Greek texts, a roman numeral sig-
nifying book or volume is followed by "chapter numbers." Other texts are
divided simply into sections. In references to Nag Hammadi texts, however, roman numerals indicate the codex number in which a tractate
occurs; the next arabic number is the page; and subsequent arabic numbers indicate the lines on the page.

[1] See C. Meyers, *Discovering Eve: Ancient Israelite Women in Context* (New York: Oxford UP, 1988), 3-23. Meyers uses socio-archaeologi-
cal analysis of the iron-age settlement in Israel to argue that Gen. 2-3 must
be interpreted from the perspective of villages organized around the household rather than from that of a hierarchical, militant and partriarchal
society. "Eve" is the co-equal, helper, whose fertility and labor are necessary to survival of the people, not the wife/mother/daughter subordinated to male aggression.

[2] See Elaine Pagels, *Adam, Eve and the Serpent* (New York: Random
House, 1988); idem, "Adam and Eve, Christ and the Church: A Survey
of Second Century Controversies Concerning Marriage," *The New Tes-
tament and Gnosis: Essays in Honour of Robert McL. Wilson*, ed. A.H.B.
Logan and A.J.M. Wedderburn (Edinburgh: T. & T. Clark, 1983), 146-
75; idem, "Exegesis and Exposition of the Genesis Creation Accounts in
Selected Texts from Nag Hammadi," *Nag Hammadi, Gnosticism, and Early
Christianity*, ed. Charles W. Hedrick and Robert Hodgson, Jr. (Peabody,
MA: Hendrickson, 1986), 257-85; idem, "Pursuing the Spiritual Eve:
Imagery and Hermeneutics in the *Hypostasis of the Archons* and the *Gos-
pel of Philip*," *Images of the Feminine in Gnosticism*, ed. Karen L. King (Phila-
delphia: Fortress, 1988), 187-206; idem, "Adam, Eve and the Serpent in
Genesis 1-3," *Images of the Feminine*, 412-23; and Gedaliahu A. G.
Stroumsa, *Another Seed: Studies in Gnostic Mythology*, Nag Hammadi Stud-
ies 24 (Leiden: E. J. Brill, 1984), 17-70.

[3] Largely the result of Augustine's influence in the theological controversies of the 4th and early 5th cents. C.E. (see Pagels, *Adam, Eve*, 98-
150).

⁴ J.P. Fokkelman, "Genesis," *The Literary Guide to the Bible*, ed. Robert Alter and Frank Kermode (Cambridge: Harvard UP, 1987), 44ff. Fokkelman uses the poetic bits as keys to a structuralist analysis of the composition of Genesis. He avoids the source-critical solution, which attributed the two accounts to different traditions which were ineptly combined at some later point. Apparent contradictions in Gnostic texts initially generated similar attempts at source criticism. Scholars who acknowledge the essentially mythic character of the gnostic materials accept repetition and even apparent contradictions as part of the overall pattern of the text. Cf. the discussion of earlier source theories in Michel Tardieu, *Trois Mythes Gnostiques: Adam, Éros et les animaux d'Égypte dans un écrit de Nag Hammadi (II,5)* (Paris: Études Augustiniennes, 1974), 21, 30-33.

⁵See Thomas Tobin, *The Creation of Man: Philo and the History of Interpretation*, Catholic Biblical Association Monograph Series 14 (Washington: Catholic Biblical Association, 1983).

⁶See John Dillon, *The Middle Platonists* (London: Duckworth, 1977), 158-60.

⁷Pagels notes that for the first three centuries of the Common Era, Christian commentators treat Gen. 1-3 as a tale about human free will and the acquisition of virtue ("Genesis 1-3," 416). However, the role of free will in determining moral responsibility is balanced by Philo's understanding of the pervasive operation of the Word as a manifestation of divine Providence. This tension is characteristic of all Platonists in the period (see Dillon, *Middle Platonists*, 166-68).

⁸ Philo takes a different approach to this question in *Questions on Genesis* I.8. There the molded *Adam* is placed in Paradise, not the one made in God's image (see Tobin, *Creation*, 108-34, 172-74).

⁹ Dennis R. MacDonald, *There Is No Male and Female: The Fate of a Dominical Saying in Paul and Gnosticism*, Harvard Dissertations in Religion 20 (Philadelphia: Fortress, 1987), 30.

¹⁰ E.g. *Poimandres, Corpus Hermeticum* I. 12-15; likewise Dillon, *Middle Platonists*, 176.

¹¹ MacDonald, *No Male and Female*, 27.

¹² Dillon (*Middle Platonists*, 175) notes the Pythagorean origins of this account of the soul. Strobaeus preserves a passage of *Haustafel* in which the father represents the rational power; the mother, desire; and the young son, spiritedness (Gk. *thymos*). The son sometimes obeys the father, sometimes the mother.

[13] Dillon, *Middle Platonists*, 177-78.

[14] Philo would find the debates among paleo-anthropologists over whether or not a particular set of hominoid remains represents the "Eve," ancestress of *homosapiens*, quite beside the point.

[15] The goal of the life of virtue is the vision of God attained by the few who become wise. See Tobin, *Creation*, 34, 135-47.

[16] Tobin, *Creation*, 109 n. 42. *Questions of Genesis* I.24 makes it clear that Philo knows several other interpretations of the creation of woman. He does not attempt to reconcile the disparate views attached to the narrative. Eve is only integrated into his larger understanding of *Genesis* through allegorical interpretation.

[17] See Birger Pearson, "Jewish Sources in Gnostic Literature," *Jewish Writing of the Second Temple Period, Compendia Rerum Iudaicarum Ad Novum Testamentum*, Section Two, ed. Michael Stone (Assen: Van Gorcum and Philadelphia: Fortress, 1984), 441ff.

[18] Pearson, "Jewish Sources," 453-57; Stroumsa, *Another Seed* 19-28.

[19] Christian gnostic teachers would employ polemic against the "Jewish creator god" to attack orthodox Christians as the latter came to identify their cause with support for the creator god of Moses. Pearson comments, "There is some irony, too, in the fact that Christianity, which had made its own moves away from its Jewish roots, was compelled to reaffirm the basic pro-cosmicism inherent in Jewish monotheism," (Pearson, "Jewish Sources," 444-45).

[20] B. Pearson offers this reading in "The Figure of Norea in Gnostic Literature," *Proceedings of the International Colloquium on Gnosticism, Stockholm, August 20-25, 1973*, ed. Geo Widengren (Stockholm: Almqvist & Wiksell and Leiden: E. J. Brill, 1977), 143-52.

[21] So Ross Kraemer, "A Response to Virginity and Subversion," *Images of the Feminine*, 262ff.

[22] Pagels, "Genesis 103," *Images of the Feminine*, 414-15.

[23] Pagels consistently uses the explicitly Christian gnostic Valentinian teacher of the second century C.E. as the framework for understanding gnostic exegesis. The detailed treatment of Philo's exegesis (e.g. Tobin, *Creation*) has shown that the author may incorporate divergent traditions and principles into the exposition of a particular text. Systematic principles only apply to those sections in which an author explicitly works out a new level of interpretation.

[24] Pagels, "Pursuing the Spiritual Eve," 191-99.

[25] Pagels, "Genesis 1-3," 414ff.

[26] Pagels, "Genesis 1-3," 415ff.

[27] See Stroumsa, *Another Seed*, 1-4.

[28] Walter Burkert, *Structure and History in Greek Mythology and Ritual* (Berkeley: U of California P, 1979), 1-4.

[29] Pagels, "Spiritual Eve," 190. Other commentators have recognized the affinity between this allegorical story of the soul and the tradition of Greek novels as well as the variations on the tales of the separated lovers found in Jewish writings like *Joseph and Aseneth* and *Tobit* (see Maddalena Scopello, *L'Exégèse de l'Âme. Nag Hammadi Codex II,6*, Nag Hammadi Studies XXV [Leiden: E. J. Brill, 1985] 45-48).

[30] Burkert (*Greek Mythology*, 6-7) proposes a sequence based on the following five functions: (1) leaving home the girl is separated from childhood and family; (2) idyll of seclusion; (3) rape, the girl is violated and impregnated by a god; (4) tribulation, she is severely punished and threatened with death by parents or relatives; and (5) rescue, having given birth to a boy the mother is saved from death as her son takes over the power to which he is destined.

[31] Tobin, *Creation*, 162-67.

[32] Dillon, *Middle Platonists*, 163-65.

[33] See the wisdom poem warning her of dangers found at Qumran, 4Q184 ("The Seductress" in G. Vermes, *The Dead Sea Scrolls in English*, 3rd ed. [Baltimore: Penguin, 1987] 240ff).

[34] Meyers, *Discovering Eve*, 72-73.

[35] Perhaps this image of Eve has been shaped by Ancient Near Eastern stories of the Wisdom goddess (Meyers, *Discovering Eve*, 91).

[36] Meyers, *Discovering Eve*, 91ff.

[37] Pagels, "Pursuing the Spiritual Eve," 190.

[38] See Richard A Horsley, "Spiritual Marriage with Sophia," *Vigiliae Christianae* 33 (1979): 2-40.

[39] Also *Migration of Abraham*, sec. 99-102; quoted from Horsley, "Spiritual Marriage," 35.

[40] Horsley, "Spiritual Marriage," 37.

[41] The imagery of recovered virginity plays a major role in the gnostic *Exeg. Soul*. The fallen soul is compared to a womb turned inside out, which must be restored as part of the process of salvation (CG II. 131, 13-123,1; translated in James M. Robinson, ed., *The Nag Hammadi Library in English*, 3rd ed. [San Francisco: Harper & Row, 1988], 194; see Scopello, *L'Exégèse de l'Âme*, 72-75). The operation is associated with a baptismal ritual. It is probably thought to be similar to circumcision and

to purify the individual by destroying fleshly pleasures (so Scopello, *L'Exégèse de l'Âme*, 74).

[42] See M. Gilbert, "Wisdom Literature," *Jewish Writings*, 283-311.

[43] Translated by F. Wisse in *Nag Hammadi Library in English*, 118.

[44] Tobin, *Creation*, 37.

[45] Tobin, *Creation*, 42ff.

[46] So Tobin, *Creation*, 36ff.

[47] So Tobin, *Creation*, 50-55.

[48] Tobin, 54ff, 172-76.

[49] See Pheme Perkins, *The Gnostic Dialogue* (New York: Paulist, 1980) 60-63, 91-94.

[50] Jean Magne, "Ouverture des Yeux. Connaissance et Nudité dans les Récits Gnostiques du Paradis," *Vigiliae Christianae* 34 (1980): 289-90, 298. A very similar description of the beauty of the tree along with a positive affirmation that Adam and Eve did gain wisdom from eating it appears in *1 Enoch 32* (Magne, "Ouverture des Yeux," 298).

[51] Eph. 5:21-33 appears to have been formulated in opposition to the ascetic rejection of sexuality often associated with the understanding of the union of Adam and Eve as a spiritual marriage (see Pagels, "Adam, Eve, Christ and the Church," 149ff., 154-55).

[52] See Klaus Koschroke, *Die Polemik der Gnostiker gegen das kirchliche Christentum*, Nag Hammadi Studies XII (Leiden: E. J. Brill, 1978), 93-96.

[53] Pearson, "Jewish Sources," 457.

[54] The only major addition to the narration is the assertion that the creator called the serpent "devil" when cursing it (47,6). The serpent was commonly identified with the devil in this period (Wis. 2:24; *Life of Adam and Eve* 12; *2 Enoch* 31; Rev. 12:9); see B. Pearson, "The Testimony of Truth," *Nag Hammadi Codices IX and X* Nag Hammadi Studies XV, ed. B. Pearson (Leiden: E. J. Brill, 1981), 162.

[55] An expanded version appears in *Orig. World* 120, 26-29, as well as in Jewish versions like the *Targum Pseudo-Jonathan* (Pearson, "Testimony of Truth," 162ff).

[56] An attribute of the devil in Jewish traditions (Wisd. 2:24), where envy over Adam's special status leads the devil to refuse a divine command to worship this being "younger than himself" and then to seek to destroy humanity (*Vit. Ad. Eve* 12-17). Pearson ("Testimony of Truth," 163) notes that Plato's *Timeus* 29E explicitly denies that the creator is envious.

[57] This detail is expanded in *Hypostasis of the Archons* (CG II. 90,20-

21) and *Orig. World* (CG II. 119,26). Gen. 3:9 frequently posed difficulties for interpreters (see Philo, *Leg. All.* III. 52; *Qu. Gen.* I. 45; Pearson, "Testimony of Truth," 164).

[58] Koschorke, *Die Polemik*, 95.

[59] See Albrecht Dihle, *The Theory of the Will in Classical Antiquity* (Berkeley: U of California P, 1982) 42-47.

[60] Dihle, *Will*, 72-89.

[61] Dihle, *Will*, 90-93.

[62] See Pearson, "Melchizedek," *Nag Hammadi Codices IX and X*, 58-59. A variant of the tale may be that found in *Orig. World* (CG II. 117, 2-28).

[63] Pearson, "Melchizedek," 58ff., 69.

[64] Stroumsa, *Another Seed*, 18ff.

[65] Translated by B. Layton in *Nag Hammadi Library in English*, 164. Turning herself into a tree evokes Greek myths of the goddess Daphne, another example of the structural pattern identified by Burkert (see B. Pearson, "She Became a Tree — A Note to CG II. 4:89, 25-26," *Harvard Theological Review* 69 [1976]: 413-15). In the gnostic case, the male savior is a heavenly consort, Seth or the Immortal Man, while the "pure seed," the gnostics, are offspring of the threatened goddess. Also see Michel Tardieu, *Trois Mythes Gnostiques* (Paris: Études Augustiniennes, 1974), 129-130.

[66] Tardieu, *Trois Mythes*, 35-36.

[67] See Matthew Black, *The Book of Enoch or 1 Enoch* (Leiden: E. J. Brill, 1985), 124-25.

[68] Black, *Enoch*, 124.

[69] Tardieu, *Trois Mythes*, 90-91, 104 n. 126.

[70] Pearson, "Jewish Sources," 453-54.

[71] *Apocry. Jn.* develops this mytheme by invoking the idea of "two spirit," a good and evil one. The Watchers could not have seduced the women unless they had appeared to be human. They create a counterfeit spirit, the anti-type of the divine Spirit, which they introduce into humanity.

[72] Stroumsa, *Another Seed*, 23.

[73] Stroumsa, *Another Seed*, 26.

[74] Stroumsa, *Another Seed*, 27ff.

[75] Stroumsa, *Another Seed*, 37-38.

[76] See Michael Williams, *The Immovable Race*, Nag Hammadi Studies XXIX (Leiden: E. J. Brill, 1985), 125-27.

[77] From Williams, *Immovable Race*, 127.

[78] Williams, *Immovable Race*, 127-30.

[79] Stroumsa, *Another Seed*, 43-45.

[80] See Tardieu, *Trois Mythes*, 102-106; Pheme Perkins, "Sophia as Goddess in the Nag Hammadi Codices," *Images of the Feminine*, 97-102.

[81] Tardieu, *Trois Mythes*, 88.

[82] Stroumsa, *Another Seed*, 62-65.

[83] Stroumsa, *Another Seed*, 152-58. According to Epiphanius (*Pan.* 25.2.4) the Barbelo gnostics held that the heavenly Barbelo (divine Mother) caused the archons to spill their seed in order to recover her lost power (Stroumsa, *Another Seed*, 65). In his anti-Manichaean writings, St. Augustine frequently mocks the Manichaean stories of the seduction of the archons (see Elizabeth A. Clark, "Vitiated Seeds and Holy Vessels: Augustine's Manichean Past," *Images of the Feminine*, 395-99). Manichaean "hearers" like Augustine were apparently encouraged to practice primitive forms of contraception to ensure that sexual intercourse did not produce children (Clark, "Vitiated Seeds," 395).

[84] The pair appear in a Nag Hammadi text, *Gospel of the Egyptians* CG III. 57, 18-22) as the parents of the angels who rule over the constellations and planets.

[85] Stroumsa, *Another Seed*, 148-52.

[86] See Frederick Wisse, "Flee Femininity: Antifeminity in Gnostic Texts and the Question of Social Milieu," *Images of the Feminine*, 297-307.

[87] Wisse ("Flee Feminity," 305) rightly rejects attempts to make this saying more acceptable to modern sentiments by alleging that it calls for a return to a primitive androgynous state or expresses condemnation of Peter's misogynist attitude.

[88] Tobin, *Creation*, 110.

[89] MacDonald, *There Is No Male and Female.*, 53.

[90] So Stroumsa, *Another Seed*, 39; Pagels, "Adam and Eve, Christ and the Church," 159-61. Rather than distinguish among the aeon Life, the Spirit, and Eve, Pagels assumes that in Valentinian sources they are all images of each other. Consequently, she fails to note the extent to which Valentinians limit the role of "Eve." Valentinian exegetes focus on the story of Wisdom and the fall of the soul into matter (see MacDonald, *No Male and Female*, 54).

[91] On the role of the Spirit in *Gos. Phil*, see Jorunn Buckley, "The Holy Spirit is a Double Name," *Images of the Feminine*, 218-227.

[92] Buckley, "The Spirit is a Double Name," 219.

[93] Stroumsa, *Another Seed*, 35.

[94] Translated by G. W. MacRae in *Nag Hammadi Library in English*, 279.

[95] As in Stroumsa, *Another Seed*, 35.

[96] Anne McGuire, "Virginity and Subversion: Norea Against the Powers in the *Hypostasis of the Archens*," *Images of the Feminine*, 244-48, 257.

[97] MacDonald, *No Male and Female*, 101.

Three:

Rachel and Leah:
Biblical Tradition and the Third Dream of
Dante's Purgatorio

Jayne Blankenship

In Dante's *Purgatorio* powerful dreams occur at moments of crucial emotional and spiritual transition. Dante dreams three such dreams in *The Divine Comedy*—all of them in this second Canticle —and each marks an important stage in his journey toward apprehension of the divine. The third of these dreams occurs in Canto XXVII after he has passed through the flames which purge a soul of lust and before he enters the Earthly Paradise. It concerns the biblical sisters Rachel and Leah. Christian exegetical tradition has consistently assigned to Rachel the role of "exemplar of the contemplative life" and to Leah, "exemplar of the active live."[1] And Dante critics have followed this model in their commentaries from medieval times to the present.[2]

The attribution, however, is puzzling in light of the women's personalities as presented in the books of Genesis and Jeremiah. Genesis shows Rachel herding sheep, running, marrying Jacob (after her father's trick substituting Leah), overcoming infertility, fleeing with her husband, stealing her father's household idols, tricking him, and finally dying in her second childbirth. Jeremiah shows her intervening from the grave on behalf of the enslaved Israelites, winning from God the promise to restore them one day to their own land. There is nothing anywhere to suggest contemplation or anything but vigor and activity. Although Leah bears more children than Rachel, she is narratively portrayed as less active than her sister, not more.

This essay contends that the labeling, which is clearly misleading, originated with a highly forced translation of the women's Hebrew names in St. Augustine's *Contra Faustum*. Unquestioningly perpetuated thereafter, the mistranslation colored and confused the use of the characters by later writers such as Dante. In the *Purgatorio* Dante utilizes both the erroneous interpretation he received and also the biblical "facts" to create a new paradigm for resolving the longstanding dilemma about active vs. contemplative modes of religious expression. Critics have noticed only his use of the received interpretation of Rachel and Leah and have failed both to recognize that this tradition is erroneous and to see how he corrects for it, weaving the two approaches into a new concept of enhanced activism.

This article will present the third dream in the context of the two previous dreams, look at critics' remarks about it, compare it to the biblical sources, examine the history of the active/contemplative dichotomy, demonstrate Augustine's mistranslations, and return to a careful reading of the dream itself in order to reveal more clearly its function in *The Divine Comedy*.

* * *

The third dream in Dante's *Purgatorio*—like the two which precede it—occurs just before dawn. This is the time, Dante tells us, when dreams are thought to be divinatory ("At that hour close to morning . . . when, free to wander farther from the flesh and less held fast by cares, our intellect's/envisionings become almost divine" [IX, 13, 16-18]).[3] Venus, the planet of love, is rising:

> It was the hour, I think, when Cytherea, who always seems aflame with fires of love, first shines upon the mountains from the east, that, in my dream, I seemed to see a woman both young and fair; along a plain she gathered flowers, and even as she sang, she said: "Whoever asks my name, know that I am Leah, and I apply my lovely hands to fashion a garland of the flowers I have gathered. To find delight within this mirror I adorn myself; whereas my sister Rachel never deserts her mirror; there she sits all day; she longs to see her fair eyes gazing as I, to see my hands adorning, long: she is content with seeing, I with labor. [XXVII, 94-108]

Dante's first dream (Canto IX) followed a day of hard climbing up the lower slopes of Ante-Purgatory. There, souls who repented late or neglected their duties wait aimlessly to be allowed to move on. In that dream Dante is snatched up by a lightning-terrible golden eagle and is carried up through the air to the sphere of fire, which scorches and awakens him (IX, 19-33). The eroticism of the dream is exactly that of Ganymede seized by Jove or Tithonus by Aurora, who are mentioned in the dream's preamble. Francis Fergusson and Mark Musa discuss how "childish" and "unformed" Dante's love is at this point. Dante has absorbed the sensuous passivity of Ante-Purgatory and functions as a victim. He cannot consciously move forward on his own, but requires divine assistance to transport him from a place of static waiting to a place where a healing kind of punishment can begin.[4] The flames in this dream prepare Dante for the actual fire through which he will have to pass in Canto XXVII before he dreams of Rachel and Leah—the fire which purges souls of lust.

Dante is terrified not only by the violence of the dream but by waking in a place different from where he fell asleep. He cannot understand what has happened to him, and Virgil must explain. While he was sleeping, St. Lucia has come through the flowers[5] and carried him far up the mountains to the Gate of Purgatory proper.[6] Then she has indicated the entryway to Virgil, with her eyes (IX, 52-63). The gesture is appropriate for St. Lucia because she was Lucy of Syracuse, a fourth-century martyr who, according to popular legend, gouged out her eyes after a suitor admired them. They were then miraculously restored, more beautiful than before. She became thereby the patron saint of those suffering impaired vision.[7] Through his need for her, Dante identifies himself as someone with limited understanding—someone who can move forward in the journey of spiritual growth only with assistance from outside his conscious self. This is the kind of assistance which dreams supply.

In Dante's second dream, a misshapen speech-impaired woman with "eyes askew"—the opposite of the eagle and Lucia in this respect—is transformed by Dante's gaze into an elegant, eloquent siren. He nearly falls under the spell of her song until another woman—"alert and saintly"—shows herself and scornfully calls on Virgil (Reason). Virgil then tears open the siren's clothes, exposing her rotten belly, and its stench awakens Dante (XIX, 7-33). This dream differs from the first dream in several ways. First, it expresses a mature male eroticism—Dante is drawn to the siren ("the coloring that love prefers" [XIX, 14] and "she / began to sing so, that it would have been / most difficult for me to turn aside" [XIX, 18]).[8] Second, Virgil himself appears in the dream—marking Dante's internalization of Virgil's wisdom and his growing ability to use it in his own behalf. And third, Dante tries on his own to understand it.[9]

The dream is like the first in that grace again comes to his assistance in the form of the "alert and saintly" lady. Singleton and Mandelbaum both fail to identify her,[10] but since the divine being who helped Dante before was St. Lucia, and since the word "saintly" is used, it is not unlikely that she is here again. Were she Beatrice, Dante would recognize her, and were she Mary, more would be made of her. It is completely appropriate that the saint in charge of helping mortals to see helps Dante here by calling upon his reason (Virgil) to reveal the rot beneath the siren's false beauty. The siren, in turn, prefigures a second siren—Leah in Dante's third dream—the Leah who represents, it is said, the active life.

Dante's second dream, therefore, marks a significant advance over the first, primarily because Dante is no longer a passive victim. That it was such a close call, however, has made him downcast and thoughtful, and, much as he wishes to accept the dream's invitation to abandon worldly concerns for more spiritual ones,[11] he is afraid to enter the lust-purging fire presaged in the Eagle dream. Virgil's reminder that only "this / wall stands between you and Beatrice" (XXVII, 35-6) gives him enough courage to follow his guide into the flames. There he longs for molten glass as something that could cool him off (XXVII, 50-1) but is drawn through the pain by a voice of light, singing: "*Venite, benedicti Patris mei*" (XXVII, 58). These are the words with which Christ will greet the just at the Last Judgment (Matt. 25-34).[12] The true attraction of this song stands in direct contrast to the siren song of earthly and sensuous attachment in Dante's second dream. Weakened by his ordeal and by the coming darkness, Dante now lies down on one of the rock stairs leading to the next level—like Jacob with his pillow of stone at Bethel—and falls asleep.

At first reading, Dante's third dream is the most straightforward and easy to comprehend of the three.[13] Dante dreams in the persona of Jacob, considering his two wives. On a literal level, the dream appears to endorse Leah's position as the "active" type. She is described as "young and fair," she gathers flowers, she has lovely hands, she makes a garland of the flowers, and she draws satisfaction from seeing herself adorned with her handiwork. Rachel, on the other hand—so Leah says—only sits in front of her mirror all day gazing at her own eyes—she never accomplishes a thing and therefore must be less desirable.

This is the simplest possible interpretation. No one follows it—presumably because it would appear to be inconsistent with the larger theme of *The Divine Comedy*, which concerns Dante's developing powers of contemplation of the divine. It is not difficult to argue against the interpretation of Leah as better by using the text of the dream itself (see below, pp. 79-80), but I have not seen any such arguments. Instead, most critics dealing with the *Purgatorio* have seen this dream as merely recapitulating the tradition. Generally, they hurry over it, citing the customary "types" and not interpreting it at all. William Anderson, for example, writes:

> In a third dream he sees two ladies, one gathering flowers who sings out that she is Leah and her sister Rachel who never stirs from gazing in her glass. She is the active life and her sister the contemplative. At daybreak they ascend the stairs and here Virgil halts to discharge his final duty.[14]

Or, like Mandelbaum, they give it brief attention:

> Rachel, the younger sister of Leah, signifies the contemplative life. Jacob was given Leah (symbol of active life) in marriage before he was allowed to marry Rachel (see Gen. 29:16ff). [15]

Some, like Singleton, discuss at length the allegory of the dream, but again claim Rachel's pre-eminence as contemplative because the tradition says so, without demonstrating why, textually:

> There has been no difficulty understanding the meaning of the dream in itself, of course. Leah and Rachel must signify respectively the active and the contemplative life. The problem is rather how the dream applies in the subsequent action of the poem. . . . Perfection in the active life must precede perfection in the contemplative. It is a matter of progression from a lower to a higher kind of life. . . .[The] goal is a summit of perfection in both the active and the contemplative orders of life, the contemplative being the higher of the two and the "final" goal.[16]

Singleton himself admits, "Dante studies do not appear to have come to any very sure view of the answers on these points."[17]

Critics such as these, who side with Rachel, are partly right — Leah is not entirely to be trusted—but they are right for the wrong reason. The point is not that Dante will have to choose between the active and contemplative versions of the just life, but rather the opposite: he will *not* have to choose.

The problem with the traditional interpretation of this dream arises when a reader wonders just how Rachel and Leah illustrate contemplative and active traits in the Bible. A careful reading of the Jacob-section of Genesis fails to produce any evidence of Rachel as contemplative. She herds sheep, meets Jacob at the well, runs to tell her father Laban, wins Jacob's love, and marries him;[18] she is barren at first and envies Leah her children; she argues with her husband and provides him with her maid as a surrogate so that she may adopt; she names and presumably cares for the two sons which result; she bargains a night of her husband's company to Leah in trade for Leah's fertility-enhancing mandrakes and then bears a son herself (Joseph); she supports Jacob's decision to flee her conniving, greedy father, and as they leave, steals her father's household idols;[19] she then boldly tricks Laban when he pursues the group by secreting the idols in a camel's saddle bags, sitting on them, and using her monthly period as an excuse for not getting up when questioned (Genesis 28-31);[20] she follows Jacob and the others to meet Esau and bows to him (Genesis 33); she conceives again, labors hard, names her child Ben-Oni / Son-of-My-Woe (though Jacob changes it to Benjamin), and dies. She is buried there on the road to Ephrat (Genesis 35:16).

Similarly, in Jeremiah Rachel intercedes posthumously on behalf of the Israelites being led into Babylonian slavery past her grave, and wins from God a renewed promise—where the patriarchs had failed—to restore them one day to their land (Jeremiah 31:15-16).[21] There is no evidence whatsoever, no anecdote or label, to suggest contemplation or vision or anything but vigor and activity.

In addition, the name Rachel in Hebrew (RHL) means "ewe."[22] Since it is by means of the selective breeding of Laban's sheep that Jacob is able to build a herd of his own, this name is quite powerful.

Leah, on the other hand, is not as active, narratively, as Rachel. She bears seven children, it is true, and names them; but however busy that makes a woman in actuality, the story and the names she gives her offspring (and those of her maid) reveal her nature as one who mainly waits and tries to please thereby:

(Leah's first four sons)

> Reuben / See, a Son!
> . . . now my husband will love me!
> Simeon / Hearing
> YHWH has heard that I am hated
> Levi / Joining
> Now this time my husband will be joined to me
> Judah / Giving-thanks
> This time I will give thanks to YHWH[23]

(Her maid's sons)

> Gad / Fortune
> What fortune!
> Asher / Happiness
> What happiness. For women will deem me happy.[24]

(The son she bears after Jacob sleeps with her as a result of the mandrake deal)

> Issachar / There - Is - Hire
>> God has given me my hired wages.

And then:
> Zebulon / Prince
>> God has presented me with a good present, this time my husband will prize me—for I have born him six sons![25]

All this is not to say that Leah is an unsympathetic character. Indeed, it is hard not to feel the fullness of her pain as the despised one. But she is passive: she allows herself to be substituted for her sister in Jacob's wedding tent;[26] she receives Jacob's seed; she goes along with Rachel's mandrake-trade and the decision to flee; and she, too, bows to Esau. An argument could be made in favor of her receptivity, but the Bible doesn't make it and neither does Dante.

In addition, her name, "Leah," means "weak" in Hebrew (L'H),[27] and a word with the same meaning—"ra kot"—is used to describe her eyes (Genesis 29:17). *A Hebrew and English Lexicon of the Old Testament* defines "ra kot" as "delicate, weak, of eyes."[28] Weak vision might be construed to indicate either a lack of contemplative capacity or, Dante aside, an inclination towards it (the viewer being less distracted); but it certainly does not suggest activity, and neither does anything else the Bible tells us about Leah. These typological ideas did not come from the Old Testament. Where, then, did they come from?

* * *

The history of the contrasting and paired types of the active and contemplative in the Western tradition, as traced by Sr. Mary Elizabeth Mason, begins with pre-Christian Greeks such as Plato and Philo. Among early Christian writers, Origen, in the third century, first compared the New Testament figures of Mary and Martha as representing contemplative and active types, respectively.[29] This is one

possible source of the Rachel-Leah role assignment. Early Christian interpreters frequently saw Jacob as pre-figuring Christ.[30] Jesus' preference
for Mary, the contemplative, was seen to parallel Jacob's preference for
Rachel, who by virtue of consistency had to represent contemplation as well. Her character in the Biblical story was almost beside
the point.[31] Seen from this perspective, an inaccurate interpretation
was forced onto the earlier text from a desire to make it consistent
with the later one.

But this is not the only explanation. St. Augustine (354-430),
Bishop of Hippo and formerly a contemplative himself, provided
later Christian exegetes with what came to be viewed as the clas-
sic presentation of the *vita contemplativa* and the *vita activa*. In his
Contra Faustum, he addresses the issue through the figures of Leah
and Rachel directly:

> Two lives are held out to us in the Body of Christ—the one
> temporal, in which we labor, the other eternal, in which we shall
> continue the delights of God. . . . Even the names of the
> women teach us to understand that. For it is said that Lia is
> interpreted 'Toiling,' but Rachel 'The Beginning Beheld' or
> 'The Word by Which is seen the Beginning.' Therefore the
> action of human and mortal life, in which we live by faith, doing
> many laborious works, is Lia. . . . But the hope of eternal
> contemplation of God, which has a sure and delightful
> understanding of the truth, is Rachel.[32]

The source of Augustine's Hebrew translations is not clear ("it
is said"), but that he did not personally read Hebrew is certain.[33] The
linking of "Leah" with the active life through "toiling" is under-
standable (if not forgivable) because, as indicated earlier, the Hebrew "L'H" means "weak," and it is "weak" in the sense of "tired out."
So one could envision a connection: tired out from working. But
the Biblical text never actually shows her working, so this interpretation is difficult to credit.

The translation of RHL as "The Beginning Beheld" or "The
Word by Which is seen the Beginning" is even harder to understand. Indeed, it is mystifying from any standpoint other than that
of a highly forced breaking up of unrelated words and then plugging

them together to form "Ra-chel." Yael Feldman theorizes that it might have been derived as follows: the first syllable of the word "ra'ah," which means "saw," could have been joined with the last syllable of "he hel," which means "began."[34]

This kind of exegetical maneuver was far from unknown in both the Midrashic strategies of the rabbis and the scriptural manipulations of the early church fathers.[35] It was also the kind of interpretive virtuosity which Augustine's own times and congregation admired. The more subtle and far-fetched the interpretation, in fact, the more lauded was the interpreter.[36] However stunning Augustine's dialectical subtlety might have seemed to his immediate audience, to twentieth-century text-oriented sensibilities it is highly distressing. We are compelled to say that Augustine used a flawed translation. And the generations of scholars who followed him and reverently took his word for almost everything dutifully repeated his mistake.

Pope Gregory the Great (540-604), for example, accepted in passing Augustine's attribution of the active mode to Leah and the contemplative to Rachel, and Thomas Aquinas followed Gregory's precedent. He diverged from Gregory, however, by seeing the active and contemplative *not* as "successive but interacting stages of growth in the interior life of an individual"[37] but as either 1) *aims* of the practical and speculative intellect (whether one's inclination is to contemplate divine truth or to help one's neighbors), or 2) the set of exterior actions flowing out of that attitude.[38]

The latter, exterior aspect came to be overstressed by Aquinas' interpreters primarily because of the evolution of the external forms of the religious orders. In Gregory's time there was but one mode of living the religious life: the monastic. But by Thomas's time—and Dante's—monks could focus *either* on pursuing spiritual perfection within the monastery *or* on works of the apostolate.[39] The emphasis on deciding between those lifestyles led readers to apply the labels "active" and "contemplative" more and more rigidly to external actions alone.[40]

The frame of mind which sees this quandary is the frame of mind which Dante possesses as he falls asleep on the eve of his third dream. The first dream (about the eagle) showed him being chosen for a vocation of spiritual ascent by a powerful force outside his personal consciousness. The second dream (about the siren) showed him developing conscious powers of discernment— trying to pick a proper goal. The third dream shows him trying to decide how best to pursue the spiritual goal he has chosen. Part of him still thinks in the "either/or" terms attributed to Aquinas. This is the conventional mind of his youth and of his times—a mind which values good deeds and sees contemplation, while holy, as preventing acts of social amelioration. It is the approach represented by Leah and reflected in her use of the typological catch-words "vedere" and "ovrare" ("seeing" and "labor"; XXVII, 108).

That Dante the writer wishes Dante the dreamer not to be taken in by the apparent attractiveness of the simple active life is revealed by a close reading of the text. In the first place, he raises a warning flag with "I seemed to see" ["mi parea . . .vedere"] (XXVII, 97). He doesn't write "I saw" but stresses instead the "seemed," which ought to remind the reader of the last dream-woman who seemed good to him—the rotten-bellied, crooked-eyed siren. "Proceed with caution," this phrase says. The next line calls her "young and fair"— a second "credibility alarm" when we learn, two lines further on, that this is Leah. Leah in the Bible is neither young nor fair. It is *Rachel* who is both young and "fair of form and fair to look upon" (Genesis 29:17). Leah is the older sister and she has weak eyes. This is all we know of her physical attributes, but given the importance of lustrous eyes as a primary standard for beauty in middle eastern countries, it can be inferred that she was not attractive.[41] Like the siren, Leah is singing, and also like the siren, she introduces herself: "Whoever asks my name, know that I'm Leah" (XXVII, 100). (Compare the siren's "'I am,' she sang, 'I am the pleasing siren,'" [XIX, 19].) The parallel is then made absolutely unavoidable by the rhymes she uses —"smaga," "vaga," "appaga" (XVII, 104, 106, 108)—which are virtually the siren's exact words: "dismago," "vago," "l'appago" ("leads astray," "wandering" or "desirous," and "satisfy" [XIX, 20,22,24]). Obviously, the reader is meant to understand that Dante the writer believes there is a certain danger in the message Leah brings, however appealing it might seem to Dante the dreamer.

Leah's song is one of self-congratulation: she calls her own hands "lovely" and feels superior to Rachel because of her own worthy labor (XXVII, 108). That labor is adorning herself with the flower garland she has made; she does this in order "To find delight within this mirror" (XXVII, 103). The kind of active life she represents, in other words, is one whose motivation is to feel good about oneself.

Her description of Rachel is also revealing—but what it reveals is more about Leah herself. It is important to notice that Leah is the only figure really "in" the dream. Rachel is present only by virtue of Leah's description and is highly vulnerable, therefore, to her sister's subjective, and weak-eyed, characterization. Leah attacks Rachel for never deserting her mirror, for sitting there all day and gazing at her own fair eyes (XXVII, 105-6). Not only is there no mirror in the biblical story, but the one thing all the different sinners in the *Inferno* had in common was that they all found fault with others. Leah does the same. And she projects onto her sister her own unconscious desires —to be pretty (i.e. to have fair eyes), to be able to see well with those eyes, and to be able to see herself, literally, in a mirror. Leah has tried to make a virtue of her necessity—"she [Rachel] is content with seeing, I with labor"—but it really hasn't worked. She doesn't understand that the purpose of self-analysis (seeing herself in the mirror) is the recognition of one's own inadequacies. She thinks it is to admire oneself. Nor does she comprehend the even deeper function of contemplation—beholding the divine. This undercutting of Leah would seem to justify the traditional evaluation of Rachel. But as Dante offers nothing positive here to support a choice of Rachel, it would seem that he is not content with the commonplace interpretation of the two. What, then, is he doing in this dream?

A clue is offered by what happens after Dante wakens. First Virgil tells him, "Today your hungerings will find their peace" (XXVII, 115). Energized, Dante climbs the stairs as if he had wings (XXVII, 123).[42] At the highest step, Virgil declares that Dante has now reached the place where he can "rest or walk until the coming of the glad and lovely eyes" (XXVII, 136-37). That is, he can be contemplative or active, can follow Leah or Rachel—it doesn't really matter. His pleasure now can be his guide—he does not have to worry about which way to act or live. His will has now grown "free, erect, and whole" (XXVII, 140-42) and no longer threatens to lead him in the wrong direction. He may look at the sun which shines upon his brow, and rest or walk among the grass and flowers of the Earthly Paradise he has reached. The question—which is better: active or contemplative, Rachel or Leah? — was the wrong question. This is as far as Virgil, representing the best which classical culture has to offer, can lead him.

But Dante's personality is unfolding into something larger, and the dream marks this change. Neither Leah nor Rachel, as shown therein, is sufficient as a way of life. It is time to meet Matilda, whom Leah pre-figures, and for Dante to comprehend that he can indeed "trust [her] looks" (XXVII, 45). He will no longer be drawn to something which is not good for him.

Like Leah, Matilda is singing and gathering flowers. She is also entwining them (XXVII, 68).[43] But unlike Leah she is not adorning herself with them or criticizing others. She is worshipping, at peace. She, in turn, will lead Dante to his longed-for Beatrice, who has been pre-figured by Rachel in the dream. And Beatrice herself, whom Dante thought to be the goal, will then, with Bernard's help, lead him on to God.

Dante's vision ultimately expands to withstand the divine light, but not before his physical eyesight is blinded by the dazzling radiance of St. John (XXV, 118-120, 138), who interrogates him on love. Then Beatrice's gaze dispels the "chaff" from his eyes, and like Paul or, more pertinently for this poem, St. Lucia, Dante can now see even better than before.

The souls Dante has encountered in Paradise so far are the souls of contemplatives like Benedict and Peter Damian and Bernard himself—contemplatives who returned to active life. Similarly, when he sees Beatrice enthroned, Rachel is at her side (*Paradiso* XXXII, 7-8). This is the second direct reference to Rachel in *The*

Divine Comedy, the first having also placed her at Beatrice's side (*Inferno* II, 100-102). Jacoff points out the symmetry of this placement in the second and second-to-last cantos of the poem, with the dream falling in between.[44] The parallelism underlines the importance of what Rachel represents.

This is not merely the contemplative Rachel of the exegetical tradition but the deeply caring Rachel who actively intercedes with God on behalf of the Israelites who are being led off into Babylonian exile, as recounted in Jeremiah 31:15.[45] Nor is Beatrice, who has consistently gazed at God in beatific contemplation, simply a contemplative. She too, has been active— saving Dante's soul. By choosing these particular figures to represent the most blessed souls, Dante is declaring his acceptance of contemplation of the divine as the highest form of human activity, but not as a lifestyle. At his core, he remains an activist, but it is a deeply generous kind of activism which he advocates.

Appropriately, the last mortal Dante sees enthroned as a patrician of the Empyrean before beholding the Eternal Light himself, is none other than St. Lucia (XXXII, 135-8). Opposite Adam, "Lucia sits, she who urged on your lady / when you bent your brows downward, to your ruin." Insight, vision, contemplation—everything the patron saint of eyesight represents—have led Dante, inevitably, to love. And that love, just as inevitably, has led him to the "enhanced activism" of writing *The Divine Comedy.*

* * *

The critics who have considered Dante's third purgatorial dream have done so, for the most part, within the same mental paradigm that Dante the Pilgrim dreamed it—traditional and pressured by the binary need to choose. Even Augustine, the source of confusion about what Rachel and Leah represent, was caught in it, as were the critics who followed him. All have been guilty—indeed, no one is ever completely innocent—of what Meir Sternberg calls "illegitimate gap-filling." In works of great complexity, such as the Bible and *The Divine Comedy,* the piecing together of information "gaps" between what is overtly stated and what the reader senses the

text "means" is almost never easy. Any interpretation gains credibility precisely in the degree to which it organizes the maximum
number of textual elements into the most cohesive patterns. "Illegitimate gap-filling" is the formation of an hypothesis based on the
reader's subjective concerns or general preconceptions rather than
on the textual details themselves.[46] This appears to have happened
to the Rachel and Leah story, both in the case of Augustine's original gloss of Genesis and in the critics' subsequent acceptance of his
interpretation. Instinctively, as a writer, Dante restored to the story
what the preachers and critics had taken from it.

The three dreams of *The Divine Comedy*, like Jacob's dream of
the ladder, are all symbolic manifestations of divine grace in action.
Something perceived as outside ourselves draws us into union with
God, which in turn educates our sympathies so that we can live
kindly with the people here. What counts is the inner orientation
toward the divine. Out of that, in time, the rest will come.

When Dante dreams his final dream, he is like Jacob wrestling
with the angel on the banks of the Yabbok. He is ready for a major
change in his relationship with God. The men have with them,
respectively, two ways and two wives, but they do not need to
choose. Out of Leah and Rachel together are born the twelve tribes
of Israel. And out of the active and contemplative casts of mind—
in succession and alternation—are born the true acts of expressive
love in which Dante locates man's reason for existence.

Notes

[1] For a tracing of the history of the general typology, see Mary Elizabeth Mason, *Active Life and Contemplative Life: A Study of the Concepts
from Plato to the Present* (Milwaukee, WI: Marquette UP, 1961). Rachel
and Leah are discussed on 32-5.

[2] Dante's son Pietro, for example, echoed by Jacopo della Lana, says
Leah represents the active life of the Old Testament. And Benevenuto
da Imola, also from the fourteenth century, claims Rachel stands for the
contemplative life. (The three are cited in Joan M. Ferrante, *The Political Vision of the Divine Comedy* [Princeton: Princeton UP, 1984], 244-45.)

In the current literature, Allen Mandelbaum heads his translation of the canto in question with the gloss, "Dante's sleep and dream of Leah, exemplar of the active life, and Rachel, exemplar of the contemplative life" (*Purgatorio*, 249). He remarks in his notes, "In Christian exegesis of the Bible, Leah is often interpreted as a symbol of the active life, the life dedicated to good works . . .and Rachel as a symbol of the contemplative and speculative life" (*Purgatorio*, 387). (All quotations from *The Divine Comedy*, unless otherwise indicated, are from Mandelbaum's translation: Volume I, *Inferno* [1980]; Volume II, *Purgatorio* [1982]; Volume III, *Paradiso* [1984], [New York: Bantam Books, 1984]. Canto numbers refer to the *Purgatorio* unless the text specifies another canticle. For clarity, when other translations and their accompanying commentaries are cited, the footnote will indicate the translator, not Dante, as author.) See also Rachel Jacoff, "The Tears of Beatrice: *Inferno* II" (*Dante Studies*, ed. Anthony Pellegrini [Albany: State U of New York P, 1982, appeared 1987]), 5 and 11, and Charles S. Singleton, trans., *Purgatorio: Text and Commentary* (Princeton: Princeton UP, 1973; Bollingen reprint, 1982), 387. All page references to Singleton are for the *Commentary* section of this volume, unless otherwise indicated.

[3]Singleton points out that it was a common idea that false dreams occurred before midnight, and true dreams after (*Purgatorio*, 181).

[4]Francis Fergusson, *Dante's Drama of the Mind: A Modern Reading of the Purgatorio*,(Princeton: Princeton UP, 1953), 34-6; and Mark Musa, *Dante's Purgatory*, trans. with notes and commentary (Bloomington: Indiana UP, 1981), 104. Musa states that it is the violent sexual impulse itself which transports mortals from an earthly to a heavenly place. Perhaps that is what a tremendous erotic impulse is—the earthly expression of (a) God's love for us. Perhaps it is the inverse, as well.

[5]Singleton also points out (*Purgatorio*, 185) that Petrocchi's text has a comma after "*dormia*," instead of after "*addorno*," which makes Lucia's approach, rather than Dante's sleeping, be on the flowers. He prefers the other meaning, but put in context with the later "flower women"—Leah and Matilda—I find the latter much more convincing.

[6]It should be noted that few critics have rested content with Virgil's interpretation of the eagle as Lucia (the name means "light"). They have claimed it represents Exodus, St. John, Rome, empire, divine justice—all subordinate, perhaps, to its reputation in medieval bestiary as capable of renewing itself every ten years by soaring into the sphere of fire (Peter Armour, *The Door of Purgatory: A Study of Multiple Symbolism in Dante's*

Purgatorio [Oxford: Clarendon P, 1983], 125; and Fergusson, *Dante's Drama of the Mind*, 34-6). In addition, the eagle was supposedly the only creature which could stare directly into the sun. (Dante writes in the *Convivio* [III, XII, 7]: "No object of sense in all the universe is more worthy to serve as a symbol of God than the Sun.") That Dante's transport here is accomplished by figures expressing great powers of sight should be kept in mind when looking at his use of the weak-eyed Leah in the third dream, and remembered, too, when he rises in Paradise with Beatrice, the only character in *The Divine Comedy* who can gaze directly at the blinding radiance of God.

[7]Musa, *Dante's Purgatory*, 104. Also Singleton, 186, and Mandelbaum, *Inferno*, 348. There is, of course, a long poetic tradition equating eyesight and deeper perception. Besides, this is not Lucia's first appearance in *The Divine Comedy*. Early in the *Inferno* Virgil explains how Mary, in heaven, took pity on Dante and sent Lucia, "enemy of every cruelty" (II, 100) to Beatrice, who in turn sent Virgil (Reason) to guide Dante out of his problems. So without Lucia, he would still be stuck, emotionally, in "the shadowed forest," where the poem began.

[8]Singleton cites Momigliano's comments on the allure of the siren's song: repetition of "*Io son . . . io son*" ["*I am*, she sang, "*I am* the pleasing siren" (XIX, 19)], the alliterative "M's," the echoing of "*mar*" ["sea"] and "*marinari*" ["sailors"], and the softness of "*piacere*" ["pleasure" and "piena" ["full"] (*Purgatorio*, 449-50). Bear in mind, as well, the three rhymes used: "*dismago*," "*vago*," and "*l'appago*" (XIX, 20, 22, 24), for, as Ferrante points out, they appear in the third dream, too (*The Political Vision of the Divine Comedy*, 245).

[9]Fergusson, *Dante's Drama of the Mind*, 107-8.

[10]Singleton, *Purgatorio*, 452 and Mandelbaum, *Purgatorio*, 36.

[11]Warren Ginsberg, "Dante's Dream of the Eagle and Jacob's Ladder," *Dante Studies* (1982), 51.

[12]Mandelbaum, *Purgatorio*, 387.

[13]Musa calls it the "briefest and least ambiguous of Dante's dreams" (*Dante's Purgatory*, 298).

[14]William Anderson, *Dante the Maker* (London: Routledge and Kegan Paul, 1980), 261.

[15]Mandelbaum, *Inferno*, 348. This note is to Canto II, *Inferno*, where Dante first mentions Rachel. See footnote 2 for his note on the dream itself.

[16]Singleton, *Dante Studies 2: Journey to Beatrice* (Cambridge, MA:

Harvard UP, 1958), 109, 110, 115.

[17]Singleton, *Journey*, 110.

[18]This is after having been forced to give place to the surreptitious substitution of her older sister Leah one week earlier —a "just-desserts" twist on Jacob's own deceiving of his father Isaac into thinking he was his brother Esau. (Jacob has already worked seven years to win Rachel. Now, with both her and Leah as wives, he must work another seven years for his father-in-law). The theme of trickster-tricked continues when Rachel gets even with her father.

[19]This was probably more to foil his efforts to trace them prophetically than to reform him, but the latter is possible too, especially with reference to Jacob's taking up everyone's household gods in the general confusion following the revenge of Dinah's rape and the Israelites' departure for Beth El. Louis Ginzberg explains how these idols were supposedly made. The head of the firstborn male baby was cut off and salted and anointed with oil. Then 'the name' was written on a small tablet of copper or gold, which was inserted into the head under the tongue. The head was then placed in the house, with lights before it. The owner bowed to it and it spoke to him on the subject requested. (*The Legends of the Jews*, 7 vols. [Philadelphia: Jewish Publication Society, 1911-38], 371-2.) Julian Jaynes theorizes on the nature of this "speech" in *The Origin of Consciousness in the Breakdown of the Bicameral Mind* (Boston: Houghton Mifflin, 1977). It is his opinion, convincingly argued, that such idols were used to trigger auditory hallucinations—the messages for which passed along a large nerve-group connecting the right brain with the auditory areas of the left brain. At times of stress or in a trance state induced by the use of these household idols, it is conceivable that people actually heard voices. Because the "voices" originated in a non-conscious part of the brain, they were attributed to the gods. This capacity, Jaynes says, may still appear in schizophrenics (106-7, 201-2).

[20]Nahum Sarna points out that, given the Israelites' attitudes on menstrual impurity, this act was one of willful defilement and demonstrated Rachel's scornful rejection of her father's religious practices. *Understanding Genesis: The Heritage of Biblical Israel* (New York: Schocken Books, 1966, rpt; 1970), 201.

[21]"Thus saith the LORD:

A voice is heard in Ramah,

Lamentation, and bitter weeping,

Rachel weeping for her children;

She refuseth to be comforted for her children,
Because they are not.
Thus saith the LORD:
Refrain thy voice from weeping,
And thine eyes from tears:
For thy work shall be rewarded, saith the LORD;
And they shall come back from the land of the enemy.
And there is hope for thy future, saith the LORD;
And thy children shall return to their own border."

[22]Benzion C. Kaganoff, *A Dictionary of Jewish Names and their History* (New York: Schocken Books, 1977), 40. See also Alfred J. Kolatch, *Dictionary of First Names* (Middle Village, NY: Jonathan David Publishers, 1980), 454; and Kolatch, *The Name Dictionary: Modern English and Hebrew Names* (New York: Jonathan David Publishers, 1967), 274. Kolatch notes here that "ewe" is the symbol of purity and gentility.

[23]Everett Fox, *In the Beginning: A New Rendition of the Book of Genesis*, trans. with commentary and notes (New York: Schocken Books, 1983), 118. The traditional English names, as supplied in his footnotes, have been substituted for the Hebrew.

[24]*Ibid.*, 120.

[25]*Ibid.*, 121. Leah bears a daughter too—Dinah—but Fox does not comment on the name.

[26]In this regard, *The Midrash Rabbah on Genesis*, trans. H. Freedman, vol. 2 (London and New York: Soncino P, 1983), 653, comments: "This Leah leads a double life [lit. her hidden (life) is not like her open one]: she pretends to be righteous, yet is not so, for if she were righteous, would she have deceived her sister?"

[27]Kolatch, *Dictionary of First Names*, 404; and *The Name Dictionary*, 239. A *Hebrew and English Lexicon of the Old Testament*, ed. Francis Brown, S.R. Driver, and Charles A. Briggs (Oxford UP, 1906; reprint 1951) uses "be weary," 521.

[28]Francis Brown, et al. *A Hebrew and English Lexicon*, 940. "Ra kot" is repeated later in the story, as well, when Jacob tells Esau (the brothers having finally been reunited) that he must move slowly because "the children are *weak*" ("ra kim"; same root, masculine form), "and I must think of the sheep and livestock with their young" (Genesis 33:13). Robert Alter has discussed the Bible's use of thematic key words in *The Art of Biblical Narrative* (New York: Basic Books, 1981), 148-9; and Fox devotes the entire first section of the preface of his translation of Genesis

to a discussion of the importance of such wordplay, which Buber and Rosenzweig, in their German translation of the Bible (1925-61), called *Leitwortstil* (*In the Beginning,* xi - xx). While there is not here a verbatim repetition of L'H, there is definitely a constellation of words also meaning "weak" or "soft," which reinforces the image. Also note that James Hastings, ed., A *Dictionary of the Bible Dealing with its Language, Literature and Contents,* vol. 3 (New York: Charles Scribners Sons, 1900), 88-9, mentions that Gray (*Hebrew Proper Names,* 96) and W.R. Smith (*Kinship,* 119) accept the meaning "wild cow" for Leah (as does Fox), but argues that the context and etymology of the word both clearly favor the meaning "weak."

[29]Mason, *Active Life and Contemplative Life,* 25. In her discussion of Origen (18-25) she condenses J. Danielou, *Origen* (New York: Sheed and Ward, 1955), 293-314.

[30]Origen laid great stress on allegorical, almost anti-textual, interpretations of scripture. See Susan A. Handelman, *The Slayers of Moses: The Emergence of Rabbinic Interpretation in Modern Literary Theory* (Albany: State U of New York P, 1982), 69-99.

[31]*Encyclopedia Judaica,* vol. 10 (Jerusalem: Macmillan, 1971), 1490. The parallels were frequently made in medieval Christian iconography too. Medieval thinkers simply did not place Biblical characters in their historical contexts but understood them to apply to New Testament and later events.

[32]St. Augustine, *Contra Faustum* XXII 52; PL 42, 432, trans. Mary Elizabeth Mason, and quoted in *Active Life and Contemplative Life,* 32. To be sure that Mason's translations were not where the error lay, I also checked *Augustine's Reply to Faustus the Manichaean* in Philip Schaff, ed., *A Select Library of the Nicene and Post-Nicene Fathers of the Christian Church,* IV: St. Augustin, *The Writings Against the Manichaeans and Against the Donatists,* (Grand Rapids, MI: William B. Eerdmans Publishing Co., 1956), which reads: "It is said that Lia means suffering and Rachel the First Principle Made Visible, or the Word which makes the First Principle Visible. The action, then, of our mortal human life, in which we live by faith, doing many painful tasks without knowing what benefit may result from them to those with whom we are interested is Leah, Jacob's first wife. And thus she is said to have weak eyes. For the purposes of mortals are timid, and our plans uncertain. Again, the hope of the eternal contemplation of God with a sure and delightful perception of truth is Rachel. And on this account she is described as fair and well-formed. This the

beloved of every pious student, and for this he serves the grace by God, by which our sins, though like scarlet, are made white as snow" (292). "Suffering" represents a slightly different emphasis from "toiling," but the argument linking it to weak eyes— that we suffer because we cannot know (see) what fruit our actions may or may not bear—seems equally as strained in supporting the assignment of the active life to Leah.

[33]See Peter Brown, *Augustine of Hippo: A Biography* (London: Faber and Faber, 1965), 257; and John-Baptist Reeves, "St. Augustine and Humanism," in M.C. D'Arcy (et al.) ed., *A Monument to Augustine: Essays on Some Aspects of His Thought Written in Commemoration of His 15th Centenary* (London: Sheed and Ward, 1930), 140.

[34]Yael Feldman, Professor of Hebrew at Columbia University, telephone conversation with author, 25 May 1987.

[35]For an example of the former, see the *Midrash Rabbah* on Genesis 33:1 ("And Dinah the daughter of Leah went out"), 735-6. The Midrash links Dinah's "going out" to Leah's "going out" to Jacob after trading the mandrakes to Rachel ("And Leah went out to meet him" Genesis 30:16). Then claiming, "as the mother so the daughter," the Midrash concludes that if Dinah had never gone out, she would not have been raped, and all the chaos resulting from her brothers' revenge on her rapist's people also would not have happened. Not only is this blaming of the crime on the victim classically sexist; it is also an inexcusable extrapolation from the actual text. For discussions of Patristic "revisional interpretation" see Handelman, *The Slayers of Moses*, 88, and Erich Auerbach, *Mimesis: The Representation of Reality in Western Literature* (Princeton: Princeton UP, 1953), 48.

[36]Brown, *Augustine of Hippo*, 254-5.

[37]Mason, viii.

[38]*Ibid.*, 82-84. Mason locates Aquinas' ideas in the *Summa Theologica*, IIa-IIae.

[39]*Ibid.*, 93.

[40]*Ibid.*, 103-4. There was, of course, not only a very large body of commentary intervening between Augustine and Dante but continuing thereafter, as well. An example from the fourteenth century—Jacobus de Voragine's analysis of the name "Cecilia" as an appreciation of St. Cecilia—illustrates both the Augustinian linking of Leah with work and also the general method of free-associative amplification for one's own purposes which had become the interpretive style: "Cecilia comes from *coeli lilia*, lily of Heaven, or from *coecis via*, a way unto the blind, or from

coelum, Heaven, and *lya*, one who works. Or again, it is the same as *coecitate carens*, free from blindness, or comes from *coelum* and *leos*, people. For Cecilia was a heavenly lily by her virginity; or she is called a lily because of the whiteness of her purity, the freshness of her conscience, and the sweet odour of her good renown. She was a way unto the blind by her example, a heaven by her unwearying contemplation, a worker by her diligent labour. Or she is called a heaven because, as Isidore says, the philosophers asserted that the heavens are revolving, round, and burning. Thus Cecilia was revolving in that she went around in her good works; she was round in perseverance, and burning with charity. She was also free from blindness by the splendour of her wisdom, and a heaven of the people, because in her, as in a spiritual heaven, the people had Heaven set before their eyes for their imitation; for they saw in her the sun, the moon, and the stars." Jacobus de Voragine, *The Golden Legend*, trans. G. Ryan and H. Ripperger (New York: Longmans Green, 1941), 689. Note that de Voragine also manages to see Leah as contemplative.

[41] *Encyclopedia Judaica*, 10:1526.

[42] Just as Dante's falling asleep on the stone step recalled Jacob's pillow of stone at Bethel, so the steps again recall the Jacob story—specifically his dream of a ladder stretching from earth to heaven, with messengers of God going up and down on it and with God himself standing over him, promising to him and his descendants the land on which Jacob lies; promising, too, care and protection until he be brought back to that soil (Genesis 28: 12-17). (This promise He repeats to Rachel regarding the enslaved Israelites.) The figure of Jacob's ladder has long been an emblem of the stages of mystical knowledge—indeed, Dante uses it outright in Canto XXII of the *Paradiso* as he ascends with Beatrice from the sphere of Saturn to the Empyrean, from the world which can be known with the senses to a universe knowable by intellectual contemplation alone. But the parallels with Jacob go further still. Like Jacob, exiled from his family by Esau's rage at having been tricked out of his birthright, Dante, too, is banished—a political exile from Florence. Like Jacob, he will have to work and learn humility. And also like Jacob, Dante will discover, in exile, a means of reaching a state of grace—the composition of this great poem. See Ginsberg, "Dante's Dream of the Eagle and Jacob's Ladder," 42, 49-51.

[43] A "joining" kind of activity, perhaps illustrating a blend of the active and contemplative. A possible historical referent for the figure of Matilda is Matilda, the countess of Tuscany. Donizo's contemporary life

of Matilda, *Vita Mathildis*, ed. Luigi Simeoni (Bologna: Zanichelli, 1930-4) describes her fight for the Church in its struggles against empire. Donizo calls her "another Martha" for her actions and "another Mary" for her concern with the faith, thus setting her as a model for combination of the active and contemplative modes. For this and more on Matilda, see Ferrante, *The Political Vision of the Divine Comedy*, 247-8.

[44]Jacoff, "The Tears of Beatrice," 3-4.

[45]See note 21. Jacoff astutely demonstrates the grammatical evidence for this identification. The Jeremiah passage employs the present participle ("Rachel *weeping* for her children"). Similarly, Dante uses the present participle in each of his three references to Beatrice's tears in *The Divine Comedy* ("*lacrimando*" twice and "*piagendo*" once). Rachel is seated beside/paired in contemplation with Beatrice. See "The Tears of Beatrice," 5. The Babylonian connection is further supported by Marcia L. Colish, who quotes a letter from Dante to the Italian Cardinals likening Rome to a widow adverting to the Babylonian captivity. *Epistola* 8 (May or June 1314), trans. Toynbee, in *The Mirror of Language: A Study in the Medieval Theory of Knowledge* (Lincoln: U of Nebraska P, 1968), 187.

[46]Meir Sternberg, *The Poetics of Biblical Narrative* (Bloomington: Indiana UP, 1985), 188-89.

Four:

Job's Wife, Walter's Wife, and the Wife of Bath

Ann Astell

The biblical wife of Job speaks only once. Seeing her afflicted husband reduced to sitting, ulcerous and silent, upon a dunghill after losing in rapid succession his property, his children, and his health, she asks him, "Dost thou still continue in thy simplicity? Bless God, and die" (Job 2:9: "Adhuc tu permanes in simplicitate tua? Benedic Deo et morere").[1]

That single, enigmatic utterance has earned Job's wife a prominent position in misogynist literature,[2] a position secured for her by Saint Gregory the Great's influential sixth-century commentary, *Moralia in Iob* (595 A. D.). While Job himself briefly reproves his wife, "Thou hast spoken like one of the foolish women" (Job 2:10: "Locuta es quasi una ex ineptis mulieribus"), Gregory goes on at length to explicate her offense. Gregory not only associates Job's wife with Eve as the archetypal temptress; he links her voice to the feminine speaking of poetry itself in its imagistic power to move, delight, and (mis)instruct. That Gregorian linkage of misogyny and poetry in the *persona* of Job's wife enables her, as we shall see, to become an important self-image for Geoffrey Chaucer, who refashions her in *The Canterbury Tales* in the double form of Alisoun of Bath and patient Griselda. Chaucer uses the stories of these two Joban wives to dramatize his own troubled relationship to his literary inheritance, to authorship and authority, especially the Latinate *auctoritas* investing clerical writings like Gregory's commentary on Job.

According to the Gregorian reading of Job's wife, Satan employs her as his instrument within an unfolding plan aimed at Job's destruction. Unable to break Job's heroic steadfastness with misfortune ("tribulationibus frangat"), the Adversary attempts to weaken him rhetorically: "persuasionibus molliat."[3] Turning to subtler means ("ad subtilia tentandi argumenta"), Satan targets Job as a second Adam and seeks in Job's wife another Eve ("ad Euam recurrit").

Indeed, Gregory finds in the wife's speech a direct echo of Eve's temptation of Adam: "verba sua Eua repetit" (III.viii, 123). As a repetition of the trial in paradise, the exchange between Job and his wife becomes charged with an eroticism not apparent in the literal meaning of their words. Gregory, in fact, overdetermines the carnal *sensus* of the scriptural letter, emphasizing the intimacy of the relationship between the speakers. Eager to scale the walls of Job's besieged soul, Satan takes the heart of the woman ("cor mulieris") as a kind of ladder ("quasi scalam") and uses her affection to reach the heart of the man ("qua ad cor viri ascendere"). Physically wounded and stripped bare ("exterius nudum"), Job stands vulnerable before the one closest to him—her whose words have the power to pierce his heart with the force of love: "dum uis amoris cor perforat" (III.viii, 122). The Old Enemy moves the wife's tongue ("antiquus hostis linguam mouit uxoris") and incites her to speak tender blandishments: "per verba blandiens loquitur."

Gregory thus identifies the wife's words very closely with her body and its carnal allurements. Limited by a carnal understanding, she speaks words of a bad persuasion ("verba malae persuasionis"), foolish words that justify the Pauline prohibition against female teachers: "Docere autem mulieri non permitto" (1 Timothy 2:12). Literally linked to the body and its passions—especially love, hope, anger, and fear—she represents allegorically the weak members of the Church (III.xx, 138: "speciem . . . carnalium in Ecclesiae sinu positorum"), and tropologically, the fleshly thoughts provoking the mind: "uxor quippe male suadens est carnalis cogitatio mentem lacessens" (III.xxxii, 154).[4]

Job responds to his wife's outcry with a reproof, encouraging her to accept both sorrow and joy as a gift from God's hand. The narrator approves his answer with the comment: "And in all these things Job did not sin with his lips" (Job 2: 10). Chapter 2 thus concludes with an echo of the final verse of Chapter 1: "In all these things Job sinned not by his lips, nor spoke he any foolish thing against God" (Job 1:22).

The neat Gregorian juxtaposition of Job's controlled and orthodox speaking against his wife's carnal rhetoric threatens to collapse when, at the beginning of Chapter 3, Job himself, after a long period of brooding silence, voices the same sentiments his wife had expressed, cursing the day of his birth and praying for death. Gregory, however, defends Job's spiritual *logos* against the literal *pathos* of his language, insisting that not everything in Scripture can or should be taken at face value. Gregory admits that, read superficially ("si superficie tenus attenditur"), Job's words are reprehensible as a blasphemous malediction ("maledictio"). Since that reading would, however, contradict the scriptural praise of Job's virtue, it must be false. The text *ad litteram* presents a stumbling block only to require a deeper, allegorical consideration of his words. Such an allegoresis exonerates Job, revealing that he actually speaks out of right judgment ("ex rectitudine iudicis"), moved not by wrath but tranquil with true teaching: "non est ira commoti sed doctrina tranquilli" (IV.i, 165).

Gregory, then, underscores the emotive carnality of the wife's discourse while denying altogether the carnal dimension of Job's despairing outcry, its ungoverned passion. Allegory justifies and renders orthodox the hero's apparent "maledictio," whereas allegory, in the wife's case, only confirms her speaking to be "male suadentis verba" (III.viii, 123). In either case, emotive language, the imagistic vehicle of passion and poetry, is marked as feminine, literal, and carnal—a form of speaking divorced from the *logos* of eternal wisdom (III.viii, 122: "a sapientiae aeternitate separavit") and redeemed only through subordination to the higher, masculine doctrine enunciated in allegorical interpretation. Even as Job corrects his wife and leads her to truth ("III.viii, 122: "ad doctrinam sanctae eruditionis misit"), Gregory justifies Job's cursing through allegoresis.

Gregory's misogynist reading of Job's wife had a long afterlife in the Middle Ages. As Lawrence Besserman observes, a strong iconographic tradition represents Job "on his ashpile or dunghill, flanked by his wife and Satan, who berate him and beat him, respectively, or we find scenes of the flagellation of Job by his wife and Satan paired with scenes of the Flagellation of Christ."[5] The Middle French *La Pacience de Job* actually rewrites the scriptural version of the story, assigning all the long, complaining speeches to the wife, not Job. In that play the wife nags and verbally abuses Job, reproaching him for (among other things) withholding some of his gold from her.[6]

In fourteenth-century England the devastation wrought by outbreaks of the plague stimulated new interest in the story of suffering Job. William Langland, for instance, singles out Job as a figure of the Christian poet, the minstrel of God, who with a fool's wisdom sings the praises of the Lord in the midst of calamity.[7] Geoffrey Chaucer, as we shall see, also turns to the tale of Job and the interpretive tradition surrounding it in an attempt to clarify his own self-portrait as an artist. For Chaucer, however, the key figure in the story is not Job but Job's wife—she whose speaking is irreducibly carnal, feminine, alluring, and poetic. Chaucer recognized, as Lee Patterson puts it, that "the voice of the poet is inescapably aligned with that of women."[8] Indeed, Chaucer parallels the difficulty of his own authorial self-definition in relation to the fatherly authority of "olde bookes"[9] to the struggle of women to achieve an authentic identity in a misogynist culture where their life-stories have been to a large extent predetermined and prescribed. When Job's wife reappears in *The Canterbury Tales* in the doubled form of Alysoun of Bath and patient Griselda, Chaucer uses the opposition between the two to explore rival ways of transforming and translating the authoritative inheritance that is his as a poet, theirs as women.

That clerical inheritance bequeathed two generic forms of the story of woman: that represented by "the book of wikked wyves" (III.685) and that embodied in "hooly seintes lyves" (III.690), the secular and sacred legends of good women. Through the Wife of Bath's response to misogyny, Chaucer articulates the ambivalence he feels as a male artist burdened with the *translatio* of an established, but morally limited and limiting, genre. The Wife's strategy is Chaucer's. Rather than deny the antifeminist charges lodged against her, Alisoun concurs with them and uses them to construct her autobiography. She embodies the books her husbands read. As Patterson phrases it, "she presents herself as a nightmare of the antifeminist imagination, a woman who not only exemplifies every fault of which women have been accused but pre-empts the very language of accusation" (678). In doing so, she gradually lays bare the "unacknowledged but insistent feminist subtext" contained in the "aggressively antifeminist texts" (Patterson 659) she quotes.[10]

Early in the Prologue Alisoun presents herself as the reincarnation of Job's wife. Even as the tongue-lashing biblical *uxor* subjected Job to flagellation, Alisoun boasts, "myself have been the whippe" (III.175). She prides herself on her ability to swear and lie and nag (see III.227-28). When her old husband (one of the first three) grows weary with her insults, she exhorts him to play the part of patient Job, even as she enacts the role of Job's wicked wife, the role prescribed for her by time-honored male fears and negative expectations:

> "Com neer, my spouse, let me ba thy cheke!
> Ye sholde been al pacient and meke,
> And han a sweete spiced conscience,
> Sith ye so preche of Jobes pacience.
> Suffreth alwey, syn ye so wel kan preche."
> (III.433-37)

The Wife, like Job's Wife, can also turn harsh scolding into erotic blandishments, as her long history of sexual alliances makes abundantly clear. She summarizes her own account of five marriages and habitual "walkynge out by nyght" (III.397) with the astrological observation: "Gat-tothed I was, and that bicam me weel; / I hadde the prente of seinte Venus seel" (III.603-04).

The Friar is quick to read the Gregorian subtext in the Wife's autobiography, and he exhorts her not to preach: "And lete auctoritees, on Goddes name, / To prechyng and to scoles of clergye" (III.1276-77). Alisoun, like Job's wife, after all, is a dangerous rhetor, speaking words of a bad persuasion ("verba malae persuasionis") that repeat Eve's temptation. The Friar also points to the demonic implications of the Wife's Joban discourse when, as Penn Szittya has shown, he parodies the Hag-turned-Beauty of the Wife's Tale in the figure of the shape-changing Green Yeoman.[11] The "gay yeman"

(III.1380) confesses that he is "a feend" (III.1448) who, in league with other devils, torments men for the sake of gain: "Witnesse on Job, whom that we diden wo" (III.1491). The Wife, then, reads her own life-story (which, in turn, is read by the Friar) as Gregory reads the biblical figure of the Wife of Job. Only at the end of the Prologue, when Alisoun describes the torment she feels when Jankyn, the husband she loves, reads aloud to her from his "book of wikked wyves" (III.685), does the male complicity in (and partial responsibility for) her actions stand clearly exposed. Even as the Wife textualizes her horrific life-story out of misogynist sources, thus confirming their authority with her experience, her clerk-husband's supply of negative female *exempla*—beginning with Eve—have their formative (or rather, deforming) influence on Alisoun, who is forced (and has been forced) to listen to them. If, as Alisoun declares, "it is an impossible / That any clerk wol speke good of wyves" (III.688-89), then the same antifeminist discourse that *describes* her behavior has, in the first place, *prescribed* it for her.

Thus, in the course of the Prologue, the "wo that is in mariage" (III.3) becomes not only the proverbial woe of husbands, but also the memorable misery of an Alisoun who has been instructed in wifely wickedness by clerks. That gradual shift in focus transforms "the antifeminist surface" with which the Wife "has covered over a tale of male deficiency" (Patterson 657) into a mirror in which both men and women can see themselves more clearly as common victims of a wicked book, the cultural text that authorizes both misogyny in men and husband-hating in wives, the torn codex over which Jankyn and Alisoun fight and through which they are reconciled in mutual forgiveness.

In making the wicked book itself his subject, Chaucer effectually reauthors it, departing from his source through the distance provided by the Wife's voice. Her reading of herself echoes Jankyn's reading of her and, in the process, exposes and undermines the clerkly tradition that promotes that sort of self-definition by women, that authorizes the Wife of Bath to be another Wife of Job. The appropriation of misogynist writing about women by a woman thus fictively parallels and literally accomplishes Chaucer's own artistic translation and transformation of the "book of wikked wyves" as a genre.

The Clerk of Oxenford's response to the Wife of Bath enables Chaucer to represent his own struggle with the opposite form of female biography, the legends of good women. In retelling the tale of patient Griselda, the Clerk takes on a task analogous to the penitential narration imposed on Chaucer the poet by the God of Love. Commanded to make "a gloryous legend / Of goode women" (*Legend*, G Prologue, 473-74) and thus atone for recording Criseyde's infidelity, Chaucer answers a charge similar to the Wife's complaint to the Clerk about clerical misogyny. Both *The Clerk's Tale* and *The Legend of Good Women* show a keen awareness that "the literary tradition of feminine virtue . . . is itself part of the male tyranny it relentlessly chronicles" (Patterson 689), since the greatness of its heroines depends for its proof upon the testing of men—a stance that perpetuates men's vice, justifies, and even necessitates it:

> And telle of false men that hem betrayen,
> That al here lyf ne don nat but assayen
> How manye wemen they may don a shame . . . .
> (*Legend*, G Prologue, 476-78)

Like the Wife of Bath, who bows to clerical authority only to undermine it, the Clerk calls attention to Petrarch ("FrAunceys Petrak"), the *auctor* of his tale, and superficially adheres to the "olde book" he has inherited as a narrator: "I wol yow telle a tale which that I / Lerned at Padowe of a worthy clerk" (IV.26-27). At the same time, however, the Clerk alters the literal terms of the narrative, so much so that it can no longer support Petrarch's interpretation of it. As Mary Carruthers notes, all the lines that Chaucer adds to his source "explicitly deny a connection between [Walter] and the God which Petrarch belatedly introduced in order to moralize his version of the story."[12]

In widening the gap between letter and allegory, the Clerk effectively challenges a tradition that records male cruelty and then allegorizes it, justifying it as godlike. Once again, Chaucer grounds his critique of his literary inheritance in the biblical Book of Job. Conscious that the Gregorian tradition exonerates Job of cursing and blasphemy ("maledictio") through a systematic allegoresis of what is literally offensive, Chaucer draws a bold parallel to Petrarch's vindication of Walter. Petrarch compares Walter to God Who, within a Joban cosmic scenario, tests His saints only to increase their glory. The Clerk's on-going narratorial commentary, on the other hand, presents a Walter "whose own evil makes an allegorized devil unnecessary,"[13] a Walter whose cruelty, within a revised Joban scheme, likens him not to God, but to the devil. The Clerk thus answers the Friar's demonic reading of the Wife of Bath with an interpretation of Walter as the Adversary.

Already in his introduction of Walter the Clerk levels a narratorial judgment against the "markys" (IV.64) for his self-centered interest in hawking and hunting at the expense of neglecting other duties: "I blame hym thus" (IV.78). Intent on fulfilling his "lust present" (IV.80), Walter resists the "servage" (IV.147) involved in fulfilling civil and marital responsibilities. Indeed, he clings so firmly to his lordly "liberte" (IV.145) that he chooses a peasant woman, Griselda, for his wife and binds her by a vow to permit him "al [his] lust" (IV.352, whether it causes her pleasure or pain (IV.353: "do yow laughe or smerte").

When Walter becomes obsessed with the wish "his wyf t'assaye" (IV.454), the Clerk exclaims against him and against men (like Petrarch) who approve Walter's course of action: "What needed it / Hire for to tempte, and alwey moore and moore, / Though som men preise it for a subtil wit?" (IV.475-79). Again and again the Clerk denies the necessity of proving Griselda's virtue: "O nedelees was she tempted in assay!" (IV.621). He even interrupts his narrative to address his female auditors: "But now of wommen wolde I axen fayn / If thise assayes myghte nat suffise?" (IV.696-97). The tale's "inner audience," the people of Saluzzo, are scandalized by Walter's murderous actions, his "crueel herte" (IV.723), and the narrator echoes that opinion, recording Walter's "crueel purpos" (IV.734, 740) in counterfeiting a papal bull to authorize his divorce.

The same narrative voice that undermines the Petrarchan allegoresis of Walter's actions as Godlike (IV.1141: "herkneth what this auctour seith therfoore")—by emphasizing their needless cruelty—explicitly labels the clerical interpretation of Job as an instance of patriarchal propaganda:

> Men speke wel of Job, and most for his humblesse,
> As *clerkes*, whan hem list, konne wel endite,
> Namely of *men*, but as in soothfastnesse,
> Though *clerkes* preise wommen but a lite,
> Ther kan *no man* in humblesse hym acquite
> As *womman* kan, ne kan been half so trewe
> As *wommen* been, but it be falle of newe.
> (IV.932-38, stress mine)

Chaucer's Clerk separates himself from this tradition through a complex restaging of the Job story. Griselda is not merely, as many have observed, a Job in female form; she is more properly seen as Chaucer's bold reinvention of Job's wife. The Clerk presents Griselda (via rhetorical *copulatio*) as a woman fit to be Job's wife, a Marylike New Eve at the side of a New Adam.[14] Whereas Gregory compares Job to an unfallen Adam and Job's wife to a fallen Eve, Chaucer's Clerk represents Job's wife (in the person of Griselda) as Mary, turning "Eva" into "Ave." In important additions to his source, the Clerk compares Griselda's presence in Janicula's poor household to God's "grace" sent "into a litel oxes stalle" (IV.207). Assuming the posture of Mary at the hour of the Annunciation, Griselda kneels to hear "what was the lordes wille" (IV.294). As Walter's wife, she cares for the people with so much wisdom, strength, and goodness "[t]hat she from hevene sent was, as men wende, / Peple to save and every wrong t'amende" (IV.440-41). Later, her baby daughter about to be seized by Walter's henchman, she prays like Mary at the foot of the cross: "Fareweel my child!" (IV.555).

Griselda shares, and surpasses Job, in the fortitudinous patience for which he is the biblical *exemplar*. As Carruthers puts it, "Griselda is virtuous. . . . Hers is the integrity of a prisoner who refuses to break under torture."[15] Echoing Job's own heroic words (Job 1:21) at the moment when Walter divorces and dismisses her, Griselda declares with unbroken dignity: "'Naked out of my fadres hous,' quod she, / 'I cam, and naked moot I turne agayn'" (IV.871-72). The substitution of "fadres hous" for the biblical phrase, "mother's womb," underscores the patriarchal origins of her affliction, having been given in marriage by her father Janicula to the high-born husband who dispossesses her of her clothes, her virginity, her children, and her home. As Walter tells her, "It liketh to youre fader and to me / That I yow wedde" (IV.345-46).

The leitmotif of Griselda's silence—"ne in thys tyme worde ne spak she noon" (IV.900)—builds through repetition into a thematic statement that not only parallels and surpasses Job's famous silence in the face of overwhelming sorrow, but also displaces the supposedly feminine rhetoric of emotive complaint onto her male attendants. As Besserman has noted, Griselda's father, not she, repeats the despairing "maledictio" of Job (Job 3:1):

> Hir fader, that this tidynge herde anoon,
> Curseth the day and tyme that Nature
> Shoop hym to been a lyves creature.
> (IV.901-02).[16]

At the same time, the Clerk-narrator of Griselda's tale frequently intrudes on her behalf, bespeaking the pain he imagines her to feel: "I trowe that to a norice in this cas / It had been hard this reuthe for to se; / Wel myghte a mooder thanne han cryd 'allas!'" (IV.561-63).

When Griselda herself speaks (in key Chaucerian additions to his Petrarchan source), the literal surface of her discourse typically conforms to the subservience demanded of her by Walter, while thinly veiling an ironic "maledictio," a subversive allegory. When, for instance, Walter announces his intention to dispose of their newborn son, Griselda denies the grief she feels, even as she expresses it:

> . . . Naught greveth me at al,
> Though that my doughter and my sone be slayn—
> At *youre* comandement, this is to sayn.
> I have noght had no part of children tweyne
> But first siknesse, and after, *wo and peyne*.
> (IV. 647-51, stress mine)

Later, when Griselda declares her intent not to remarry after having been "swich a lordes wyf" (IV.839), the passage superficially
honors Walter, even as it registers, at another level, sharp reproach.
A similar double-edge inheres in her paraphrase of Canticles 8:6
("Fortis est ut mors dilectio") when she tells Walter, "Deth may
nought make no comparisoun / Unto youre love" (IV.666-67).[17]

When Chaucer dramatizes through the Clerk his own struggle
to deal with the constraints imposed on him by an authoritative
source (Petrarch) and genre (the legends of good women), he presents a fictive situation in which failure becomes a victory. Not only
does the Clerk's retelling fail to support Petrarch's allegory of a godlike Walter (and thus challenges the generic justification of male
tyranny via allegoresis), but that same failure explicitly undercuts
the exemplary nature of the tale as a lesson in virtuous female subservience to domineering husbands.[18] As the Clerk puts it, "This
storie is seyd nat for that wyves sholde / Folwen Grisilde as in
humylitee, / For it were inportable, though they wolde" (IV.1142-
44). Addressing the men ("lordynges!") in his audience, the Clerk
advises them not to put women to the test in the hope of finding
another Griselda. He repeats the same message in the supposedly
ironic context of the envoy: "No wedded man so hardy be t'assaille
/ His wyves pacience in trust to fynde / Grisildis, for in certein he
shal faille" (IV.1180-82).

The Clerk only superficially assumes the misogynist position
that denies the possibility of heroic female virtue; at a deeper level,
he criticizes all the would-be Walters in his audience, all those who
justify their cruel testings as an idealistic search for female perfection, who act like Satan while playing God. That "Grisilde is deed,
and eek hire pacience" (IV.1177) is not surprising, given the tor-

tures to which men like Walter have subjected her. That Griselda lives as an authentic female hero depends, as Chaucer demonstrates, on rereading and rewriting her story to articulate its silences and thus discover in it new meaning. The poet must align with the feminine voice and allow Griselda to speak.

When Chaucer's Clerk reifies both Walter's cruelty and Griselda's immense suffering, the tale itself becomes a powerful tale of conversion. Unlike the Petrarchan Walter whose tyranny is only apparent, not real, the Clerk's Walter undergoes a dramatic change of heart when he takes the swooning Griselda into his arms: "'This is ynogh, Grisilde myn,' quod he; / 'Be now namoore agast ne yvele apayed'" (IV.1051-52). The scene, with its Job-like restoration of lost happiness, recalls the repentant Jankyn at the side of his book-beaten Alisoun, and the chastened rapist-knight in the Wife's Tale, enjoying at last the embrace of the tutelary lady whose physical transformation mirrors his own inward changing.

Whatever the sharp, initial division between the generic forms of female biography—misogynist and hagiographic—Chaucer's separate reworking of each leads, in the tales of the Wife and the Clerk, to a startling common ground between the two and a distinct narrative convergence. The Wife's strategy is, to be sure, much different from Griselda's, but both creatively redefine the roles assigned to them and effect the conversion of the men they love. The Wife's alter ego, the Loathly Lady of her story, celebrates the *gentillesse* that is apparent in Griselda's noble virtue, the *gentillesse* that "cometh fro God allone" (III.1162), not from social standing. Both the Loathly Lady and Griselda long for and experience a Cinderella-like *translatio* that is likely, perhaps, only in fairy tales and romances, but conceivable even in the cruel world where rapes, beatings, and murders make heavenly dreams all the more necessary. As Chaucer affirms, to change the literary forms that function as social *exempla* is to admit the chance for happy endings, both fictive and real.

The Clerk's playful "song" (IV. 1176), recited "for the Wyves love of Bathe" (IV.1170), encourages her and "al hire secte" (IV.1171) to enact the nagging role assigned to Job's wife, rather than the patient part of a Job-like Griselda. Playing the poet's part, the Clerk sings "Lenvoy de Chaucer" in an artistically self-conscious linkage of both Griselda and Alisoun and the two genres (of praise and blame) used to shape their life-stories. Indeed, he advises the Wife to avoid a Petrarchan rendition of her misogynist biography: "Ne lat no clerk have cause or diligence / Ĩo write of yow a storie of swich mervaille / As of Grisildis pacient and kynde" (IV.1185-86).

At a first reading, the Clerk's "game" ("lat us stynte of ernestful matere") ironically encourages Alisoun to act in a manner that he, in fact, disavows. Another reading detects *ironia* in the rhetorical cover of a "game" and finds "ernestful matere" (IV.1175) in the Clerk's literal message: "Ye archewyves, stondeth at defense" (IV.1195). In a world of Walters, after all, women like the Wife of Bath have at least a fighting chance for survival because they know how to "Ekko" (IV.1189) the misogynist language of men with a covert "maledictio." For women to speak their own language, however, requires them (and poets like Chaucer) to hear what Griselda, "so discreet and fair of eloquence" (IV.410), is saying in her Joban silence.

Notes

¹ I use the Douay-Challoner translation of the Vulgate into English. For the Latin text I quote the version used by Gregory the Great in his commentary on Job, in consultation with *Libri Hester et Iob* in *Biblia Sacra Iuxta Vulgatam Versionem*, Vol. IX (Rome: Vatican, 1951). The expression "bless" ("benedic") is a biblical euphemism for its opposite, "curse."

² Scripture itself records that misogynist reading in the Book of Tobias (2:10-23). The virtuous Tobit, blinded and persecuted, is first explicitly compared to Job by the narrator and then subjected to scolding by his wife Anna. Early evidence of a comic representation of Job's wife appears in the Greek *Testament of Job* (1st century B. C.). For a treatment of that work, see Lawrence L. Besserman, *The Legend of Job in the Middle Ages* (Cambridge, MA: Harvard UP, 1979), 41-51; Neil Forsyth,

The Old Enemy: Satan and the Combat Myth (Princeton: Princeton UP, 1987), 234-35.

³ Gregory the Great, *Moralia in Iob Libri I-X*, ed. Mark Adriaen, CCSL 143 (Turnhout: Brepols, 1979), III.viii, 121. Hereafter all citations from this edition are given parenthetically. St. Thomas Aquinas briefly echoes Gregory's reading of Job's wife in his scholastic commentary, *Literal Exposition on Job*, trans. Anthony Damico (Atlanta, GA: Scholars P, 1989), 94-95.

⁴ Gregory observes that weak-minded people who fail to hold fast to God's will ("Deo intentione") under trial, are deservedly called women (III.xxi, 141: "non immerito mulieres uocantur"). Elsewhere Gregory explains that "woman" is used in Scripture either to designate a member of the female sex or to refer to "frailty" in men and women alike. See *Moralia* XI.xlix.65.

⁵ Besserman, 4.

⁶ See Besserman's discussion, 99-103.

⁷ Langland depicts Job as a man who sang in his sorrow, and "Alle his sorwe to solace thorw that song turnede" (*Piers Plowman: An Edition of the C-text*, ed. Derek Pearsall [Berkeley and Los Angeles: U of California P, 1979], Passus XVIII.18). Job, of course, stands as the chief biblical model for Langland's allegorical character, Patience.

⁸ Lee Patterson, "'For the Wyves love of Bathe': Feminine Rhetoric and Poetic Resolution in the *Roman de la Rose* and the *Canterbury Tales*," *Speculum* 58 (1983): 695. Subsequent references to this essay are parenthetical.

⁹ Geoffrey Chaucer, *The Canterbury Tales*, in *The Riverside Chaucer*, 3rd ed., ed. Larry D. Benson (Boston: Houghton Mifflin, 1987), VII, line 1974. All quotations of Chaucer's works are taken from this edition and cited hereafter parenthetically. Chaucer's early works (*The Book of the Duchess, The House of Fame, The Parliament of Fowls*) all fictionalize the poet Chaucer's response to "olde bookes" (Cicero, Ovid, Virgil), and the same self-reflexivity characterizes his later works (*The Legend of Good Women, Troilus and Criseyde, The Canterbury Tales*). See Lee Patterson, "'What Man Artow?': Authorial Self-Definition in *The Tale of Sir Thopas* and *The Tale of Melibee*," *SAC* 11 (1989): 117-175; Ann W. Astell, "Chaucer's 'Literary Group' and the Medieval Causes of Books," forthcoming in *ELH*.

¹⁰ See also Mary Carruthers, "The Wife of Bath and the Painting of Lions," *PMLA* 94 (1979): 209-22; W. F. Bolton, "The Wife of Bath:

Narrator as Victim," in *Gender and Literary Voice*, ed. Janet Todd (New York: Holmes and Meier, 1980).

[11] See Penn R. Szittya, "The Green Yeoman as Loathly Lady: The Friar's Parody of the Wife of Bath's Tale," *PMLA* 90 (1975): 386-94.

[12] Mary Carruthers, "The Lady, the Swineherd, and Chaucer's Clerk," *Chaucer Review* 17 (1983): 229. Carruthers argues that Chaucer's version closely resembles Boccaccio's earlier rendition of the Griselda story.

[13] Edward Condren, "The *Clerk's Tale* of Man Tempting God," *Criticism* 26 (1984): 107. See Peggy Knapp's comment on Condren's unusual, but plausible, reading ("Griselda and the Patient Clerk," in *Chaucer and the Social Contest* [New York and London: Routledge, 1990], 132). See also Harriett Hawkins, "The Victim's Side: Chaucer's *Clerk's Tale* and Webster's *Duchess of Malfi*," *Signs* 1.2 [1975]: 339-61).

[14] For a study of Marian imagery in the Tale, see James I. Wimsatt, "The Blessed Virgin and the Two Coronations of Griselda," *Mediaevalia* 6 (1980): 187-207.

[15] Carruthers, "The Lady, the Swineherd, and Chaucer's Clerk," 230. This reading, of course, militates against the view held by some that Griselda is a passive victim. See, for instance, Donald H. Reiman ("The Real *Clerk's Tale*; or, Patient Griselda Exposed," *TSLL* 5.3 [1963]: 356-73), who calls Griselda "pathetic rather than virtuous" and casts aspersions on her "intelligence" and "moral sensitivity."

[16] See Besserman, 112.

[17] For a detailed discussion of Griselda's "dialogic re-envoicing" of Walter's discourse, see Lars Engle, "Chaucer, Bakhtin, and Griselda," *Exemplaria* 1.2 (1989): 429-59. See also William McClellan's response to Engle in that same issue, 499-506.

[18] For a treatment of exemplary uses of the Griselda story, see Charlotte C. Morse, "The Exemplary Griselda," *SAC* 7 (1985): 51-86.

Five:

Holoferne's Textual Impotence: Discourse vs. Representation in Du Bartas' "La Judit"

Catharine Randall Coats

"La Judit" is the first play in a trilogy Guillaume Salluste Du Bartas entitled the *Muse chrestienne* (1572). The title of the collection is significant, for it, along with the dedication to the pious, Evangelical Marguerite de Navarre, demonstrates the poet's program. He intends to combat the notion held by Ronsard, and the Pléiade, that poetry may be essentially pagan, and to mandate an exclusively Christian art of writing. This appears to be a bold, iconoclastic attempt, for Du Bartas is a Calvinist, and John Calvin found inefficacious any writing that was not a derivation or repetition of the divine Word.[1] Through our examination of "La Judit," we may see how Du Bartas resolves this apparent dilemma: by proclaiming a Christian textuality that undercuts, or overwhelms, his initial eloquence. This, he feels, is desirable, so that the Biblical Word may always and everywhere prevail. His word, if it is unmotivated by God, is as unsuitable and blasphemous as that of the pagan Holoferne in "La Judit." Du Bartas reacts against Holoferne, who represents the notion of image-oriented rather than scripturally attentive writing. It is by explicitly writing himself into his story as Judit (who, in like fashion, reads herself in the biblical stories she turns to) that Du Bartas can in any way legitimize his writing. Through such a strategy of *mise en abyme*,[2] or inscription, both Judit and Du Bartas come to be mere actors in a greater drama: the one penned by the supreme author, God. Thus Du Bartas acts as a faithful Calvinist exegete when he composes "La Judit."

He begins "La Judit" with an invocation to God, "la muse chrestienne." This undermines Du Bartas' own work and turns it over to the Lord. God will be the author and actor in this play:

> Fay rayer ton Esprit
> Sur mon esprit aveugle, et dore cest escrit . . .
> Tel qu'ores ma plume orine
> Traite divinement matiere si divine.
> (I, v. 19-12)

"La Judit," Du Bartas claims, is the first "juste poème [qui] ayt traicte en nostre langue des choses sacrées" (dédicace 7). Yet Du Bartas tempers this audacious assertion immediately; he does not pretend, despite his reputation as a Protestant apologist, to be any authority: 'je renvoye . . . à ceux qui ont employé beaucoup plus d'huile et de temps à feuilleter les volumes sacrez que je n'ay faict encore" (dédicace 8). Thus, from the very first words he pens, Du Bartas renounces authorship. "La Judit" seems, rather, to derive its impulse from the biblical story of which Du Bartas appears the mere transcriber. He is a vessel for its transmission, animated (as we shall see is later the case with Judit) only by the divine will, and not his own: "d'un transport tout sacré fai-moy grossir le coeur / Des rais de ton Esprit mon esprit illuminé" (II, v.5-7), he beseeches God. The possible comparison of his spirit to a book which another, greater author will rubricate ("illumine") introduces the textuality motif that underlies the entire play: the act of writing—whether and how it can be sanctioned—is obsessively examined here.

Creation and textuality are intimately linked elsewhere in Du Bartas' *oeuvre*. It is significant that the action of "La Judit" unrolls in six days, as does Du Bartas' chef-d'-oeuvre, *La Sepmaine*, in which each book mirrors the acts of God on each day of creation. Thus, Du Bartas creates his text by imitating God's genesis of the world. In the same way, the character of Judit as we encounter her at the beginning of the play is at yet unformed; by the end of the sixth day she has been shaped to function as God's instrument (as has been Du Bartas in his writing).

In forming his text, Du Bartas adheres closely to the biblical story to demonstrate his subordination to God. The Hebrews, besieged by the pagan king Holoferne, doubt their ability to withstand his military might. They hold a council to determine how to repulse the pagan host, but internal contention prevents them from arriving at a decision (Book I). Meanwhile, back in camp, Holoferne is spotlighted. He asks an adviser to tell him about the Hebrew people. His discourse thus already is determined by that of God's chosen people; it will ultimately be overcome by Judit, their representative (Books II-III). As the time for battle approaches, Judit retires to her tent to seek solace in reading the Old Testament. In a crucial turning point both for the drama and for Du Bartas' conception of himself as a writer, Judit is emboldened by the examples of Hebrew heroines that she finds in Scripture. Indeed, she is enraptured, uplifted in a mystic state during which the process of God's molding of her as this instrument begins (Books III-IV). She is then inspired by God to go to Holoferne, to seduce him, and to kill him. Accordingly, she bedecks herself extravagantly, knowing that pagans prefer ostentation in their idols. She proposes to delude the king into worshipping her beauty in an idolatrous fashion and then find the opportunity to slay him (Book IV). Holoferne is instantly enamored of her. More significantly, he is silenced by her. Enthralled by an image, he abandons the dynamic, military discourse that had formerly characterized him. Judit's speech, which defines and belittles Holoferne, takes center stage (Book V). As night falls, the festival Holoferne has held in Judit's honor comes to an end. Alone with Judit, he passively allows himself to be deceived by her appearance ("l'homme écervelé . . . / Se laisse ainsi tromper . . ." [V, 63-7]). Lulled to sleep, he is beheaded by Judit, who thus effectively disassociates herself—a sacred instrument—from him, a profane and blasphemous being. Judit returns to the Hebrew camp to inform them of their salvation which she, through God, has written upon Holoferne's body with her bloody knife, and which Du Bartas, as Judit, has registered in his text.

The struggle between Judit and Holoferne epitomizes the conflict Du Bartas experiences concerning his act of writing. He intends to establish a program of sacred writing distinct from that of the Pléiade, in which the typical luxuriance of fleshly images, earthly celebration, and mythological motifs prevail, and which proposes to exalt a poet-*vates* through a *furor* that enables his writing. Du Bartas wishes to remove the focus from the writer and return it to its only legitimate source, God.[3] He wishes to make of all writing a sort of *credo*, as he does in *La Sepmaine*:

> Or donc avant tout temps, matière, forme et lieu,
> Dieu tout en tout estoit, et tout estoit en Dieu,
> Incompris, infini, immuable, impassible,
> Tout-Esprit, tout-lumière, immortel, invisible,
> Pur, sage, juste, et bon. Dieu seul. . . .   (I, v. 25-29)

The Pléiade poets, by concentrating their efforts on the perfecting of human art, are not worshipful. Du Bartas proposes to overcome their influence by dialectically opposing Judit who, in an anachronistic leap, represents for Du Bartas Christian writing and reliance on the Word, and Holoferne, who incarnates the pagan concept of representation or adoration of images. The manner in which Judit ultimately disarms Holoferne is predicated on the ruse of deploying a representation that lures the idolator. She beats him with his own weapons. Indeed, her alluring disguise is composed of Petrarchan conceits illustrative of the sensual poetry of the Pléiade.[4] The extensively reworked Petrarchan motif of the mistress progressively delineated as though in a *blason*, her body parts composed of jewelry and precious stones, lends itself well here to Judit's purpose, for such an appearance all too readily recalls the pagan custom of elaborately dressing idols in extravagant and costly apparel. In addition, poets such as Ronsard frequently emphasized the physical, carnal qualities of their lovers. Judit adopts the same expedient in her approach to Holoferne.

Holoferne, duped by this strategy, reveals himself to be a superficial character. Judit, however, is unified and univocal because she is fashioned by God, inspired by him to act out a script with which he supplies her (just as he pens the words of which Du Bartas' pages are composed). The sole purpose of Judit's rhetoric is to reveal Holoferne's misguidedness while she progressively saps the strength of his discourse. She then fills the void which remains with God's voice which speaks through her. In this manner, Du Bartas as a writer testifies to the absolute precedence of biblical inspiration over any personal or literary motivation.

God's preeminence is shown through the agents he chooses. Judit, a devout, retiring, and bookish widow, is an unlikely conduit for divine vengeance, yet her very weakness is an essential counterfoil to the manifestation of God's limitless capabilities. The fragile vessel she constitutes has parallels, as well, with Du Bartas, who writes only to undo his verse and to disclaim his act of authorship, returning his work to God. Du Bartas articulates a crisis of writing: "Ma main tremble d'horreur et comme de coutume / Sur mon sacre fueillet ne sçait guider ma plume" (III, v. 239-44, Baiche). Yet, like Judit, when he joins himself with God through his entreaty, the success of his poem is guaranteed: "Guide ma plume lasse, enflemoy de courage / Et fay qu'à ton honneur j'acheve cest ouvrage" (III, v. 250-52, Baiche). At the same time, Du Bartas reveals his Calvinist theological and literary bias for narrative over description, postulating a legitimate, Word-oriented form of writing in opposition to image-focused pagan expression. The narrative of "La Judit" becomes the path "pour guider l'esleu au salut destiné."[5] For the Calvinist writer, only divine inspiration can correctly motivate writing. Du Bartas mandates "la possibilité d'aller au-delà de l'espace physique . . . [et] tache d'entrer dans les espaces abstraites de la théologie."[6] Rather than attempt to make one's own gods through description, human writing must give itself over to God to become the written-upon, just as Judit must abdicate her self-doubt in order to be inhabited by the divine will. When Judit beheads him, Holoferne becomes the object upon which God's will is starkly inscribed; it is literally carved upon his body by Judit's knife and written into the text as God's vengeance upon those who seek to thwart him. With his death, his textually enacted impotence is complete. Powerless to seduce Judit, his speech forever stilled, Holoferne is utterly vanquished by his own failure to hear and recognize the Word of the Lord. The once-powerful conqueror succumbs to a mere woman just as, Du Bartas seems sure, the profane poetic inspiration of the Pléiade will be overcome, through his feeble agency, by the "muse chrestienne." God's warning to Holoferne, early and obliquely addressed to him in the text, is realized: "je suis cil qui est, seul fut et seul sera / Cil qui de rien fit tout et qui, fort, réduira s'il veut le tout en rien" (II, v. 127-33, Baiche). If Holoferne only had had ears to hear! Pagan, he had only eyes to see, and what he saw deceived him.

It is necessary that Holoferne be rendered passive and power-less in order that God's potency prevail. Du Bartas expresses this need in an image that betokens the superimposition of one discourse on another to efface the former: "je veu dessus cuivre graver à jamais" (III, 84) to eradicate impious utterances and deeds. Through the medium of Judit, this is precisely what he will do in the course of the play. In this way, Du Bartas' literary creation conforms to the constraints of Calvinism: he does not create a wholly new work, but rather modifies and magnifies the Bible, erasing the pagan element (Holoferne) from sacred history. He is truly the tool with which God writes a narrative of salvation. He creates by yielding to God's Word:

> Esprit, d'ou tout esprit prend mouvement et vie . . .
> Espan sur moy ta grace
> Affin qu'à ton honneur ceste oeuvre je parface.
> (III, 259-64)

Because it is necessary that the self be relinquished in order that God's Word not be obstructed, throughout the drama the is-sues of speech and self-presentation, of reality and illusion, are cru-cial questions that prompt the narrative. While Judit may be initially divided as to her worthiness and ability to act in God's plan, once she prays—that is, turns her personal discourse over to God—all is set right, and she is made whole. Indeed, she becomes an emblem of salvation; in her can be *read* the favorable outcome of both *La Judit* and of Hebrew history:

> Que si par le passé l'on peut conjecturer
> Les choses à venir, nous devons espérer
> D'elle nostre salut; et mesme son visage
> Ja-desjà nous praesage [le salut]. (IV, 316-20)

"Discours" can have two meanings as Du Bartas conceives it. There is human discourse, which may or may not be pagan narration, and which is never valued. Distinct from this discourse is the utterance of the divine Word. In Du Bartas' *La Sepmaine*, for instance, God's speech interpenetrates the poet's writing; God covers the text, motivating and endorsing it.

> Ainsi qu'un bon esprit, qui grave sur l'autel
> De la docte mémoire, un ouvrage immortel,
> En troupe, en table, au lict, toujours pour toujours vivre,
> Discourt sur son discours et nage sur son livre,
> Ainsi l'Esprit de Dieu sembloit. (I, 289-94)

Judit's discourse derives from that of the Lord. Holoferne, on the other hand, is a braggart, mouthing vainglorious pronouncements. His words strut across the page toward the future glory he paints for himself but never attains, for these words are swallowed up by Judit's stronger discourse. Significantly, in his first appearance, Holoferne is inarticulate; he abdicates his presentation speech in which the audience would ordinarily be informed about his character. Instead, he asks Amon, one of his trusted chiefs, to recount the history of the Hebrews. This foreshadows the supplanting of his own historical aspirations by that very people he proposes to conquer. God then alters Amon's pagan perspective, supplying him with new words and causing him to utter involuntarily the truth about the Hebrews' privileged status in history:

> Car bien qu'il fut payen de naissance et de loy,
> Sa langue démentant et son coeur et sa foy
> Discourt des faits hébrieux si sainctement
> d'autant que cest Esprit . . .
> Est le saint orateur qui dicte sa harangue. (II, 21-30, Baiche)

The Hebrews' salvation is thereby already determined within the narrative. Judit will serve only to validate, and activate, the contract between God and his elect which Amon, the "payen non-payen" (II, 44), his speech dictated by God, is compelled to express:

> Mais s'ils n'ont poinct enfreint la sacrée alliance
> garde-toy de toucher
> Un peuple que Dieu . . . tint si cher. (II, 368-70)

Enraged, Holoferne threatens to kill Amon for his *truthful* recounting, which Holoferne calls false. It is his fatal flaw to be unable to distinguish truth from falsehood. He unjustly orders, "Meurs, meurs donques, meschant, de ta langue faussaire / Et de ton double coeur reçoit le deu salaire." (II, 425-7)

Similarly, Holoferne's inability to read signs correctly arises from his belief in appearance; his idolatrous mentality predisposes the adoration of the visual. Were he to link appearance with Word, he would be saved, but he has been totally cut off from the integrity of the Biblical Word, and so ascribes to appearance a power it does not have. He isolates images as though they were totalities of incarnate meaning. Venerating the picture instead of what it means, he builds his being upon nothingness. When Judit attires herself to appear before Holoferne, she artfully presents herself as a gaudy, bejewelled object of adoration; her limbs are those of a statue, and her beauty is inhuman, like that of a goddess:

> Son grand front plus poli qu'une pièce de glace
> D'un ébène excellent deux cerceaus deliés
> Sur deus astres brillantz sont dextrement pliés.
> Son col ressemble un pilier d'ivoire, ou bien d'albastre
> Et son sein est si blanc que tout l'ost idolâtre
> Idolâtre après lui. (IV, 345-65)

It is clear that the Hebrews, and Du Bartas, deem the natural state of the pagan, and of Holoferne, to be that of an idolator, for the adjective "idolâtre," used as a description of "tout l'ost" becomes a reality, a verb of (deluded) action: "idolâtre après lui." Holoferne's immediate worshipful response can indeed be equated with the absolute submission one shows to an idol. It is unmitigated by any healthy suspicion that this Hebrew woman so suddenly and inexplicably arrived in his camp should not be trusted. He reacts to Judit as an *image*, and so is eventually helpless before the onslaught of her *discourse*. The misleading 'inspiration' Holoferne believes he finds in Judit's appearance is as unfathered, Du Bartas implies, as is any writing not founded in the Word. That is, writing that is not scriptural in content, focus, and idiom poses an obstacle to the perception of truth. It blocks the Word, just as images, inadequate representations of real things, inhibit access to true perception. It is for this reason that, when Du Bartas is occasionally tempted to yield to artifice and to the blandishments of poetic "making," he rebukes himself: "muse, tu perds le temps . . . / Va retrouver Judit" (V, 191-2).

Du Bartas further illustrates the need for scripturally based writing by associating the Pléiade and Petrarchan cliché (among other such conceits) of the wounding glance cast by the mistress's eye with Judit's duplicitous semblance: "le seul regard d'une femme l'effraie / Et lui navre le sein d'une incurable playe" (IV, 481-88). He thus equates the snare of Judit's beauty with his definition of unfounded and deceitful writing.

Judit's first encounter with Holoferne immediately reveals how she will proceed to render him physically powerless before her sexuality, and textually impotent when confronted with her unprecedentedly strong discourse. She appears as a glittering idol: "le pourtraict de l'estrangere dame / Estant le seul objet du louche oeil de [Holoferne]" (V, 5-6, Baiche). Judit paints a deceptive picture for Holoferne with her words, flattering him to falsely persuade him of his eventual triumph:

> Ton seul nom chassera les plus vaillantes troupes;
> Devant toi les hauts monts abaisseront leurs croupes;
> Les fleuves devant toi les ondes tariront. (IV, 409-13)

Believing in the false representation his idol's words have generated, Holoferne lies enraptured in the coils of Judit's rhetoric. A nefarious Scheherezade, Judit's defense and offense are textual and reside in the stories she tells and in the pronouncements she makes. Already her discourse begins to enact the silencing of Holoferne's voice, as well as prefiguring his murder: "Jadis il commandoit à maint prince et maint roi / Et ores à soi-mesme il ne peut donner la loi" (IV, 493-4). Judit has caused a reversal. Infatuated by her, Holoferne has become an utterly passive being. He acknowledges this, incapable of rectifying it:

> Hélas! Hélas! dit-il, faut-il donc que je vive,
> O change malheureux! Captif de ma captive?
> Mais est-ce vivre, hélas! (V, 40-2)

This lamentation seems almost to prepare the ease with which Judit kills Holoferne. It is as though he has already renounced life. Unknowingly, he calls, figuratively, on the Hebrews to exact the very vengeance with which the play will literally end:

> Changés donques, Hebrieus
> Changés en ris vos larmes;
> Triomphez de mon ost, de moi . . .
> Je ne suis plus celui dont le nom seulement
> Causoit a vos soldats un gele tremblement;
> Mais je suis celui, dont le coeur jadis brave
> Est or serf d'une serve, et d'une esclave esclave.
> (IV, 419-24)

The doubly stated "esclave" follows upon and undoes the gender distinction preserved between "serf" and "serve," symbolizing through its possible feminine attribution the overpowering of Holoferne's male identity by Judit. That is, "esclave," designating Holoferne, is stated without a determiner, seeming to indicate that it is governed by the preceding "une."

Holoferne admits himself *displaced* by the passion she has ignited in him: "je ne suis plus celui. . . ." Judit's discourse invades and redetermines all space. Inarticulate because image-oriented, Holoferne wishes that he could display his heart, on which he believes his love to be written, to Judit. The fact that Holoferne now carries on his heart his love for Judit, and no longer harbors there the marks of the overweening ambition that had once characterized him, demonstrates how he has already been altered and weakened. It is significant that he cannot give voice to these words of love but rather seeks to display them, again demonstrating his dependence on representation.

> Que n'ay-je, transparent,
> Mon sein comm' un cristal, pour lui rendre apparent
> Le tourment de mon coeur, et pour lui faire lire
> Ce que par trop aimer ma bouche ne peut dire. (III, 541-5)

He is frustrated in his attempt because Judit's discourse proposes to write itself upon that same space. The knife with which Judit will kill Holoferne will create for the victim an anti-representation; it will carve *her* murderous inscription upon him, overlaying and eradicating what he had thought written there.

Holoferne is overcome by Judit's strategies of *inventio*. Judit wraps him in the treacherous threads of her speech:

> La vefve . . .
> Invente cent delais et faisant, cauteleuse,
> Discours sur discours
> Le sot tyran abuse. (V, 169-72)

The overlapping layers of discourse serve two purposes: they reinforce the strength of Judit's own speech, adding recital upon recital to form a solid narrative block, and they convey the sense of an oppressive, wordy weight bearing down upon Holoferne's own neutralized speech.

While telling him lies, Judit leads Holoferne to a higher truth, one he will experience only in death: that God's vengeance shall be enacted and that the Word shall be restored. Holoferne's being knows no such truth; he is composed entirely of lies:

> Les bravaches gens-d'armes
> Mentent le plus souvent parlant de leurs faictz d'armes.
> (V, 440-442)

In comparison to the bewitching effect of Judit's speech, his vaunting descriptions of military prowess are flimsy indeed, especially since we have already been assured by Amon, and by the Hebrews' emblematic reading of Judit's symbolic presence, of the outcome of the play. God's discourse has asserted its ascendance from the outset. In addition, Holoferne can only recount that which has already occurred; with Judit's arrival, Holoferne's ambitions to seize the future have been quelled, and he now lives only in his past exploits. He is incapable of pursuing his goals because of the prohibitive power of Judit's presence: "Mais las! madame, / je suis ore bien loing de mon intention" (V, 342-3). Similarly, in a recapitulation of a battle, he recalls issuing a series of orders to his army ("Vengés, courrés, faictes . . ." [V, 445-55, Baiche]), but these imperatives went unheeded. Holoferne's discourse, now in the present as well as in the past, has been rendered impotent. "Achève ton discours," Judit tells him (III, 437, Baiche), meaning, simply and brutally, "die." Having relegated Holoferne to the past tense, Judit now appropriates the future tense; she incarnates it, for it is a future the Hebrews will possess: "Nous devons esperer d'elle nostre salut" (IV, 322).

Salvation, Du Bartas affirms as a Calvinist iconoclast, comes not through the illusion of reliance on image but rather through the return to the divine Word and its textual recording that Judit exemplifies. Her character is in every way vitalized by the Spirit. Du Bartas underlines the correspondences among Judit's sorrow, writing, and divine inspiration:

> Et cependant Judit, qui verse incessamment
> De ses yeus deus ruisseaus, tesmoins de son tourment, Employe
> ores le temps en prières ardantes:
> Empolye ores le temps en prières ardantes:
> la prière lui sert pour pousser son Esprit . . .
> Jusques au plus haut ceil . . .
> Et le feuillet sacré, pour y trouver dedans
> Convenable remède. (III, 416-39)

The images of superimposition recall Du Bartas' paradigm of writing quoted earlier in this essay, in which God overlays the writing of the poet. The tears Judit weeps are both witnesses and writing agents; they impel her to turn to the Bible to *read herself into* the examples she finds there. Thus, her tears, which trace ('verse') down her face the verses through which Du Bartas will render her an instrument of God's Word, metaphorically announce Du Bartas' textual strategy. In it, like the figure of etching on copper, he will use writing to layer over and eradicate that which is pagan. Judit's face is similarly transformed by the tears that cover it. The Spirit, which also inspires Du Bartas, causes Judit to turn to a text for consolation and for models of other women recorded in Scripture who have enacted God's will in history. The triumph already transcribed in the Bible becomes for Judit an activated *exemplum*. She will live out that which she reads. The example she reads compels her to act. The faithful, salvific nature of such writing contrasts with Holoferne's superstitious self-abasement before an idol, and reveals the divine source of strength in which Judit's acts, and Du Bartas' writing, are grounded. Human writing, according to Du Bartas, is inadequate; like Judit, he needs the divine Spirit to breathe the Word into him:

> Esprit . . .
> Guide ma plume lasse, enfle-moy le courage
> Et fay qu'à ton honneur j'achève cet ouvrage.
> (III, 247-52, Baiche)

As Judit turns to the Bible for guidance, she finds examples of past heroines of Israel whose courage she desires to imitate; but her human nature, the "chair," "vient par mille discours son dessein empescher" (III, 438). This is a resumé of the drama that will transpire between Holoferne and Judit, in which her word, divinely inspired, will prevail over his pretentious and profane speech. Before Judit can be God's vessel, she must be purified. Consequently, Judit experiences a spiritual schism and battles within herself ("cependant que Judit avec Judit débat" [III, 445]) until the Lord suppresses her fearful voice, supplanting it with his own in an archetype of the operation of divine inspiration. As Judit scans the Book, a wind stirs the pages, then flattens them precisely where Jael's divinely sanctioned murder of the pagan king Sisera took place:

> Un ventelet s'esmeut qui ce fueillet abat
> Et le suivant descouvre: affin que Judit lise
> Comme Jahel remit le sainct peuple en franchise,
> Cest exemple dernier si fort accouragea
> La craintive Judit. . . . (III, 446-51)

That God intends Judit to read, and ruminate upon, this example is made clear in the passage's wording. The "ventelet" only rises "*affin que* Judit lise." The customary biblical term for the Holy Spirit, *ruach* or wind, makes the connection more explicit: the Spirit comes to vivify the letter. Judit, Du Bartas' literary alter ego, acts as he would: like a true Calvinist, adhering to a personal doctrine of spiritual inspriation. He feels commanded by God to "guider l'esleu au salut destine" (VI, 185) just as Judit is ordained to save Israel.

As Du Bartas feels authorized by his elect Calvinist status to read his poem's existence as biblically prefigured, Judit reads the act she has not yet performed as it is foretold in the Bible. Animated by God's Word, Judit asserts herself in an active manner which she will sustain throughout the drama. She breaks the council's indecision, places them in a passive role, and takes the weight of the Hebrew's history upon herself:

> Je veux, dit-elle alors, si Dieu m'est favorable,
> Desassiéger ce fort par un coup mémorable.
> Ne n'enfoncés plus oultre, attendés seulement
> De mon hardi dessein l'heureux evenement. (III, 505-8)

Judit is now explicitly conjoined with God. Through the rupture introduced in the following verse by the identification of the speaker, her name is clearly associated with "I am," the Hebrew term for God: "*Je suis*, dit-elle alors, / Fille du sainct Jacob . . ." (III, 329-30, Baiche).

It is essential that Judit, as Du Bartas in his writing, separate sacred from profane. Holoferne's stranglehold on the holy people can only be broken through Judit's agency, as she recognizes:

profaner l'hospitalité saincte?
Ce n'est pas la profaner; plus saincte elle sera
Quand pareille ma main les saincts garentira.
(V, 108-110, Baiche)

When she strikes Holoferne, Judit utterly disentangles the unholy
alliance: sacred history is separated from Holoferne's pagan grasp,
just as his head is severed from his body: "l'âme fuit en Enfer, le corps
choit sous le lict / Et la teste demeure en la main de Judit" (IV, 140-
6). The isolator is now an image for Judit's manipulation as Judit
holds up his head as a trophy. Exposed to the derisive contemplation of Israel, Holoferne is a type of anti-idol. As Judit has posed as
an idol to gull Holoferne, Holoferne has failed to adequately interpret the representation with which she lured him, accepting it at
surface level, without perceiving the powerful discourse it harbored.
Now the Hebrews act as iconoclasts, wreaking their vengeance upon
their former persecutor. The dismembering of Holoferne's body figures the silencing of Holoferne's voice which Judit had achieved in
the narrative. Now, the Hebrews

pèlent son menton pasle, esgratignent sa face,
Crachent dessus son front, arrachent de sa place,
La langue, qui souloit mesme oultrager les cieus.
(V, 204-89)

The epithet "autre" is used to designate Holoferne, marking
an alienation between victor and victim and conveying the impossibility of ever reconciling sacred and profane discourse. The opposition of Judit and Holoferne, then, mirrors the fracturing of human
and divine communication and posits the fundamental man-God
separation of which Du Bartas, in his attempt to sacralize the suspect tools of literary expression, is constantly aware. In their hal-
lowed mission, Judit and Du Bartas pit themselves against a secular,
profane "other": the fiction, or lie, which Holoferne embodied. In
this sense, the narratives of both Holoferne and Judit undergo
kenosis, or emptying-out, in the text. This is a phenomenon com-

monly experienced, for instance, by the Old Testament prophets who, in order to be rendered fit to articulate the divine message, first must abandon their self-hood. Similarly, while Judit overpowers Holoferne's discourse to erase it, her ability to superimpose her narrative, silencing his, is in no way due to human capabilities but rather to God's power. Du Bartas ultimately disclaims authorship in "La Judit." In his writing, "God has ceased to be a signified, becoming purely a signifier, the mark of a truth henceforth absent from discourse." [7]

As God is the focus of the text, Judit's selfhood must be textualized progressively. That is, as a human being her existence becomes less significant than her effectiveness as a symbol in the overall, on-going literary economy of God's saving acts in history. She is narrated by others in the course of the drama in ways that display her as both an agent in, yet distinct from, the story in which she is told. For instance, two soldiers see her leaving the city and *interrupt* the drama to furnish the reader with information about her life. Endowed with God's purpose, her life has become *separate* from them: She is something they narrate, something we read. They conclude:

> Je t'ay brièvement récité
> Les beaux faicts de Judit, sur qui nostre cité
> Tient ses deux yeux. Mais je ne puis te dire
> Quel chemin elle tient, ni à quoi elle aspire.
> (IV, 317-20)

An instrument of the divine will, Judit is no longer predictable in human terms. And, similarly, the unfolding of the text will map the displacement of human interpretation by divine determination.

The status of "La Judit" as the liminary work in the *Muse chrestienne* indicates that Du Bartes views the play as a program for his writing. [8] The explicitly biblical subject, the silencing of the poetic voice before the divine utterance, and the determination to eradicate profane elements in favor of a "poésie saincte" are all components of the project. Judit's masquerade as an idolatrous image may be linked to Du Bartas' distrust, as a Calvinist, of the would-be enclosure of divine presence within an object.[9] Judit's real mode of action is that of discourse, vehicle of the potency of God's Word over the static image. Her discourse is "stronger" than Holoferne's because it is single-minded in intention: God is her source and legitimation, while Holoferne and the pagan band are diverse and divided because ungrounded:

> Un pré n'est au printemps si bigarré de fleurs
> Diverses en odeurs, en effects, en couleurs,
> Que l'ost est bigarré de bandes differentes
> en langues, meurz, habitz, en armes et en tentes,
> Si que le vieil Cahos. . . . (II, 10-17, Baiche)

The straightforward enunciation of divine Word asserts itself over passive, descriptive poetry occupied with secular or profane matters. The textualized impotence which Holoferne suffers in Judit's presence epitomizes Du Bartas' discrediting of any writing that is not biblically sanctioned. The poet must confess his debt to God and offer himself as a channel for God's purpose. In this way, Judit becomes much more than a symbol of Du Bartas' literary creation. Rather, the focus is displaced from the author to the *true* source, and she comes to represent God's dynamism. Holoferne can thus be read as a token of the impotence which threatens Du Bartas as writer *unless* he gives voice to a divine pre-text (just as Holoferne had to be rendered passive and die in order to remove all resistance to the Word embodied in Judit). Like Holoferne, whose narration alters radically from a future orientation to being enmired in the past, Du Bastas' text was only ever his in the past: it now belongs to God. The writer's literary strategies have yielded to theological claims.

The final scene in which Judit dances her triumph assimilates her further to the Calvinist paradigm of writing: she is like the Psalmist as she sings to God's glory. She insists that only God could have written the outcome of this drama. As Judit ends her song, Du Bartas ends his:

Icy Judit achève, icy
J'achève aussi, ayant
Regracié la divine merci,
Qui mon oeuvre a daigné jusqu'à la fin conduire.
(V, 349-53)

Momentarily agitated by a strong, divine wind, they are now incorporated into the text of salvation which God writes.

Notes

¹ For a more extensive development of this argument, see Catharine Randall Coats, *Subverting the System: d'Aubigne and Calvinism* (Kirksville, MO: Sixteenth Century Essays and Studies, 1991).

² Cf. Lucien D. Allembach, *The Mirror in the Text*, trans. J. Whitely (Cambridge: Cambridge UP, 1989).

³ Terence Cave, *Devotional Poetry in France: 1570-1613* (Cambridge: Cambridge UP, 1969), 109.

⁴ Cf. "Avis au lecteur" in Guillaume Salluste Du Bartas, "La Judit," ed. crit. Andre Baiche (Association des publications de la faculte des lettres et sciences humaines de Toulouse, 1971). Consult also the other edition used: Du Bartas, *The Works of Guillaume Salluste Du Bartas*, ed. Urban T. Holmes, Jr. (Chapel Hill: U of North Carolina P, 1938). This edition is used throughout the text, unless otherwise indicated by the inclusion of the designator "Baiche" at the end of the citation.

⁵ Du Bartas, "La Judit," ed. Baiche, 129.

⁶ Luzius Keller, *Paligene, Ronsard, Du Bartas: trois études sur la poésie cosmologique de la Renaissance* (Berne: Francke, 1974), 113.

⁷ Michel de Certeau, *Heterologies: the Discourse of the Other*, trans. Brian Massumi (Minneapolis: U of Minnesota P, 1986), 109.

⁸ F. Braunrot, *L'Imagination poétique chez Du Bartas* (Chapel Hill: U of North Carolina P, 1973), 86.

⁹ As in the Catholic doctrine of transubstantiation.

Six:

Jephthah's Daughter: The Parts Ophelia Plays

Nona Fienberg

Although in *Hamlet*'s early acts, Laertes, Polonius, and Hamlet all treat Ophelia as if she were no more than the object of their various desires, by the fourth act she has made herself the play's subject.[1] She disrupts the court with her unruliness, inserting her vision of the world into the play. Only the fact that Ophelia encodes her disruptiveness in ballads, riddles, floral garlands, and pantomime has veiled her presence in productions and readings tied to monologic discourse. Feminist readings of culture, however, draw into the center discourses that have been marginalized. Gertrude, the only other woman in *Hamlet*, herself begins such a process. When Ophelia drowns after slipping from the margins of an offstage brook, Gertrude brings the vision of Ophelia's last acts onto the center of the stage, visualizing and interpreting her life and death both for the King and Laertes, and for the play's audience. Gertrude's elegy offers the fullest woman-centered reading of Ophelia's life in the play. Ophelia plays many parts as she substitutes her own desires and mysteries for those which Hamlet hermetically articulates when he describes her as Jephthah's daughter.

The story of Jephthah and his daughter makes a brief appearance in one of Hamlet's puzzling exchanges with Polonius. As Polonius introduces the arriving players, "the best actors in the world," Hamlet interrupts his praise:

> **Hamlet.** O Jephthah, judge of Israel, what a treasure
> hadst thou!
> **Polonius.** What treasure had he, my lord?
> **Hamlet.** Why,
> 'One fair daughter, and no more,
> The which he loved passing well.'
> **Polonius.** Still on my daughter.

Hamlet. Am I not i'th'right, old Jephthah?
Polonius. If you call me Jephthah, my lord, I have a daughter that
I love passing well.
Hamlet. Nay, that follows not.
Polonius. What follows then, my lord?
Hamlet. Why,
'As by lot, God wot,'
and then, you know,
'It came to pass, as most like it was.'
The first row of the pious chanson will show you more, for look
where my abridgement comes. (2.2.393-410)[2]

Hamlet alludes to a contemporary ballad which retells the
story in Judges 11:

Have you not heard these many years ago,
Jeptha was judge of Israel?
He had one only daughter and no mo,
The which he loved passing well:
And, as by lott,
God wot,
It so came to pass,
As Gods will was,
That great wars there should be,
And none should be chosen chief but he.[3]

The allusion remains a riddle wrapped in an enigma. Is Polonius a
"Jephthah"? What does "follow" from that reference? What does it
mean to Hamlet to suggest the analogy between Ophelia and
Jephthah's daughter?

The story of Jephthah, the Judge of Israel who vowed in return for a military victory to sacrifice to God "whatsoever cometh
forth of the doors of my house to meet me" (11:31), has held a fas-
cination in the Western tradition.[4] As it is told in Judges 11, when
Jephthah returns from success in battle both Jephthah and the
Bible's reader experience a shock, "and behold, his daughter came
out to meet him with timbrels and with dances and she was his only
child; beside her he had neither son nor daughter" (11:34).[5]

Jephthah explains his vow, lamenting that she has brought him so low and caused such great trouble. His daughter assures him that indeed he must honor his promise to God, but requests that before she is sacrificed she be permitted several months in the mountains with her maiden friends to lament her virginity. When she returns, Jephthah fulfills his vow. Thereafter the maidens of Israel honor Jephthah's daughter with a communal retreat each year.

Even in this spare outline, the story is disturbing. In Israel's earliest history, when God called upon Abraham to sacrifice his son, the test and the threat are there, but God intercedes before Isaac is killed. Where is God's intercession for Jephthah's daughter? But as the Bible tells us more, the story becomes more problematic. Jepthah's own origins are obscure; our first introduction to Jephthah tells us that he was a Gileadite, a mighty man of valor, but "the son of an harlot" (11:1), who remains unnamed. Because of his mother's marginality, he is cast out to make his way without family support. Because he has a reputation as a ruffian, the people of Israel call upon him reluctantly to lead their cause. His vow to kill the first crea-ture to meet him at the doors of his house if he won his battle is itself ambiguous. The Hebrew can be translated either "whosoever" or "whatsoever." Did he think he'd come upon a dog? Further, the example of Abraham and Isaac had long ago taught Israel that hu-man sacrifice was not part of a relationship with God. Then, since the story makes no mention of a wife and explicitly tells us that Jephthah has one daughter "and no more," who else might Jephthah have suspected would be the first to greet him but his daughter? Fi-nally, if this unnamed daughter will submit to her father, what are the two months in the hills for? Why does he grant her this time with her maiden friends?

Feminist cultural criticism addresses some of these questions by demonstrating the link between the historical stage of state for-mation and the regulation of female sexuality. In Judges, a time of political confusion follows closely upon the conquest of Canaan.[6] Jephthah's vow, then, can be seen as a bargain with God to con-firm patriarchal power through female sacrifice. Jephthah's power depends upon the absence, negation, and death of the female, particularly those closest to him: mother, wife, and daughter. When his daughter greets him with dance and music, Jephthah directs at his daughter his anger that he must sacrifice her. The oppressor blames the victim. In so doing, he commits himself to the male-centered plot of competition, conflict, destruction, and female sexual regulation in the interest of state formation.

Jephthah's daughter only elliptically poses an alternative woman-centered plot involving community, marriage, and birth. She does speak, first to say that he should not perjure himself before God,[7] and then to request her time in the hills. In her community of women friends, she will lament her powerlessness in the patriarchal world. In addition, by separating herself physically from the society and by associating herself solely with women, this nameless daughter of an unnamed mother may achieve a measure of autonomy for two months. She laments her exclusion from the sequence of a woman's life—maiden, wife, mother—which validates her in that context as a contributor to the continuing life of her community. So her time in the mountains substitutes for the violently suppressed woman's plot. Instead of the woman's comic plot, celebrating the continuation of life through birth, Jephthah's plot triumphs. She returns to be sacrificed in flames. The ritual lament of the women of Israel expresses the female community's sense of loss not only for Jephthah's daughter, but also for all lost women's stories.

By the time this story reaches Hamlet, it is no longer set in its biblical context. When Chaucer alludes to the Jephthah story at the end of "The Physician's Tale" of Virginius and Virginia, he does so with the weight of the biblical text behind Virginia's plea:

> "Thanne yif me leyser, fader myn," quod she,
> "My deeth for to compleyne a litel space;
> For, pardee, Jepte yaf his doghter grace
> For to compleyne, er he hir slow, allas!
> And, God it woot, no thyng was hir trespas,
> But for she ran hir fader first to see,
> To welcome hym with greet solempnitee." (238-244)[8]

Here, Chaucer's Virginia identifies herself with the biblical daughter as she pleads her case to Virginius. In contrast, Hamlet alludes to a popular ballad as he suggests his fear that Polonius is ready to sacrifice Ophelia to his ambitions, while Ophelia herself is absent. While the ballad contains the essential ingredients of the female sacrifice consolidating the state, the play introduces differences. Polonius is a court advisor, not a warrior. He has a son (whom he is also capable, in his malicious ignorance, of destroying). And Ophelia bears neither no name, nor, like Chaucer's Virginia, merely the feminized name of the father.

In the disturbed, highly competitive court environment of *Hamlet*, the allusion suggests Ophelia's innocent complicity in the competition for political power. While both Jephthah and Polonius are ignorant that they have set up the sacrifice of their daughters, Jephthah's unnamed daughter acquiesces in her father's victimization of herself to confirm his power. In contrast, Ophelia's submission to Polonius is only temporary. Once his death and her madness free her, she creates a new way to compete for attention, advantage, and privilege in the court of Denmark. It is as if Jephthah's daughter had returned from her two months in retreat with her woman friends to insert her own neglected agenda on the political scene. So Ophelia interferes in and subverts the corrupt court world of Denmark. Finally, she dies "in her own defense" as the gravedigging Clown of Act 5 speculates with a percipience he does not dream of.[9]

This essay suggests cultural resonances between the politically unstable time of Judges in Israel's history, the political confusion in *Hamlet*'s Denmark, and the anxiety over succession in late-Elizabethan England. Through such cultural resonances *Hamlet* articulates issues left unspoken in the story of Jephthah's daughter. In disturbed states, political uncertainty prompts the regulation of female behavior. Because of the political disturbances in and around Denmark, Ophelia becomes a pawn of her father's ambition and of the male competition for power. Laertes, Polonius, and Hamlet all hedge her about with reminders of the sexual double standard. Despite their efforts, she develops from her status as a victim of those court politics to become also an author of a potentially different story, a woman's story. In spite of Laertes' and Polonius' efforts to make her "no loved one: o-philia" and "no daughter: o-filia," she fills that empty space with her presence. She preoccupies the court, insisting that she be heard while she lives and impinging on the dynamics of court competition in her dying and death.[10]

If we keep in mind that Ophelia's ambitions, not just Hamlet's, have been frustrated by the late events in Denmark's court, then we will be able to understand more fully her responses to her brother and father's cautions about Hamlet's love, and to Hamlet's strange behavior. The only woman to whom Ophelia might look to understand a woman's position in court society is the Queen. Like Ophelia's, Gertrude's sexuality prompts male attempts to control her. Between the two women, father, brother, son, and brother-in-law all design to control female sexuality to serve their ambitions. Gertrude, in marrying Claudius, grants legitimacy to his rule, thus undermining Hamlet's hope for immediate power. When Hamlet rails against his mother's sexuality, then, he is in part venting his anger at the nature of her political power, which derives from her physical nature, her body. Only through this marriage to Claudius does she remain Queen. So in Hamlet's objections, sexuality is also political. Similarly, when Laertes and Polonius caution Ophelia against sustaining her relationship with Hamlet, sexuality is also political. They do not know that their resentment and attempts to regulate Ophelia's sexuality derive from their jealousy of her access to so powerful a figure as Hamlet. Instead, they base their interference on the double standard, a less apparently political motivation. In so doing, they subvert her potential to become part of a politically powerful marriage. Through their strictures on her, they prevent her from aligning herself with Hamlet as they curry favor with the party of Claudius. So they seek to cut off Ophelia's access to Hamlet. Instead, her body becomes Polonius' to use for his political advancement, as he stages her appearance to lure Hamlet to reveal his love-madness. Not like a Jephthah, but like a Lot, he prostitutes his daughter for his political advantage; Hamlet's ballad suggests the reference to the Lot story: "as by lott, God wot."[11]

As long as Ophelia plays the part of Polonius' political instrument, she speaks with a muffled voice of confusion, fear, and doubt.
She does not know what to think, believe, or do. Soon after Laertes
has told her to fear Hamlet, she reports to Polonius, "My lord, I do
not know,/ But truly I do fear it" (2.1.85-6). When Polonius asks if
she has given Hamlet any hard words of late, her response is "no,
but yes,"

> No, my good lord; but as you did command
> I did repel his letters and denied
> His access to me. (2.1.108-110)

When Ophelia returns Hamlet's love favors, the timing makes it
look like what it is: a power play. Her brother and father compel her
to abandon Hamlet when his fortunes are down, as if she were looking for advancement elsewhere, casting her lot with another can-
didate.

In one extended speech, however, Ophelia reveals her articulate command of court politics. When she laments the overthrow
of Hamlet's "noble mind" and the fall of his political prospects, her
cry of loss is for her own ambitions as well as his. She has aligned
her hopes with his expectations:

> And I, of ladies most deject and wretched,
> That sucked the honey of his music vows,
> Now see that noble and most sovereign reason
> Like sweet bells jangled, out of time and harsh,
> That unmatched form and feature of blown youth
> Blasted with ecstasy. O, woe is me
> T'have seen what I have seen, see what I see!
> (3.1.155-161)

In the ten blank verse lines ending in a couplet Ophelia commands
the stage and our attention. Even as she has internalized that negation of herself into a cipher as demanded by Laertes and Polonius,
"O, woe is me," she also fills the wooden O of the Globe with her
presence. She has seen the blasting not only of Hamlet's fortunes,

"Th'expectancy and rose of the fair state," but also the marriage plot Hamlet's "music vows" led her to expect.

Although Laertes and Polonius tell Ophelia that marriage with Hamlet would be a political impossibility, the marriage plot remains a hope for Gertrude throughout the play and forms the bond between the two women. As Claudius and Polonius plant Ophelia to trap Hamlet, Gertrude comments:

> And for your part, Ophelia, I do wish
> That your good beauties be the happy cause
> Of Hamlet's wildness. So shall I hope your virtues
> Will bring him to his wonted way again,
> To both your honors. (3.1.38-42)

This plot resurfaces periodically throughout the play, an alternative to the dominant plot of destruction. When Ophelia reappears following her long absence after "The Mousetrap" and her father's casual slaughter, she insists that Gertrude see her. While offstage she has used the liberties her madness, like Hamlet's, affords her to show herself to the strange Gentleman. Just as offstage she has defied male strictures to seclusion and opened herself up to his eyes and interpretation, onstage she demands Gertrude's attention. Despite Gertrude's reluctance, "I will not speak with her" (4.5.1), she finally grants Ophelia the privilege of the court.

Before, she had been enclosed in her closet sewing, so that Hamlet would know he could find her there to perform for her the pantomime she reports to Polonius in 2.1.77-100. Now she has become unpredictable, a wanderer, and subject to the searching gaze of strange gentlemen. When her hopes of advancement through marriage to Hamlet are dashed, Ophelia becomes a kind of player, like those she watched when we last saw her. Then, watching the players intrude on the court world to tell their truth, Ophelia had been admonished by Hamlet, "Be not ashamed to show, he'll not shame to tell you what it means" (3.2.135). At her next appearance on stage, she, like a wandering player, comes to hold a mirror up to the court.

When Ophelia enters, she no longer speaks with her earlier voice of submission to Laertes and Polonius. Instead she uses a range of voices, many of which are subversive. First, she sounds like a proud, importunate courtier, "Where is the beauteous majesty of Denmark?" (4.5.21). She commands attention in much the same way Laertes does upon his entrance less than one hundred lines later when he demands, "Where's the king?" (4.5.112).

Laertes' entrance so obviously threatens insurrection that it may be too easy to overlook the parallels between their competing political claims, his assertive and explicit, hers subversive and encoded in mad woman's language. Both entrances are preceded by forboding, "I will not speak with her" and "Alack, what noise is this?," "Attend, where are my Switzers?" Both entrances are prepared for by nameless interpreters. The Gentleman who asserts that Ophelia "spurns enviously at straws" may remind us that when Fortinbras finds "quarrel in a straw" he is inspired to invade Poland. In her way, Ophelia invades the court of Gertrude and Claudius. When a messenger interprets Laertes' arrival, he cries of rebellion and advises the King to "Save yourself." Both sister and brother articulate their disturbances about their parentage in the wake of their father's murder. Ophelia muses "They say the owl was a baker's daughter. Lord, we know what we are, but know not what we may be" (4.5.43-4). Laertes mentions their mother now for the only time in the play:

> That drop of blood that's calm proclaims me bastard,
> Cries cuckold to my father, brands the harlot
> Even here between the chaste unsmirched brows
> Of my true mother. (4.5.117-120)

Now, when Laertes asserts his rebellious power, he locates the source of that force in his "true mother." Yet he does so through vituperation that might echo the cries against Jephthah's harlot mother.

For her part, Ophelia locates the source of her power in woman's culture. Her folk songs' colloquial diction, slender trimeter and tetrameter, and familiarity may not seem threatening on the late

Elizabethan stage, where, since Marlowe, the blank verse line speaks with heroic authority. Her songs, however, introduce the protesting voice of oppressed women in society:

> By Gis and by Saint Charity,
> Alack, and fie for shame!
> Young men will do't if they come to't.
> By Cock, they are to blame,
> Quoth she, 'Before you tumbled me,
> You promised me to wed.'

He answers:

> 'So would I'a'done, by yonder sun,
> And thou hadst not come to my bed.'(4.5.58-66)

The King is as ignorant of the meaning of her ballad as Polonius was of the meaning of Hamlet's Jephthah ballad. Both Hamlet and Ophelia have access to a culture from which the other members of the court circle are excluded and in which they can find no meaning. Both Hamlet and Ophelia use that ballad culture at once to communicate their frustrations with the social order and to veil the dimensions of their rebellion against the values of this court.

After Ophelia sings, she leaves as though her performance has been decorous, "Come, my coach! Good night, ladies, good night. Sweet ladies, good night, good night" (4.5.72-3). Her audience has been, however, one of women, real and imagined; her message, no less than that Laertes more openly espouses, has been one of rebellion. Ophelia's rebellion against the double standard and its oppression of women arouses fear in Gertrude, who understands.

Just as Ophelia intrudes into the inner court circle, Gertrude intrudes into Claudius and Laertes' plotting to murder Hamlet when she brings the news of Ophelia's drowning. Although it cannot be clear how Gertrude knows the details she reveals, we are not surprised that it is Gertrude who knows. Like Ophelia, Gertrude insists on her time and the attention of the plotting men. She interrupts their machinations with the story of Ophelia's death.

Gertrude's tale of Ophelia's death allegorizes the limitations, frustrations, and aspirations of Ophelia's court career. Gertrude portrays Ophelia not as a victim of court politics but as an independent maker of texts, particularly as a woman who draws her understanding of her world from women's culture. Ophelia's texts, flower weavings, pantomime, and old songs offer a range of modes for telling alternative stories using languages different from that of the court world.

Although Laertes' "Drowned! O, where?" could readily have been answered with no more than a phrase, "in the brook," Gertrude speaks with a particularity and a precision that answer Ophelia's needs and her own. Gertrude paints a verbal picture of a different world, not in the court, but "there." In so doing, she moves that marginal place by the brook onto center stage for the space of her speech, thus offering a glimpse of the otherness that has been so little understood in this play. For Gertrude, Ophelia's last acts provide an opportunity for a woman to become a subject, rather than an object in the action.

At first, she works in small, making fantastic garlands, as we once saw her sewing in her closet:

> There is a willow grows askant the brook,
> That shows his hoar leaves in the glassy stream.
> Therewith fantastic garlands did she make
> Of crowflowers, nettles, daisies, and long purples,
> That liberal shepherds give a grosser name,
> But our cold maids do dead men's fingers call them.
> (4.7.165-170)

Ophelia's floral text is an intricate one, with an intimately encoded meaning. While Gertrude reserves it for others to interpret the garland, she does pause to list the names of flowers, to reject shepherds' names for long purples, and to insert the maidens' name, "dead men's fingers." Gertrude here privileges women's work and women's words, insisting on the alternative text she presents on Ophelia's behalf.

Gertrude then describes Ophelia playing at a coronation, as she tries to hang the garland, now allegorized as "crownet weeds":

> There on the pendent boughs her crownet weeds
> Clamb'ring to hang, an envious sliver broke,
> When down her weedy trophies and herself
> Fell in the weeping brook. (171-174)

These acts suggest Ophelia's preparation and hopes for advancement. To attribute her fall to the breaking of an "envious sliver" extends the political connotations of her pantomime. Finally, Gertrude's description of Ophelia's death recalls the last moments of her court life:

> Her clothes spread wide,
> And mermaid-like awhile they bore her up,
> Which time she chanted snatches of old lauds. . . . (174-176)

Her "mermaid-like" singing recalls Ophelia's "mad" songs, as she sustains her life after political disappointment and fall. So intricate an allegory of Ophelia's career is not accessible to Laertes or the King; the former hears only the fact and manner of her death, "Alas, then she is drowned?" (181), while the latter is concerned only with Laertes' rage. Gertrude has, however, perhaps like Jephthah's daughter's maiden friends, returned from temporary exile to interpret the meaning of the sacrificed daughter's life. Much like Ophelia's mad songs for an audience of women, Gertrude's elegy may require the complicity of women who will join her in lamenting the lost woman's story.

Although the meaning of Gertrude's allegorical elegy may only be accessible to a limited audience, she has gained her point. If Ophelia had not drowned, she might have become a pawn in the men's plotting once again, or one of the victims of the multiple murders which end the play. Then, her death would have been afforded what the other victims earn, that is either inappropriate eulogy or none at all. Instead, she "drowned herself in her own defense," and receives the 16 lines of uninterrupted appreciation Gertrude creates for her.

It is a strange allegiance, that between Gertrude and Ophelia, one that cuts across class and many apparently conflicting interests. Yet *Hamlet* traces, among its many plots, a woman's plot which aligns the only two women in the play. Although the men of the play never articulate the potential for rebellion the shared interests of Gertrude and Ophelia might unleash, they do know they fear them. They enact their fears of the women's power in their repeated efforts to control women's bodies. Gertrude, however, who has had one son "and no more," has identified in Ophelia the hopes for her future heirs and power. In Ophelia's turn to Gertrude, she releases herself from the role as victim, as Jephthah's daughter. Instead, she begins, too late, to identify her interests with those of women, in particular Hamlet's mother, who would have become, had the women's story been written, Ophelia's mother.

Notes

[1] For a discussion of the idea of the subject in feminist readings of Renaissance texts, see Carol Thomas Neely, "Constructing the Subject: Feminist Practice and the New Renaissance Discourses," *English Literary Renaissance* 18 (Winter 1988): 5-18.

[2] All references to *Hamlet* use William Shakespeare, *Hamlet, Prince of Denmark*, ed. Willard Farnham, rpt. ed. (Baltimore: Penguin Books 1971). Act, scene, line references are in parenthesis following the quotations.

[3] Bishop Thomas Percy, *Reliques of Ancient English Poetry*, ed. H.B. Wheatley, vol. I, 182-185.

[4] Wilbur Owen Sypherd, *Jephthah and His Daughter: A Study in Comparative Literature* (Newark: U of Delaware P, 1948). For a valuable psychoanalytic reading of the Jephthah story, see Robert Seidenberg, "Sacrificing the First You See," *The Psychoanalytic Review* 53 (1966): 49-62. For a literary-feminist reading of the Jephthah story, see Phyllis Trible, *Tales of Terror* (Philadelphia: The Fortress P, 1984), 98-118.

[5] *The Pentateuch and Haftorahs*, Hebrew text, English translation and commentary, ed. J.H. Hertz (London: Soncino P, 1970-1980), 667.

Hertz's commentary says of Jephthah, "his strange unhallowed vow would have been impossible under settled religious conditions. The condemnation of Jephthah's vow by the Rabbis has been re-echoed in many tongues and many lands. A thousand years later, Dante wrote in his *Paradiso*:

> Be strong to keep your vow; yet be not perverse—
> As Jephthah once, blindly to execute a rash resolve.
> Better a man should say, I have done wrong,
> Than keeping an ill vow, he should do worse.

The New Oxford Annotated Bible with the Apocrypha, ed. Herbert G. May, Bruce M. Metzger (New York: Oxford UP, 1977). This text offers this translation, "whoever comes forth from the doors of my house to meet me . . . I will offer him up for a burnt offering" (Judges 11:31).

⁶Gerda Lerner, *The Creation of Patriarchy* (New York: Oxford UP, 1986). Lerner's discussion of women in Old Testament society appears in Chapter Eight, "The Patriarchs," 161-179. Joan Kelly's work on the regulation of female sexuality in times of state formation appears in *Women, History, and Theory* (Chicago and London: U of Chicago P, 1984). See in particular her essay on "Early Feminist Theory and the *Querelle des Femmes*, 1400-1789," 55-109. On 88-90 she discusses the transition from Elizabeth's "exceptional" reign to James I's state regulation of female behavior.

⁷*The Letters of Abelard and Heloise*, trans. with an intro. by Betty Radice (Baltimore: Penguin, 1974). In Letter 6, Abelard writes Heloise, "No deeds performed by men have been greater than those of Deborah, Judith, Esther, the daughter of Jephthah who dies to save her father from perjury (Judges XI, 30)" (181).

⁸*The Riverside Chaucer*, ed. Larry D. Benson, 3rd ed. (Boston: Houghton Mifflin, 1987).

⁹Carol Thomas Neely, *Broken Nuptials in Shakespeare's Plays* (New Haven: Yale UP, 1985). The interpretation of Ophelia which has proved most helpful to me appears on 103-4 of Neely's book. I hope that this essay begins to respond to the call Elaine Showalter issues in her article "Representing Ophelia: women, madness, and the responsibilities of feminist criticism," for an Ophelia-centered reading of *Hamlet*. The article appears in *Shakespeare and the Question of Theory*, ed. Patricia Parker and Geoffrey Hartman (New York: Methuen, 1985), 77-95.

¹⁰In a later use of the Jephthah story, this one from Hobbes' *Levia-*

than, Hobbes asserts that every subject is the author of the sovereign's acts,

> And therefore it may, and doth often happen in Common-
> wealths, that a Subject may be put to death, by the command of
> the Soveraign Power; and yet neither doe the other wrong: As
> when *Jeptha* caused his daughter to be sacrificed: In which, and
> the like cases, he that so dieth, had Liberty to doe the action, for
> which he is neverthlesse, without Injury put to death.

Thomas Hobbes, *Leviathan,* ed. Macpherson (Baltimore: Penguin Books, 1968), 265-6. Hobbes' discussion of the subject's "corporall Liberty" to be the author of his actions is useful because it assumes the political significance of the Jephthah story. In addition, the corporal or physical nature of the subject's liberty becomes precisely the issue for Ophelia, as she is at first enclosed, restricted in her actions and presence, limited to the dalliance of a puppet. In contrast, her later physical freedom suggests another writer's interpretation of Jephthah's daughter's retreat in the mountains. To a late Medieval preacher that physical freedom seems an invitation to licentiousness:

> Nyce maydenhode is ylyckened to Jeptes doughter, that walkede
> aboute in the monteynes twey monthes for to wepe her
> maydenhode. So doth nyce maydenes that walketh aboute in
> medes and in fayre places ledynge daunces and syngynge, as it were
> schewynge hemselfe to lese her maydenhode. . . .
> (Sypherd, *Jephthah and His Daughter,* 11)

I thus coopt two antifeminist responses to the story of Jephthah's daughter for a feminist reevaluation of Ophelia's importance in *Hamlet.*

[11]Lerner's discussion of the story of Lot and his daughters, Genesis 19, appears on 172-3.

Seven:

"An Immortality Rather than a Life": Milton and the Concubine of Judges 19-21

Louise Simons

> "May her bones flower again from the tomb."
> —Ecclesiasticus 46.12

At the end of the Old Testament Book of Judges, Chapters 19-21, the story is told of an anonymous woman, a Levite's concubine, who meets her death one night through mob violence; indeed, the mob's action is sexually degrading as well as brutal. "With their whoredom," writes Richard Rogers, "they committed murther also," for "such like sinnes never goe alone."[1] Since most seventeenth-century biblical commentators interpreted the woman as adulterous, her death provided them with material for a providential homily. "God calls her for reckoning," states Joseph Hall, who extracts poetic justice from the chain of events, "and punishes her with her own sin. . . . Adultery was her sin, adultery was her death." Similarly, Rogers emphasizes, "For we see, that she suffred death, and that not only for her adultery, but even as it were in it."[2] Exegetically, then, the woman's horrific ordeal becomes a morally edifying illustration of trespass punished. John Milton, however, refuses the didactic convenience of using the concubine's ordeal to demonstrate divine retribution. In fact, Milton dignifies the concubine by treating her story, in its particulars as well as its larger impact, with respect for the personal suffering and conviction of its national significance. As we will see, Milton empties the nighttime episode of salacious or titillating content,[3] just as he empties it of suggestion that the mob's abominable action may in part be excusable because it works as God's instrument. It is Milton's probing interest in the woman's life and death that will be the focus of this study.

Judges 19 begins with seeming simplicity by suggesting that a domestic quarrel has taken place between the woman and the Levite,[4] who at that time is "sojourning on the farther side of the hill-country of Ephraim" (19:1).[5] Following some sort of squabble between the pair, the concubine leaves the lonely hill country where the Levite resides and returns to her father's home in the more metropolitan area of Bethlehem in Judah. Every translation is an act of imaginative interpretation, but this woman's life and death provide the translator with especially difficult problems. Much of the Hebrew wording in the last chapters of Judges is indefinite or unclear and requires a kind of free-flowing interpretation, based as often on psychological insight as on syntactical decision. At this point in the narrative, for instance, the wording used in most English translations is highly misleading. It states that the concubine "played the harlot against" the Levite "and went away from him unto her father's house" (19:2). As I will show later, the actual idea to be conveyed is not that the woman is sexually unfaithful to the man but that she becomes intransigent about remaining with him.

Even though the people depicted in Judges 19-21 take on personalities, none of them is given a name. The domestic and sexual functions of the woman are conveyed, of course, by her designation as a concubine, just as the priestly status of the man is shown by his designation as a Levite. It happens that the concubine's fate as an individual becomes intertwined with the collective fate of the Israelite tribes, and thus, although the tragic events of her life are personal, they also take on public significance. During this period in Israel's history, the twelve tribes show an increasingly urgent desire for nationalistic incorporation. Their confederation, though, takes place in uneven movements that are often difficult to follow. To further the reader's confusion, during the period of changeover from tribal autonomy to national autonomy, the sections of the Scriptures that deal with confederation cut back and forth achronologically.[6] For both these reasons—political confusion and narrative confusion—we must be cautious about drawing historical conclusions; but even so, the latter events of Judges appear to depict, at least symbolically, the enfolding of the final tribe.

Historically, the episodes recounted in Judges 19-21 take place when the scattered Israelite tribes are still operating under systems of self-government, and the narrative contains no valiant figure who can be thought of even in hindsight as a judge or leader. Instead, the section is marked by a spirit of individualism expressed even in the ordinary person. Linguistically, privatization is accomplished by means of a rhetorical reminder so often repeated that we may consider it as forming a redactive critique: "In those days there was no king in Israel; every man did that which was right in his own eyes." At 17:6 and 21:25, this entire thought is given; in 18:1 and 19:1, the first half only is stated. Since the individual tribal member ("every man") is nominated as the privileged unit of these chapters, it becomes textually significant to understand what "doing . . . right" appeared to be to the private person in those myopic, chaotic days before God's anointed saw to righting matters for the entire nation. As it happens, the concubine whose story is featured plays a sacrificial, folkloric role in the new nation's destiny. Her death becomes the crucial factor—a call to conscience—in confederating all the twelve Israelite tribes. Although the twelve clans are not united during this time, the period is transitional. They are tending toward consolidation, as eventually their coming together under a kingship is recounted in the next biblical books, I and II Samuel. The domestic troubles of the couple whose story we will be following, the Levite and his concubine, become instrumental in the process of national unification.

Formally, from the outset of Judges 19, the biblical narrative establishes its claim to widened meaning by taking note of the tribes' lack of monarchial rule ("In the days when there was no king . . ."). Throughout, the personal and domestic narrative enhances its own significance by attending to the story's various geographical locations. Finally, the moment of peripeteia takes place when the concubine's personal account recedes to the background and the imperatives of tribal redefinition become central. At this point, the woman as a suffering person has been overwritten first by the husband's and then by the tribes' use of her as a symbolic figure. In both her manifestations, as private individual and as public symbol, she appealed to the creative imagination of John Milton. Indeed, her story takes on multiple meanings in Milton's thought and in many respects threads together his diverse writings, as the Judges narrative finds its way into varying aspects of his prose as well as his poetry.

At the ending of Chapter 19, the concubine has been killed and her body hewn into a dozen pieces which are sent out to rouse the twelve Israelite tribes to justice. The horrified tribespeople, when made aware of the outrage perpetrated on the woman, say, "Such a thing hath not happened nor been seen from the day that the children of Israel came up out of the land of Egypt unto this day"; they add, "consider it, take counsel, and speak" (19:30). It seems that this is the very injunction Milton feels compelled to obey. In "speaking to" the events of the narrative, however, he makes two widely divergent interpretations. First, he links the plight of the Levite's concubine to events contemporary to his own life. In this case, the intimate picture of the woman's life elicits from Milton a kind of hermeneutics of intimacy. In advocating divorce reform, he makes use of her personal experience to soften the harshness of the term *fornication*. In a sense, I have organized my heuristics to parallel Milton's; my close reading of this portion of the text follows Milton's own type of analysis. Milton writes that even though the concubine did not indulge in "divorsive fornication," still she is termed a *harlot*. Biblical terminology, he reasons, thus shades the meaning of *fornication* to allow divorce to those who are unhappily married. It is the plight of couples held in "the bondage of canon law" that he addresses, hoping, himself, through "the rule of charity," to restore "the good of both sexes" (*YP* II, 220).

In a second kind of interpretation, Milton uses an extension of the same story to validate political repression in his own time; this he does by focusing on a different aspect of the account. In this reading of the Judges narrative, Milton considers not the problems of the oppressed individual but the wider quandaries of waging a just war. Here, he makes a broad, political, literal reading of the massacre of an entire tribe; he uses the example of harsh Israelite retaliation in a war of revenge against recalcitrant people to justify English repression of the Irish. These two contradictory hermeneutical approaches, one restorative and tender, one punitive and harsh, each emphasizing a different facet of the story, arise from Milton's varying applications of the biblical text; he is a man of contradictions, seen thus, immersed in the issues of his own lifetime.

Finally, Milton enlarges the local ordeal of the violated woman into a powerful indictment of all kinds of social, religious, and political injustice. In this reading of Scripture, Milton is neither a man seeking to justify desire for divorce nor a political reactionary to Irish rebellion. His interpretation causes the concubine's story to transcend both the mundane details of her daily existence and the grisly particulars of her violent and abusive death. This overarching interpretive use of the biblical material bespeaks Milton's preoccupation with endowing transitory, earthly life with an ultimately enduring and symbolic purpose.

I

In composition, the Book of Judges is divided into three not especially homogeneous sections. The first and third parts (Judges 1:1-2:5 and 17-21) are composed of older material that functions as a kind of bridge between its large middle portion (2:6-16:31) and Joshua, which precedes, and I and II Samuel, which follow. The next books in Scriptures, I and II Samuel, recount how the Israelites unify and regularize their system of government, moving from the heterogeneity of tribal control by patriarchal clans to the hegemony of monarchial authority by anointed kings. In Judges, a combined political and sacred concern underlies the Israelite tribes' now-and-then, here-and-there, attempts to gain the land of Canaan for themselves as God's rightful tenants. Judges opens *in medias res*: "And it came to pass after the death of Joshua, that the children of Israel asked of the Lord, saying: 'Who shall go up for us first against the Canaanites, to fight against them?'" The long midsection of Judges carries the territorial theme forward; battles are fought at various sites against local inhabitants, with the Israelite tribes usually marshaling under the command of a succession of heroes. In general, it is in this middle portion that those tribal leaders or warriors are to be found whom we somewhat misleadingly call "judges."

The last five chapters, 17-21, form a self-inclusive coda, in which the events of 17-18 are often a prelude to 19-21. For this reason, at times I include them in my general discussion. In the smaller

domestic realm, we read of households that play host to two opportunistic Levites, and in the larger political arena, we follow the continued hard-fought victories of the Israelite people in the embattled
land of Canaan. In the accelerating warfare of the final chapters of
Judges, especially in a three-part battle in which the tribes engage
in slaughter of each other, the Israelites unite to find not only military but also domestic solutions to besetting tribal problems.

In Judges 17 and 18, a Levite named Jonathan who is a na-
tive of the comfortable city of Bethlehem in Judah travels to the
far hill country of Ephraim "to sojourn where he could find a place"
(17:8). He becomes priest to a household whose altar and sacred
objects were made to reverse a curse for robbery. We see that the
Levite is not particular; he neither inquires about the origin of the
objects of worship nor scruples at joining the tribe of Dan when it,
in turn, steals the holy objects. In fact, when the opportunity arises
to minister to a Danite multitude rather than to one household
only, "the priest's heart was glad" and without ado he "turned and
departed" (18:20). The tribespeople of Dan are made easy by both
their turncoat priest, the Levite, and their graven images stolen from
the former robber. Thus "six hundred men girt with weapons of war"
feel secure in invading the fruitful land of Laish in Canaan and slaying the gentle, unsuspecting inhabitants in a brutal appropriation
of what they consider to be their own "inheritance" (18:16, 1).

The section ends by stating that the graven image appropriated by the tribe from a private household is to remain with the
Danites during "all the time that the house of God was in Shiloh"
(18:31). Shiloh, as we see, is the sacred residence of the ark of God,
and is evidently mentioned here as a true altarplace in order to contrast it with the stained Danite altar. In the final chapter of Judges,
though, Shiloh itself becomes the locale of large-scale ravishing of
women, young virgins who come out to dance in the harvest festival. Forcible entry, then, whether caused by desire for the fertile land
or for the fertile women, is an essential element of the Judges narrative. Indeed, desire for one accompanies desire for the other. The
formula of commodification works in both directions: the woman
may equal the land or the land may equal the woman, according

to different passages. In fact, after the carnage of a ferocious internecine war, when the Canaanite land-grab is temporarily not at issue, human procreation becomes this book's final preoccupation.

At the end of Chapter 17, Micah, the former robber, consecrates the Levite as his household priest and remarks innocently, "Now know I that the Lord will do me good, seeing I have a Levite as my priest." The redactor shows an evident distaste for all the self-serving characters—the thieving Micah, the turncoat priest, the plundering Danites. Chapter 18 begins the story of the brutal Danite takeover with the words, "In those days there was no king in Israel." Again Chapter 19 opens in a similar way, "And it came to pass in those days, when there was no king in Israel, that there was a certain Levite sojourning on the farther side of the hill country of Ephraim, who took to him a concubine out of Bethlehem in Judah." Directing attention to the lack of a figure of rule over the land creates a feeling of unease. Even the mention of tribal and geographical names familiar from the just-previous chapters suggests some linkage between the two Levites, the named one of 17-18 and the unnamed one of 19-21, and conveys a sense of their disjunctive wandering, in that they traverse the same terrain as they travel from place to place. Interestingly, the place names recur in somewhat scrambled order: the first Levite travels from Bethlehem in Judah to the hill country of Ephraim; the second Levite resides in Ephraim, imports his concubine from Bethlehem, follows her back to Bethlehem, and runs into trouble on the return to Ephraim.

Because, as Robert G. Boling notes, the biblical world is a male world,[7] dominated by male interests and governed by patriarchy, Judges 19 contains an unusual story. The narrative quickly turns its attention from the Levite to his concubine, who is unhappy in her lot. The story tells us that she leaves the Levite and returns home, evidently acting on her own initiative. In Scripture, when women occasionally initiate action to save men—as the midwives preserve the male children of the Israelite slaves against Pharaoh's command (Exodus 1:15-19)—their resourcefulness gains them approval.[8] The concubine's willful behavior, however, directed as it is against her society's structures, remains unratified. Perhaps her story even carries in it her implicit punishment for being headstrong. She will be victimized—"abused . . . all the night" (19:25)—almost to death and then mutilated in her death.

Moreover, the concubine's biblical account has suffered an unsympathetic translation. It seems she flees the Levite's dwelling as a result of domestic discord. The Hebrew is obscure at this point, however, and requires consideration of social, psychological, linguistic, and rhetorical factors, which include the probability of the concubine and the Levite's actions, as well as unusual verb construction and placement in the text. Translators who have misread the Hebrew have by result revised her reason for leaving, thereby placing blame exclusively on the woman: "And his concubine played the harlot against him and went away from him unto her father's house" (19:2).[9] One reason, perhaps, that the narrative's probability went unquestioned lies in the homiletic usefulness not only of the woman's infidelity,[10] but of the man's forgiveness: "By how much better this Levite was, so much more injurious was the concubine's sin," states Hall.[11] Milton is known to have owned two Bibles in English, an Authorized Version (1612 ed.) and a Geneva Bible. As a headnote to Chapter 19, both state: "A Levites wife being an harlot, forsooke her husband, and he tooke her againe." In 19:2, both say the "concubine played the whore," which is glossed in the margin: "Ebr., besides him: to wit, with others." It is this problematic translation, however, that particularly caught Milton's sympathetic attention, and he mentions it with disapproval in several of his works.

In his Divorce Tracts, Milton considers which qualities go into a good marriage, where the partners are truly meet help for each other, and which go into a bad marriage, where the partners are legally bound to each other to their misery, and what action gives an unhappy marital partner fit cause for divorce. Necessarily, Milton must turn his attentive scrutiny to Christ's sentence, "Whosoever shall put away his wife, except it be for fornication, and shall marry another, committeth adultery" (Matthew 19:9; see YP II, 329-43). Since Milton wishes to advocate the availability of divorce to cure matrimonial unhappiness, one of his jobs is to subvert the usual interpretation of Christ's words by extending the meaning of *fornication*. In *The Doctrine and Discipline of Divorce*, he belittles the legalism inherent in the notion that divorce is meant to be obtainable for "nothing but actual fornication, prov'd by witnes"; moreover, he observes that "the word *fornication* is variously significant in Scripture" (*YP* II, 334). Milton cites "men of high wisdom and reputed piety" who agree that "divorsive fornication" may exist outside the act itself of sexual unfaithfulness (*YP* II, 334). Milton actually misquotes one of his citations, Grotius' *Annotationes* (97), in developing the opinion that "fornication is tak'n in Scripture for such a continual headstrong behaviour, as tends to plain contempt of the husband."[12] Milton adds that Grotius "proves" this definition of fornication "out of *Judges* 19.2. where the Levites wife is said to have playd the whoor against him" (*YP* II, 335). In approval of Grotius and in disagreement with the reading that the concubine is a harlot, Milton also refers to Grotius' citation of "*Josephus* and the *Septuagint*, with the *Chaldaean*," which "interpret" to the concubine "only . . . stubbornes and rebellion against her husband." Continuing to dismiss the charge that the concubine committed bodily fornication, Milton includes marginalia from the Buxtorf Bible's rabbinical commentary, which refer to a marital tiff as the cause of the concubine's departure; Milton reiterates, "and to this I adde that *Kimchi* and the two other Rabbies who glosse the text, are in the same opinion" (*YP* II, 335). Indeed, in interpreting Christ's prohibition, the story of the concubine becomes Milton's proof text.

In the Judges narrative, after the concubine has been gone for four months, "her husband arose, and went after her, to speak kindly unto her, to bring her back" (19:3). The phrase "to speak kindly" is the English equivalent of the Hebrew "to speak to her heart." The wording seems to denote a tiff and not a serious breach on the woman's part of any obligation or trust. When the husband arrives in Bethlehem, the concubine "brought him into her father's house; and when the father of the damsel saw him, he rejoiced to meet him. And his father-in-law, the damsel's father, retained him" (19:3-4). The father-in-law entertains the Levite into the fifth day, even though after three days the Levite is ready to depart with the concubine. "The four months' absence of his daughter is answered with four days' feasting," even though "this feast, which was meant for their new nuptials, proves her funeral," notes Hall (289-90). Nothing in the account of the interchanges between the two men indicates, or even *suggests*, that the woman was adulterous. Milton obviously considers the gracious hospitality of the father-in-law to be a telling point, because to drive home his argument in the Divorce Tracts, he says, "*Ben Gersom* reasons that had it bin whoordom, a Jew and a Levite would have disdain'd to fetch her again." Milton then adds his own shrewd assessment of the concubine's leavetaking, "And this I shall contribute, that had it bin whoordom she would have chosen any other place to run to, then to her fathers house, it being so infamous for an hebrew woman to play the harlot, and so opprobrious to the parents" (*YP* II, 336).

Two years later when Milton writes *Tetrachordon* to "confirm" the ideas he espouses in *Doctrine and Discipline of Divorce*, he again alludes to Judges to prove that "the language of Scripture signifies by fornication . . . not only the trespas of body" (*YP* II, 672). One wider meaning, he repeats, is "also any notable disobedience, or intractable cariage of the wife to the husband, as Judg. the 19. 2" (*YP* II, 672). Milton provides his own intertextual gloss, as he harks back from *Tetrachordon* to "*the Doctrin of Divorce*" for reinforcement of his own interpretation (*YP* II, 672). In *Tetrachordon*, Milton sums up his position that the word *fornication* expressed "as the language of Christ understands it" means "a constant alienation and disaffection of mind, or . . . the continual practice of disobedience and crossnes from the duties of love and peace, that is in summ, when to be a tolerable wife is either naturally not in their power, or obstinately not in their will" (*YP* II, 673). It is the willful departure of the concubine that underlies Milton's last definition.

In addition, there is only one place in *Christian Doctrine* where Milton cites any of his own works. In that citation, he refers to the section of *Tetrachordon* which states that when Christ permitted divorce on the grounds of fornication, Christ himself meant the word *fornication* to have a broad application. "I have proved this elsewhere," says Milton in *Christian Doctrine*, "basing my argument on several scriptural texts. . . . The best text to demonstrate this, and there are many, is Judg. xix. 2: *she fornicated against him*. This was not by committing adultery, because then she would not have dared to run home to her father, but by behaving in an obstinate way towards her husband" (*YP* VI, 378). Certainly, Milton's concern to salvage the concubine's reputation is motivated by a self-interested desire to bolster his own unusual interpretation of Christ's word. But it is evident that the perplexities of her harrowing story take hold in his imagination; he writes her fate across his works.

An event in Milton's own life must be mentioned as it may enter into his thinking on the desirability of divorce. From the sketchy facts we have of Milton's first marriage, we may see a possibility that when Milton read Judges he pictured Mary Powell as the headstrong wife and himself as the long-suffering husband. The pair were married in 1642, probably in late May. She left Milton shortly after (within a month's time, as it seems) for her father's house and did not return to Milton until 1645, even though it appears she was expected back soon after the time she had left. Milton's first Divorce Tract was published on August 1, 1643. Any conjecture that might be made about his unhappiness with his own marriage or his willingness to end it has to be based on the scanty biographical information.[13] Milton's writing on the divorce issue seems to me to be based mostly, if not entirely, on disinterested conviction and not to be a reliable indicator of his personal dissatisfaction. Long after he and his wife were reunited, Milton continued to address the issue of divorce with the same vigor and firmness of conviction.

In 1654 in Milton's *Second Defense of the English People*, he returns to the divorce issue, remarking that in his previous writings he took the issue of domestic liberty as his own special province. "Hence," he writes, "I set forth my views on marriage, not only its proper contraction, but also, if need be, its dissolution. My explanation was in accordance with divine law, which Christ did not revoke. . . . Concerning the view which should be held on the single exception, that of fornication, I also expressed both my own opinion and that of others" (*YP* IV, 624-25). In reiteration of his own broad interpretation as the correct one, Milton mentions the 1646 publication of John Selden: "Our distinguished countryman Selden still more fully explained this point in his *Hebrew Wife*" (*YP* IV, 625).[14] Selden's *Uxor Ebraica* did not influence Milton's Divorce Tracts, of course, since Milton's writing preceded Selden's. Rather, Selden reaffirmed Milton's reasoning; however, since Selden was an important ally, Milton again refers to Selden's book in *Christian Doctrine* when he reintroduces the divorce issue: "Furthermore, as Selden demonstrated particularly well in his *Uxor Hebraea*, with the help of numerous Rabbinical texts, the word *fornication*, if it is considered in the light of the idiom of oriental languages, does not mean only adultery. It can . . . signify anything which is found to be persistently at variance with love, fidelity, help and society (i.e., with the original institution of marriage)" (*YP* VI, 378). Since reference to the concubine underlies and pervades Milton's work, and since her story is not exactly a Renaissance commonplace (aside from sermons, it seems not to be cited), we may reason that the story has a special significance for Milton.[15]

It may be worth noting that when Milton refers to Judges, he makes no distinction between the marital status of either a concubine or a wife.[16] He always refers to the Levite as the woman's "husband," and to the woman's father as the Levite's "father-in-law." The Bible states that the Levite "took to him a concubine." This wording, as Phyllis Trible notes, renders the Levite the subject and the concubine the object and, as Trible remarks further, shows the Levite's control and ownership.[17] Even so, the societal power of this particular man over this particular woman is not at issue. The term, *took to him*, is the usual one for marital description; it conveys no special subjugation in concubinage. It is true, the Levite had a place of distinction in the Israelite world, but this set him apart from all others and not just from the one woman. In *The Likeliest Means*, Milton remarks on the duty the Israelites owed to Levites, as a priestly class, because Levites "had no part nor inheritance in the land" (*YP* VII, 282). Indeed, what we see in Judges is not that the Levites were markedly powerful but that they were unsettled (unlanded) and were forced to scramble for their priestly positions.[18]

Although Milton and most other commentators mention the woman as wife and the man as husband, she is invariably referred to in Hebrew as either a woman or a concubine, whereas his designation as a man or a Levite is not fixed throughout. In fact, the scriptural pattern changes dramatically in verses 26 and 27 with two highly significant references. After the woman has been ravished all night by a Benjamite mob and is either dead or near death, the redactor causes the references to distance the Levite from the concubine and her ordeal, stationing him above her: in the final identifications, the Levite is referred to as "her lord" (19:26, 27).

II

In recounting the brutal scene that occurs during one night on the return journey to Ephraim, the narrative itself turns murky, or, at least, becomes difficult to follow and to place in perspective. The covering darkness, it seems, disguises not only the violent motives of a lawless mob but also the strategic motives of the biblical redactor. When we reach this eventful scene, we may see Milton's interpretive interest begin to extend beyond the personal story of the traveling couple to include the political reactions of mobs and nations, as he gathers material in support of his political ideas.

The woman's ordeal takes place on the return from Bethlehem. At the end of his fifth day as his father-in-law's guest, the Levite, now having tarried longer than he had intended, departs with his concubine and his servant. He refuses to spend the night in Jebus, which he thinks of as "the city of a foreigner" (19:12), but stops instead in Gibeah, a city of the tribe of Benjamin. He waits expectantly in the open square as the sun goes down, but by eventide no one has invited him to be a guest for the night. Finally, an old man, one who is also from the hill country of Ephraim but now residing in Gibeah, sees the Levite and speaks to him cordially. The Levite accounts for his journey by saying he is on his way "to the house of the Lord" (19:18), a statement unexplained by any other events of the narrative and perhaps only a self-serving fiction. The former

Ephraimite takes the Levite and the Levite's entourage home with him, even while suggesting some uneasy comment about their safety in the growing darkness outside in the square.

At home, the old man performs the functions of a host, and while the two men are eating, drinking, and "making their hearts merry, behold the men of the city, certain base fellows [in Hebrew: *benai belial*, or *sons of worthlessness*], beset the house round about, beating at the door" (19:22). Symbolically, the setting sun indicated trouble, and, indeed, an evil scene is about to take place. It is one that most biblical commentators gloss only briefly by referring to the "abomination" or "outrage" at Gibeah, while giving exegetical attention to identifying place names, estimating actual dates of events and number of tribe members, and noting the growing degree of consensus among the clans as they prepare for monarchy. Milton, however, alludes to the dissolute bestiality of the Benjamite mob in his prose, specifically in *Animadversions* and *Eikonoklastes* and generally in *Christian Doctrine*, and in his poetry, obliquely in *A Mask* and directly in *Paradise Lost*.

In Gibeah, the riotous mob who knock at the old man's door demand to sodomize his guest, the Levite. "Bring forth the man that came into thy house, that we may know him," they insist (19:22). Their demand and the ensuing scene reprise the events of Genesis 19, when the men of Sodom demand Lot's guests, male angels, for the same purpose. Indeed, as Burney demonstrates, the Judges episode is constructed upon the Genesis one "in so remarkable a manner as to compel the conclusion that one narrative must have been deliberately modelled on the other."[19] The Hebrew verb, *yd'*, or *to know*, makes the mob's lascivious intent clear, as does the host's response. "Nay, my brethren," he denies them, "I pray you, do not so wickedly; seeing that this man is come into my house, do not this wanton deed" (19:23). Instead, he makes the men a counter offer, "Behold, here is my daughter a virgin, and his concubine; I will bring them out now, and humble ye them . . ."—in Hebrew, the host uses "humble" as a euphemism for ravishing the women—". . . and do with them what seemeth good unto you." He finishes, "But unto this man do not so wanton a thing" (19:24). In Hebrew, the "do not" that the host uses is a negative form reserved for absolute prohibition, and "so wanton a thing" is another euphemism for sexual ravishment.

What "seemeth good" in the psychology of the mob becomes a complicated matter for the reader, perhaps, but "the master of the house, the old man" (19:22) playing host to a traveling priest is concerned that the lawless rout outside his door not bestialize a man, a Levite, a guest. The holy injunction to remember the time when the Israelites were strangers in the land of Egypt makes the host's duty to shelter and protect his guest all the more pressing; "this man is come into my house" forms his primary excuse to the boisterous crowd at his entryway. When the Benjamites do not "hearken to" the host but instead continue their demand that he deliver his guest to them for their sexual pleasure, one of the men who is inside—either the householder or else the Levite—moves to break the deadlock. One or the other thrusts out the concubine to appease the violent men who are in waiting. The Bible continues, "so the man laid hold on his concubine, and brought her forth unto them" (19:25).[20] Apparently, it is the Levite himself who takes defensive action.

The nighttime scene is murky in multiple ways. Just as the syntax is confused, so is the sexuality. It is difficult to identify "the man" who makes the final decision; did he (as host) lay hands on the other's concubine or (as guest) on his own? Further, why did the crowd order out the man, yet accept the woman? Was the concubine, as Cedric C. Brown surmises, "fobbed off" on them?[21] Erotic tension is simultaneously both released by the preservation of the Levite and heightened, or at least disturbed, by the persecution of the concubine. An omnipresent concept in the Bible is that as God creates us individuals, so the individual is the essential unit of all suffering. This we feel, certainly, as we read the concubine's story. The woman is a blasted, blighted, mute, suffering victim. Whether his hands actually thrust her out the door or not, the Levite commits a crime of faithlessness through breaking the trust that is the domestic bond.

The Judges account now turns from the two men—host and guest—back to the woman and her suffering at the hands of the Benjamites: the narrative continues with "and they knew her, and abused her all the night until the morning; and when the day began to spring, they let her go" (19:25). Milton makes various kinds of use of the swift account of the demand for one victim, the man, and the brutalizing of another, the woman. In *Christian Doctrine*, although the entire episode from Judges may figure in his list of biblical offenses against others, "Homosexuality, fornication, violation, adultery, incest, rape, prostitution, and offenses of a similar kind," Milton then specifies "Judges xix.22" as providing an example of sodomites among Israelite men, those who are the "sons of Israel" (as per Deuteronomy 23:17) (*YP* VI, 756). In Judges, these sodomites are denominated "sons of *belial*," or brutish revelers. In Milton's poetry, they reappear twice, once in *A Mask Presented at Ludlow Castle* and once in *Paradise Lost*.

A *Mask* is a courtly entertainment commissioned in 1634 by the Earl of Bridgewater, who had recently been installed as Lord President of Wales. In *A Mask*, the "sons of *belial*" are refigured by just one nighttime debauchee, Comus, the foremost anti-masque character. Comus, who is associated with drink through Bacchus, his father, is a reveler/enchanter who appears in the gloom of night outside the gates of civilized society. He is the leader of a route of monstrous followers. The direct connection between *belial*, or riot and worthlessness, and the Greek rites of *komos*, or nocturnal dissipation, is made by Milton himself in one of his notations in the Trinity College manuscript. As a possible topic for a tragedy, Milton lists: "Comazontes or the Benjaminits Jud. 19. 20 &c. or the Rioters" (*YP* VIII, 556).[22] When Milton turns to depicting "Comazontes or the Benjaminits . . . or the Rioters" in his masque, the subject matter of the scriptural encounter in nighttime Gibeah must be toned down considerably for a theatrical genre devoted to aristocratic entertainment, especially for a masque presented to a family by that family's three youngest children.

In *A Mask*, the character of Comus retains its dark, *belial*-like quality. As a nocturnal being of evil, Comus carries a suggestion of the sodomite,[23] but also as a demigod, he is a youthful figure of some appeal, a poetic reveler who entices other fallible beings with a *carpe diem* message. "Braid your locks with rosie twine / Dropping odours, dropping wine," he invites, adding that "Rigor now is gon to bed, / And Advice with scrupulous head, / Strict age, and sowr severity" (*Mask* 105-109). Thematically, the threat of rape is present, but in the main action its danger is averted by the chaste Lady and her stalwart community. The evil power of lust is evident not only to the Lady in the central action, but also to the water nymph Sabrina in one of the masque's secondary narratives. In Sabrina, we encounter a kind of mixed parallel to the molestation of the unnamed concubine of Judges. Sabrina's background includes a concubine-mother and a fatal flight that ends in drowning. She is a figure of victimization and virgin purity both, but more important is the transformation she undergoes. When Sabrina "Commended her fair innocence to the flood," she "underwent a quick immortal change, / Made goddess of the river" (*Mask* 831, 841-42). Both Sabrina and the Lady undergo a final change into immortality; the Lady becomes a spiritual bride in heaven.[24] Like her Miltonic counterparts, the biblical concubine may be understood as ultimately taking on a symbolic life also; hers is as a perpetual plea to public conscience.[25]

In the opening book of *Paradise Lost*, Milton writes that "when Night / Darkens the Streets, then wander forth the Sons / Of *Belial*, flown with insolence and wine." Milton visualizes the scene doubly, joining the episodes from both Genesis and Judges: "Witness the Streets of *Sodom*, and that night / In *Gibeah*, when th' hospitable door / Expos'd a Matron to avoid worse rape" (*PL* I.500-505). "Worse rape," which may refer to sexual abuse of the host's virgin daughter, seemingly refers to ravishment of the Levite himself. The sacrifice of the concubine in his stead has some analogue in God's sentence passed on all mankind in Book Three: "Die hee or Justice must; unless for him / Som other able, and as willing, pay" (*PL* III.210-11). In *Paradise Lost*, of course, it is the willing Son who offers himself as redeemer. The concubine may seem to be a "shadowie type" indeed, but her life pays for others. Whichever Milton had in mind as an even greater horror averted, "worse rape" of the virgin daughter or of the priestly guest, in effect he bears witness to the tragedy that occurred. Those who might expect a patriarchal hermeneutics from Milton, one that is dismissive of the woman's suffering as of less account than the man's, misread Milton's interpretation of the event. Milton recounts the horror, then refocuses on the redemption; yet he glosses the two halves equally, giving full attention to both the *before* and the *after*. The same kind of cultic myth that informs biblical narrative—in Judges, the story of the victimized woman as scapegoat or sacrifice —also charges Milton's epic poem. It is this biblical quality that Michael Lieb refers to in *Paradise Lost* as "the essentially archaic . . . the nonlogic of mythic or prediscursive thought."[26]

The concubine's function as an appeal to public intervention is well recognized by Milton. *Animadversions* is published in July 1641 as a response to Hall's *An Humble Remonstrance* of January 1641. In the question and answer format of *Animadversions*, Milton first excerpts the Hall remonstrance, often rendering Hall incomprehensible in the process, and then provides his own jibing answer. To Hall's *"Thou sufferest thy Wife* JESABEL: was shee Wife to the whole Company, or to one *Bishop* alone?"* Milton replies: "Not to the whole company doubtles, for that had bin worse then to have bin the *Levites* wife in *Gibeah*: but heere among all those . . . whom you trample upon, your good Mother of *England* is downe againe in the throng" (YP I, 713). In this passage of *Animadversions*, the concubine is figuratively equated with the ravished Church of England, which, in Milton's metaphor, is "downe" forced "againe in the throng" of bishops. The bishops, here, of course, are the evil rapists, the Benjamites.

III

Usually, daylight should signal a new beginning, but in the case of the concubine raped all through the night, the woman's agony seems to have no turning point. "The dawning of the day" finds no brightening meaning for her tragedy. Her isolation and shame imply her ostracism from the protected safety of human domestic quarters, which are, explicitly, under ownership of men: "Then came the woman in the dawning of the day, and fell down at the door of the man's house where her lord ['*dnyh*] was, till it was light" (19:26). With the new day, the narrative attention returns to the Levite, who means once more to be on the road: "And her lord ['*dnyh*] rose up in the morning, and opened the doors of the house, and went out to go on his way" (19:27). Once outside, he discovers his concubine, fallen in the doorway "with her hands upon the threshold" (19:27). He speaks to her with an evident intention of reincorporating her into his household, "Up, and let us be going."

We must pause to wonder what purpose the Levite can intend for the woman. Her main identity has been an erotic one up to this point, and she is now not only disgraced but also unfit to be a Levite's bed partner. In Miltonic imagery, the primary sign of the concubine's estrangement from the Levite is found in her empty hands reaching toward the doorway of the house: they are outstretched in vain.[27] *Handedness* is Milton's most useful symbol for union. In the separation scene in Paradise, he writes of Eve, "from her Husbands hand her hand / Soft she withdrew" (*PL* IX.385-86). And at the end of the poem, as Adam and Eve depart Eden together, he describes the pair in their new environment: "The World was all before them, where to choose / Thir place of rest, and Providence thir guide: / They hand in hand with wandering steps and slow, / Through *Eden* took thir *solitarie* way" (*PL* XII.646-49; my emphasis). In the Judges narrative in English, connectedness is indicated rhetorically—by use of polysyndetonic conjunctions which are monotonous in their pervasive repetition: *and* links the linguistic world as well as the phenomenal world; *but* dissevers them. "And her lord rose up in the morning, and opened the doors of the house, and went out to go his way; and, behold, the woman his concubine was fallen down at the door of the house, with her hands upon the threshold. And he said unto her: 'Up, and let us be going'; but none answered." Five times *and* is repeated in just this small section as the man performs common activities, until the shock of *but* intrudes into the bright, ordinary, trivial world of daylight. In the circular travel patterns of these Israelites moving about in the land, the woman's journey is short-circuited.

No other person is so "solitarie" as this fallen woman, her seeking hands outstretched on the threshold of the house. Words for dwelling places seed this narrative (in Hebrew, most often *byt* is used, for *house* or *home*), indicating the domestic nature of the episode and the sheltering protection that society offers its members. "Fallen down at the door [in Hebrew, *pth*, or *doorway*] of the house," she is completely isolated outside social boundaries. She has not taken part in the discourse until now, and at this point she is disjoined from language and from society, and rendered a cypher. Thus, when her prone body is addressed in terms of the everyday world, "up, and let us be going," the Bible says of her: "none answered" (in Hebrew, literally, "there was no answer").

It is the conjugal relationship itself which is most carefully avoided throughout the narrative. At the outset, the Levite is referred to as *'iš*, or *man*. In a somewhat unusual rhetorical construction, he is the concubine's *'iš*, her man. At the end of the concubine's life, he is called *'dnyh*, her lord. It is absence that is significant: nowhere is he called *ba'al*, the ordinary, everyday term used to indicate the masculine role of a husband, whether to a concubine or a wife (literally: *ba'al* is *master*; there is no separate word meaning *husband*). It seems to me that a teleological strategy operates under the narrative all along: the writer works to avoid the reader's censure of the Levite for what is to happen when the Levite returns to his home. All through the tale, the Levite has been, in a sense, compartmentalized from the concubine. They never converse; he does not even address her directly until she is no longer able to answer. In departing Gibeah, he changes the direction of the very narrative itself. He picks up the concubine's prostrate body from the doorstep, takes the body with him, "and when he was come into his house, he took a knife, and laid hold on his concubine, and divided her, limb by limb, into twelve pieces" (19:29). In Hebrew, the dismemberment reads: "cut her according to her bones." He sends the dozen body parts "throughout all the borders of Israel" (19:29). In economic terms, the concubine is a commodity, and seen thus, the events of this section in Judges recount the bitter fate of an expendable woman. Yet as Milton recognizes, in her death, the sacred significance of her narrative takes over, transcending the local myth of the scapegoated outcast, and the concubine becomes a powerful rallying point for morality and justice. The Miltonic pattern of interest is in revival that takes a new form, typically a spiritual form.[28] It is the Levite who brings this change, a kind of reversal, to pass.

Underscoring the folkloric element of this narrative, in which twelve body pieces is so convenient a number, the dismembered woman immediately galvanizes the tribes to action. They assemble "as one man," and they agree to take action "as one man" (20:8,11), a meaningful, repeated construction that knits a corporate entity— the assembled congregation—into a solitary being—an individual—in a Book whose measure of righteousness is taken through the singular perspective of "every man."

IV

When the clans gather together, they seem to recognize that their unstated purpose is to make war. Implicitly, the redactor acknowledges this to be so, for without explanation, the passage states that "four hundred thousand footmen that drew sword" were to be counted (20:17). The assembled tribesmen, in all their vast number, accept the Levite's account of what happened at Gibeah without question. The Levite tells them that "the men of Gibeah rose against me, and beset the house round about upon me by night; me they thought to have slain, and my concubine they forced, and she is dead" (20:5). Actually, in recounting his version, the Levite ambiguates what happened in the dark of night at Gibeah. Although the house was indeed surrounded by a debased, brutal mob, the offense they wished to commit seemed clearly against morality. The men battering the door claimed to be after sex, not slaying. The Levite says more accurately of the Benjamites that "they have committed lewdness and wantonness in Israel" (20:6). On the other hand, in fairness to the Levite's recasting of the situation, at the end of the concubine's ordeal, which was the same abusive one intended for him, the woman dies. Perhaps the Levite reads his own mortality in hers.

Significantly, when all the tribes gather to consider what action must be taken against the perpetrators of the outrage, the men of Benjamin do not join their brothers at Mizpah. Moreover, they refuse to send the offenders (*belial*) from Gibeah to be put to death, as the tribal elders decree must be done to "put away evil from Israel" (20:13). So the confederated tribes declare war on Benjamin, and after a touch-and-go battle of three parts—something of a model for *Paradise Lost*'s climactic Battle in Heaven—God finally delivers the Benjamites into the hands of their brethren. In the chapters which recount the fighting, 20-21, wholesale slaughter takes place, and the redactor chronicles the mounting bloodshed factually, without emotion.

In 1651 in *A Defence of the People of England*, Milton draws a parallel between the regicide and other deaths that became necessary to war-embroiled England in his own time and the deaths that were caused by the ancient Israelites' stern adherence to morality. Rebutting Salmasius in defense of the blood that was shed because of the Civil War, Milton demands rhetorically, "What teachings of law or religion ever instructed men to consider their own ease and the saving of money or blood or life more important than meeting the enemy? Does it matter whether the enemy be foreign or domestic? Either one threatens the state with the same bitter and ruinous destruction. All Israel saw that without much shedding of blood she could not avenge the outrage and murder of the Levite's wife; did they think that for this reason they must hold their peace, avoid civil war however fierce, or allow the death of a single poor woman to go unpunished?" (*YP* IV, 431). Milton rallies his community with the same call to redress moral wrong that the Levite chose. His plea is for justice when justice appears least easy to obtain. In *Paradise Lost*, the fallen angel Belial is in appearance "graceful and humane," and one who "seemd / For dignity compos'd and high exploit," but who is actually "slothful" and "To vice industrious." Unfortunately, Belial can "make the worse appear / The better reason, to perplex and dash / Maturest Counsels" (*PL* I. 109-15). In opposition to the slothful ease of a persuasive Belial, *consider* the plight even of the "single poor woman," Milton writes in reminder to his fellow citizens; *take counsel*, he admonishes them; and *avenge outrage and murder*, he finishes.

Because of the battle strategy used by the Israelites in Judges 20, all the women and children of Benjamin perish in flames. One outcome of their death is that the men of Benjamin are left without women to repopulate the tribe. The possible extinction of a tribe is felt as a disaster by all Israel. For this reason, many hundreds of additional tribespeople are slated to be killed. Since the men of Jabesh-gilead did not help defeat the Benjamites, their young, unmarried women are consigned to the defeated tribesmen. Twelve thousand men are dispatched to "smite the inhabitants of Jabesh-gilead with the edge of the sword, with the women and the little ones . . . utterly destroy[ing] every male, and every woman that hath lain by man" (21:10), so that their virgin daughters, four hundred young women, can be given to the surviving warrior-Benjamites. In *Eikonoklastes*, Milton makes use of this startling event from Judges. Milton upholds Parliament's role in defying Charles I over the right way to curb Irish rebellion. He claims that the king's plea for mercy for the Irish is mere pretence, and he cites Judges 21 in his defense of Parliament's action. He speaks of the right of "a Nation by just Warr and execution to slay whole Families of them who so barbarously had slaine whole Families before" (*YP* III.482). Ireland, then, metaphorically, is not divorcible from England; Ireland is to be dealt with sternly, not tenderly and with mercy. Milton's statement applies to the killing of the Benjamite women and children, to be sure, but it is a misapplication of the Jabesh-gilead section because these men had refrained from warfare and were not present at the battle preparations when a curse was placed, "Cursed be he that giveth a wife to Benjamin" (21:18). Hence, the women of Jabesh-gilead are the only ones available to marry Benjamites. Milton asks, "Did not all *Israel* doe as much against the *Benjamits* for one Rape committed by a few, and defended by the whole Tribe? and did they not the same to *Jabesh Gilead* for not assisting them in that revenge? I speak not this that such measure should be meted rigorously to all the Irish, or as remembering that the Parlament ever so Decreed, but to shew that this [Charles's] Homily hath more of craft and affectation in it, then of sound Doctrin" (*YP* III.482).

Even when the virgins of Jabesh-gilead are given in marriage, there are not enough young women for all the men, and the elders instruct the Benjamites who are left without wives: "Behold, there is a feast of the Lord from year to year in Shiloh. . . . Go and lie in wait in the vineyards; and . . . if the daughters of Shiloh come out to dance in the dances, then come ye out of the vineyards, and catch you every man his wife of the daughters of Shiloh, and go to the land of Benjamin" (21:20-21). As was mentioned previously, Shiloh is the site of God's holy ark. Just as the Danites' slaying of the gentle people of Laish was ratified by God, so the kidnapping of young women taking part in religious celebration is legitimated by tribal elders. In fact, the dancing in the vineyards is perhaps cultic, which turns abduction of the virgins into a sort of harvest time fertility rite.

Everything that is sanctioned by the elders is recorded in the Judges narrative without any sign of pity or remorse.[29] The conjunction of the need for women and the need for land—the overarching domestic and political imperatives—is played out to its ultimate ending. The injunction to "be fruitful and multiply" (which validates the appropriation of women) and the injunction to claim Israel's "inheritance" (which validates the appropriation of land) are of gravest importance to the tribes' continued existence and may seem to transcend all other concerns. Yet, indeed, the sacred is the paramount realm. This is the truth that Milton speaks to. He takes the woman's dissevered body to be an imperative call to justice. In addition, Milton conflates Justice with Truth in *Eikonoklastes*: "Truth and Justice are all one, for Truth is but Justice in our knowledge, and Justice is but Truth in our practice" (*YP* III, 583). Perhaps he has the final remains of the concubine in mind as he portrays Truth, hewn and scattered, in *Areopagitica*. In this work of 1644, just as in *Animadversions* of 1641, the bishops are figures of evil: "They are the troublers, they are the dividers of unity, who neglect and permit not others to unite those dissever'd peeces which are yet wanting to the body of Truth" (*YP* II, 550-51). In Judges, the *benai belial* are "dividers of unity" who do not carry out the dismemberment but indeed cause it.

So once again, this time in the seventeenth century, in another nation without a king, the unnamed woman may become a symbol of despoiled, fragmented, and much abused Truth. The woman whose story we have been following—the concubine who died from a long night of brutal rape—makes her appeal to our collective conscience in that special place where "every one" collectively becomes a multitude that reacts "as one" to insure justice. "Die [mankind] or Justice must," Milton declares and then renews the option, "unless for him / Som other able, and as willing, pay . . ." and Milton completes the thought, ". . . The rigid satisfaction, death for death" (*PL* III.210-12). At the finale of Judges, death rigidly adds to death, in stupefying carnage. As for the concubine, after her violent ending, she is reborn into an afterlife of remembrance. For Milton, the liminality of death is the central possibility of life.[30]

Notes

[1]Richard Rogers, *A Commentary upon the Whole Book of Judges* (London: imprinted by Felix Kyngston, 1615), 905.

[2]Joseph Hall, *Contemplations upon the Principle Passages in the Holy Story*, vol. 1, *The Works*, 10 vols., ed. Philip Wynter 1863; rpt. (New York: AMS P, 1969), 293; Rogers, 905.

[3]In a different kind of treatment of Hebrew women, John Lightfoot lingers over sexual infidelity and its humiliating punishments, in *The Temple Service as it Stood in the Dayes of our Savior* (London: R. Cotes, n.d.), 193-95.

[4]The Hebrew word *'is*, used to describe the Levite, is the generic word for *man*. *The Holy Scriptures* and most biblical commentators refer to the Levite as the woman's "husband." Phyllis Trible, however, calls the Levite "'the master' to distinguish him from the other nameless males and to indicate his power over the concubine"; *Texts of Terror: Literary-Feminist Readings of Biblical Narratives* (Philadelphia: Fortress P, 1984), 88. Although Trible's chapter, "An Unnamed Woman: The Extravagance of Violence" (*Texts of Terror*, 65-91), provides an insightful reading of this

text, it seems to me that *husband* conveys to twentieth-century readers the domestic nature of the couple's relationship. On the other hand, as T. Drorah Setel points out in "Prophets and Pornography: Female Sexual Imagery in Hosea," in *Feminist Interpretation of the Bible*, ed. Letty M. Russell (Philadelphia: Westminster P, 1985), during the time of Judges, "marriage is a property relationship . . . . There is no verb 'to marry'; a man 'takes' a woman for himself, thus transferring her possession from her father's household to his own," 89. In any event, translation of the Levite's role as either *husband* or *master* indicates a kind of stance toward the narrative on the part of the translator. I think this narrative is intended to gain power as it grows from seemingly innocuous seeds. To denominate the man as *husband* sounds more ordinary to a contemporary audience.

C.F. Burney notes that the inelegant redundancy of such phrasing as "His father-in-law, the damsel's father" (19:4) is surprising and may indicate another version of this story in which the woman was wife, not concubine. Other repetitions also suggest an alternative version; for instance, one confusing doubling in the Hebrew, which is usually understood as "took to him a concubine," may also be translated as "took to him a wife, a concubine," *The Book of Judges*, rev. ed. (New York: Ktav Publishing House, 1970), 442.

[5]Most biblical citations are taken from *The Holy Scriptures*, rev. ed. (Philadelphia: Jewish Publication Society of America, 1955). Citations of Milton's poetry are from *The Complete Poetry of John Milton*, ed. John T. Shawcross, rev. ed. (Garden City: Doubleday, 1971). Citations of Milton's prose are from *Complete Prose Works of John Milton*, 8 vols., ed. Don M. Wolfe et al. (New Haven: Yale UP, 1953-82), hereafter cited as *YP* in the text.

[6]In this matter, Martin Buber's opinion may stand for the critical consensus. As he indicates, in general the Judges events are "reported circumstantially and unclearly"; *Kingship of God* (New York: Harper & Row, 1967), 78.

[7]Robert G. Boling, *Judges: The Anchor Bible* (Garden City: Doubleday, 1975). Boling points out succinctly enough, "It was a man's world," 274.

[8]See J. Cheryl Exum, "'You Shall Let Every Daughter Live': A Study of Exodus 1:8-2:10," *Semeia* 28 (1983): 63-82.

[9]Many root confusions may have led to the misconstruing of the woman's action. One main cause is juridicial and lies in the fact that legally an Israelite woman was not permitted to divorce her husband and

automatically was considered an adulteress if she left him. In the reasoning of J. Alberto Soggin, "The responsibility for the matrimonial crisis, on which the text gives us no information, must have lain with the husband, at least in view of his later behaviour; however, the cause of the quarrel cannot have been very serious, if the wife and the father-in-law are so glad to be reconciled," *Judges: A Commentary*, tr. John Bowden (Philadelphia: Westminster P, 1981), 284.

The most important cause of interpretive confusion is the perplexing nature of the Hebrew forms, which are both obscure and rendered in unusual order and placement. Scribal error is one possible explanation. For different kinds of discussion of the difficulties in interpreting the Hebrew stylistics, see Boling, 273-74, and Soggin, 284.

[10]See, for instance, Rogers' lengthy reprobation of this concubine's sin and his general "Caveats about Whoredom," 865-67.

[11]Hall, 288; see 288-89 for dilation on the Levite's "good nature" and "mercy."

[12]According to Lowell W. Coolidge, "Milton attributes to Grotius a somewhat more positive tone than the original seems to warrant. Grotius says [those who] give fornication an extended meaning . . . take their argument from Judges 19:2," *YP* II, 335.

[13]For a brief account of Milton's first marriage, see Arthur Axelrad, *A Milton Encyclopedia*, gen. ed. William B. Hunter, Jr., 9 vols. (Lewisburg: Bucknell UP, 1979), 5:79. For a more lengthy description, see William Riley Parker, *Milton: A Biography*, 2 vols. (Oxford: Clarendon P, rpt. 1969), I: 229-40.

[14]John Selden's *Uxor Ebraica seu De Nuptiis et Divortiis Veterum Ebraeorum Libri Tres* (1646) is to be found in the Library of the British Museum.

[15]In Laurence Sterne's eighteenth-century sermon, "The Levite and his Concubine," in vols. 1 and 2 of *The Complete Works and Life of Laurence Sterne* (New York and London, 1904), Sterne follows the couple until they leave the father-in-law's house to journey back to Ephraim. At this point, Sterne turns aside: "It serves no purpose to pursue the story further," he says; "the catastrophe is horrid" (295).

[16]Although Hall condemns Israelite social systems: "The law of God allowed the Levite a wife; human connivance, a concubine," he adds that "neither did the Jewish concubine differ from a wife, but in some outward compliments: both might challenge all the true essence of marriage," 287.

[17]See Trible, 66.

[18]It is difficult to ascertain the exact professional status of Levites during this historical period. It seems most likely to me that the "sons of Aaron" were connected with such sanctuaries as the one at Shiloh, whereas the "sons of Levi," whose number included the two Levites whom we read of in Chapters 17-18 and 19-21, were less well-connected and sought their livelihood in their own region of Judah, or even in the remoter region of Ephraim where these two Levites "were sojourning." For fuller discussion of the "almost insuperable" problem of defining the Levites—perhaps they were a tribe, perhaps a class—see Burney, 436-41.

[19]For a phrase by phrase comparison, see Burney, 444.

[20]As Trible notes, the woman was seized and pushed out, seemingly in haste; see Trible, 76.

[21]Cedric C. Brown, *John Milton's Aristocratic Entertainments* (Cambridge: Cambridge UP, 1985), 67.

[22]For discussion of the linkage between *belial, komos,* and Comus, see Brown, 65-68; Louise Simons, "'And Heaven Gates Ore My Head': Death as Threshold in Milton's Masque," in *Milton Studies XXIII,* ed. James D. Simmonds (Pittsburgh, 1987), 62-64.

[23]See Simons, 61, 65.

[24]See Simons, 93.

[25]Athalya Brenner, in *The Israelite Woman: Social Role and Literary Type in Biblical Narrative* (Sheffield, England: JSOT P, 1985), describes no paradigm that fits this woman who seems neither temptress nor matriarch, not prostitute nor prophetess. Yet in effect, she becomes the fulfillment of all these four functions.

[26]Michael Lieb, *Poetics of the Holy: A Reading of Paradise Lost* (Chapel Hill: U of North Carolina P, 1981), 100-101. Lieb's discussion of the "sense of myth" underlying both Genesis and *Paradise Lost* pertains to this section of the Judges narrative also; see 100-102.

[27] In the English version that Milton would have read, the concubine is described as either dead or fallen "at the doore of the house, and her hands lay upon the threshold." Mieke Bal says the extended hands show both "request" and "accusation," in *Death and Dissymetry: The Politics of Coherence in the Book of Judges* (Chicago: U of Chicago P, 1988), 125.

[28]Milton's preoccupation with solar and Phoenix imagery unites his interest in this passage from Judges with his rendering of *Samson Agonistes* from the earlier Samson section of Judges (13-16).

[29]One conjecture is that the redactor may be showing displeasure with King Saul, who was a Benjamite. This theory, however, would not

explain why the same tone is taken when the internicine bloodbath continues even after the Benjamites are dealt with. In noting God's "ironic detachment" from the fighting and abductions that take place at the Judges ending, David M. Gunn calls the concubine "abused and divided and used as the excuse for the ensuing orgy of civil war and rape," in *The Literary Guide to the Bible*, ed. Robert Alter and Frank Kermode (Cambridge: Harvard UP, 1987), 119. Burney demonstrates the entire ending to be "manifestly unhistorical," 446. The close is not historical but didactic and literary. Closure is circular. At the beginning, God designates Judah to fight the Canaanites (1:1), and at the ending, Judah to fight the Benjamites (20:18). The horrors grow and multiply. At the beginning, the Israelites fight the Canaanites; at the ending, each other. The attack on one concubine not only *precedes* the attack on other women, but even worse, the "orgy of . . . rape" against one woman becomes "the *excuse*" for the "orgy of . . . rape" against numerous women.

³⁰ My grateful thanks to Roger Boraas for scholarly assistance, and to editors Raymond Frontain and Jan Wojcik for encouragement and editorial advice.

Eight:

Dinah and the Comedy of Castration in *Sterne's* Tristram Shandy

Raymond-Jean Frontain

"Every thing in this world," observes Tristram's philosopher father, Walter, "is big with jest,—and has wit in it, and instruction too,—if we can but find it out."[1]

One of the pregnant jokes of which the novel has yet to be formally delivered is the reason for Toby's anguish at hearing any mention of his aunt Dinah's marriage to and impregnation by the family coachman about sixty years before Tristram begins telling his tale. The scene of Toby's being tormented by his brother Walter is surely among the most memorable in the novel (I. xxi. 48-53). When Walter speaks of the family scandal in public, Toby pleads with him to stop; in private, however, he simply plugs his ears and whistles "Lillabullero" until his brother's speculations have run their course. Toby's response, then, is generally assumed to include embarrassment at the shame that his aunt's inappropriate marriage has brought upon the family, motivated by a sensitivity at once squeamish and sympathetic.[2]

A biblical analogue to Aunt Dinah's experience, first tentatively proposed by Howard Anderson and later more emphatically asserted by Melvyn New and the editors of the Florida Edition of Sterne's works, however, goes far in helping us recover Walter's allusion. "Walter Shandy may have in mind that her godparents should have remembered Genesis 34," Anderson suggests, "where Dinah, daughter of Jacob and Leah, is defiled by Shechem." New is more certain: "Walter has in mind Dinah's defilement as related in Genesis 34: 1-31." As he summarizes the episode,

> Dinah, the daughter of Jacob, is seduced by the uncircumcised Shechem, who then asks for her in marriage. Jacob stipulates that Shechem's people must be circumcised, but after they have undergone the ritual—indeed, while they are recovering from

it—Jacob and his sons slaughter them to avenge Dinah's shame.³

Surely, biblical Dinah's sexual defilement by someone not of her tribe is the kind of detail that Walter's mind would seize upon in representing his aunt's marriage to and impregnation by someone not of her social class. Curiously, however, neither Anderson nor New explores the analogy's field of reference. More provoking, although oddly appropriate in the criticism of a novel which itself depends upon a regular amount of "misreading" or misunderstanding, New's summary mistakenly says that Dinah was "seduced" by Shechem when the biblical narrative says boldly that "he took her, and lay with her, and defiled her" (Gen. 34: 2), and that "Jacob and his sons" slaughter the men of Shechem's tribe to avenge Dinah's shame when only Simeon and Levi, her two full brothers, do so, and much to their father's displeasure. Most importantly, however, neither Anderson nor New gives any indication as to why the biblical allusion should discombobulate Toby so, or why Walter should take such delight in teasing his brother with it.

The reference to biblical Dinah, I think, ultimately invites the reader to compare Shandy family history with the patriarchial history of loss and begetting narrated in the middle chapters of Genesis, the story of Dinah and Shechem acting as a submerged pattern against which many of the most important episodes in Sterne's novel are played out. Genesis 34, thus, acts as an indicator of the deep structure of *Tristram Shandy*. The ambivalent actions of biblical Dinah which precipitate the enforced circumcision and subsequent murder of Shechem make her the tragic antitype of the comic woman of appetite in *Tristram Shandy*, repeated confrontation with whom inevitably humiliates the genitally self-conscious or sexually impotent male; Shechem's misfortune is burlesqued by Toby's, Tristram's, and even the Shandy bull's impotence. Significantly, while originally a narrative of sexual violence, mutilation and death, the biblical *récit* of Dinah and Shechem functions in *Tristram Shandy* as part of a comedy of castration and regeneration. This clearly touches on the paradox which, as John Traugott insisted in 1971, Sterne criticism "ought to treat: that *Tristram Shandy* is a very gay, reassuring, and in a crazy way optimistic work, in spite of the horrible solipsism, in spite of the black humor, grim things, really terribly grim things. . . . This is a fact that criticism must take account of, . . . *how* it comes about that through this terror and absurdity and solipsism Sterne discovers something joyful."⁴

Sterne's reversal has significance beyond the paradox described by Traugott. The history of Bible interpretation, as theorists like Mieke Bal have come increasingly to emphasize, is the history of how readers "misread" the biblical narratives in order to empower their own moral/political agenda. I suspect that Sterne was delighted to be able to turn the Dinah and Shechem story against the upholders of a presumptive biblical morality, perversely "misreading" the *récit* in order to further his own *comic* moral agenda. In studying how Sterne defuses by rendering farcically the traumatizing threats of rape and castration, we will in effect be analyzing Sterne's philosophy of "*True Shandeism*," which,

> think what you will against it, opens the heart and lungs, and like all those affections which partake of its nature, it forces the blood and other vital fluids of the body to run freely thro' its channels, and makes the wheel of life run long and chearfully round. [IV. xxxii. 255]

The Biblical Drama of Castration and Beheading

As many readers recognize, the episode in Genesis 34 regularly referred to as "the story of Dinah" is hardly about Dinah at all. The story is a myth, explains Gerhard von Rad,⁵ designed to explain the prehistoric conflict by which nomadic Jews obtained grazing lands in central Palestine, and why the tribes of Simeon and Levi were later unwelcome there. (When Simeon and Levi murder Shechem and his men, their father Jacob berates them for subsequently causing his name "to stink in the land," not to mention for endangering the entire family should Shechem's allies unite to avenge his death.) In such a reading, the episode marks the turning point in their pre-recorded history when a nomadic people, attracted by the embellishments of an agricultural existence, appropriate and settle land held by others. The "rape" of Dinah, like the "abduction" of Helen of Troy, becomes a later rationalization for a war of territorial expansion.[6] Nehama Aschkenasy's feminist reading of the story reaches a similar conclusion, even while asking a very different set of questions about the text. "The main focus of the story is not the girl who has been violated, but rather the tense and complicated relationship between Jacob and some of his sons. It is not a story about a woman, but about men, with the woman the element triggering certain events but taking no active part in the actual plot that develops." A pawn in the power struggle between the Israelites and the Canaanites, as well as between Jacob and his sons, Dinah as a "real woman" is "submerged and forgotten" in "a parable about men's fight for a land."[7]

But even as a pawn controlled by the men about her in a narrative not immediately concerned with her happiness or welfare, Dinah betrays an independence that is provocative and even troublesome. What, for example, is her reason for going among the Canaanites in the first place? The narrative says simply, "And Dinah the daughter of Leah, which she bare unto Jacob, went out to see the daughters of the land" (34:1). Was she curious, as von Rad suggests, about the more stable existence of the local women, her curiosity intended by the compiler of Genesis to represent the Jews' larger desire to finally settle and cease their nomadic sojourning in place after place? Or, as the Midrash sages assert, does the repetition of the phrase used to describe Leah's earlier "going out" to the fields to invite Jacob to her bed (Gen. 30: 16) suggest a similar sexual intention on the part of Leah's daughter and, thus, imply a "like mother, like daughter" correlation?[8] "Violation" and "dishonor" are words used by Dinah's brothers, rather than by the narrator, to comment upon what transpires between her and Shechem; while they may suggest that she was raped by the local squire, they may just as likely be her brothers' derogatory epithets for her involvement in a mutually gratifying love affair of which her family disapproved on largely religious grounds because it was with an uncircumcised male. Likewise, the narrator's use of the word "defiled" may be in reference to Dinah's religious impurity rather than a description of any violent sexual use made of her. In fact, the narrator never questions Shechem's affection for Dinah, and the fact that, after killing him and his kinsmen, Simeon and Levi "took Dinah out of Shechem's house" (34: 26) may suggest that she stayed willingly with him despite the taboo of his being uncircumcised, and so had to be brought to her father's home by force.

The narrative thus admits the possibility that what is often referred to as the "rape" of Dinah was possibly not a rape at all. The idea of sexual violation, rather, may be an interpretive accommodation made by pious readers uncomfortable with the narrative's description of a biblical matriarch's too-independent behavior. It is the distance between these two narrative possibilities, I shall shortly argue, that Sterne exploits for part of his comic effect.

Aschkenasy's observation that the war fought between the Jews and the Canaanites is over the land and not the woman, Dinah's body simply being associated with the land, may raise a significant thread in the narrative's tapestry for us. Issues of sexual and agricultural fertility seem inextricably interwound in the episode, as they are in Hebrew narrative in general, creating what critical theorist E. D. Hirsch might call a "typological similarity."[9] The story is set in planting or harvesting time when the men are out working in the fields. That a practise of waylaying women at such a time existed in the pre-monarchical period is suggested by the episode in Judges 21: 16-23 wherein the Benjaminites are instructed to hide in the vineyards until the daughters of Shiloh go out to dance in the highway, and then "to catch you every man his wife" and bring her home to restore his ruined family estate. In a reverse maneuver, widowed, childless Ruth wins herself a husband when she covers herself with Boaz' skirt while he is sleeping on the threshing floor during harvest season. Such a primitive association of agricultural fertility with a woman's sexual availability may underlie Dinah's "going out" to see the women of the land during planting or harvesting time; in the narrative, control of Dinah's physical person is suggestively bound with ownership of the land.

This association of the human body with successful steward-
ship of the land is continued in the Jews' tricking Shechem into
undergoing circumcision, a sexual mutilation (to a non-Jew) which
results in the loss of his life and eventually his land. Circumcision,
of course, is required of the Jews in Abraham's covenant with God.
As God stipulated the terms,

> I will make thee exceeding fruitful, and I will make nations of
> thee, and kings shall come out of thee. And I will give unto thee,
> and to thy seed after thee, the land wherein thou art a stranger,
> all the land of Canaan. And ye shall circumcise the flesh of your
> foreskin; and it shall be a token of the covenant betwixt me and
> you. [Gen. 17: 8-11]

For the sons of Abraham, loss of part of the sexual member paradoxically ensures propagative power ("I will make thee exceeding
fruitful"), and guarantees dominion over a land that at time of
Yahweh's prophecy belonged to someone else. But this paradox
holds true only for the Jews, circumcision of their enemies conversely symbolizing a political "castration" or loss of virile power. The
Lord's delivery of Canaan to Abraham's descendents is ironically
justified later in the Jews' history in the episode under consideration
when Dinah's brothers require Shechem and his men to undergo
circumcision in order to intermarry with the Jews, and then murder them while they are prostrate with pain from the surgery. Symbolically emasculated by the ritual, they are defenseless when
Simeon and Levi attack with upraised phallus-like swords (v. 25).
The city of Hamor and Shechem is then "spoiled" (v. 27) in an action that parallels Dinah's originally having been "defiled" by
Shechem (v. 2). If the woman's body is associated with the land or
with the enclosed space of the city, then the man's penis is the sword
by which he claims and enjoys the land's fruits and city's riches.
Circumcision symbolically enhances the Jews' penile/political power,
while conversely suggesting an enemy's political emasculation.[10] We
find this association elsewhere in Hebrew narrative. As dowry for
his daughter Michal, for example, King Saul demands 100 Philis-

tine foreskins; David, who will prove himself both a successful king and a fruitful husband, extravagantly delivers 200 (1 Sam. 18: 25-27).

Freud's equation "To decapitate = to castrate"[11] may help identify the complex biblical association of the sexually seductive woman with the female who overpowers, thus emasculating, her partner which I believe is at the heart of Sterne's comedy of the sexually aggressive female and sexually impotent male. Decapitation, reasons Freud, is a displaced act of castration, the visual equivalent of the intended action whose outright representation is taboo. (We still speak of the glans as the "head" of the penis. Iconographically, the upright male torso is the visual equivalent of the erect male member, while the trunk of the body slumped on the ground after decapitation may suggest detumescence or loss of phallic power.) In Hebrew narrative, the supposedly weak female hero regularly defeats her physically superior antagonist with a wound to the head. After inviting Sisera into her tent and lulling him to sleep, for example, Jael drives a phallic tent peg through his head (Judg. 4: 17-21). Likewise, Judith seduces Holofernes with her beauty and then decapitates him with his own sword after he's lapsed into something like post-coital slumber. More subtle is Delilah's ordering that Samson's head be shaved while he sleeps, thus depriving him of his physical strength (Judg. 16: 17-20).[12] The motif is continued in Christian narrative where Herodias' daughter is rewarded for her dance with the head of John the Baptist (Matt. 14: 6-11).

Dinah's involvement, unwilling as it may be, in the circumcision and subsequent death of Shechem places her within a larger pattern of biblical women who deprive men of their sexual/political power by beheading them and thus symbolically castrating them. Of course, biblical Dinah neither beheads Shechem herself nor lures him into a trap so that others may kill him; nor is Shechem either beheaded or castrated outright. But Shechem's people lose their land and Shechem himself undergoes genital violence and subsequent loss of life for love of Dinah. There is, of course, an implicit—and at times explicit—misogyny to a cultural tradition which, even while celebrating the biblical matriarch such as Jael or Judith as the

deliverer of her people, is threatened by her as an emasculating virago.[13] In tracing the history of misogyny in literature, Katharine M.
Rogers notes that one of the reasons for "the idea that women are
animals hostile to man's idealism" is the fact that in the Christian
West, sexual desire has generally been considered degrading, thus
making the woman who excites it appear "as a seducer from virtue:
she hands man the apple, she soils his soul, she brings him down
into the mud." Rogers appropriately summarizes a discussion of biblical Dinah in the thirteenth century *Ancren Riwle* in this regard:
"because Jacob's daughter, Dinah, walked out to see the country she
was raped; and because she was raped, a great city was burned, its
prince and people were slain, and her father and brothers . . .
broke a truce and became outlaws." As the author of the *Riwle* mor-
alizes, "this evil . . . came of Dinah . . . not from her seeing
Sichem [sic]. . . with whom she sinned, but . . . from her letting
him set eyes upon her."[14]

It is to this part of the Dinah story, I believe, that Toby Shandy
responds with such painful discomfort. For sexually timid Toby,
Aunt Dinah is a daughter of Eve, like her mother responsible for a
man's fall. She is a manifestation of the succubus of antiquity whose
kiss could draw a man's breath and, in Christian times, even his soul
from his body. She is the woman of appetite whom the Middle Ages
and Renaissance believed caused a man to lose a day off his life every time she led him to ejaculate in coitus with her. She is that figure of sexual folklore, the grasping woman with the *vagina dentata*
from whom the vulnerable male must shield both his genitals and
his life.[15] She is, most immediately for Uncle Toby, the Widow
Wadman who—in the final pages of the novel, in an incident which
occurred ten years before Tristram's birth but in which all the movements of the novel climax—dared to hope to see, and even thought
to touch, the place where Toby had received his wound, so shocking Toby that he was confirmed a bachelor for the rest of his life.

The Randy Daughters of Eve and the Impotent Sons of Adam

Provocatively, while asking women to read the chapter on Walter's theory of noses without allowing their imaginations to be carried away by the devil and so to think of something other than the nose whenever he refers to the size of a man's olfactory organ, Tristram resorts to Rabelais' metaphor of Tickletoby's mare astride whom no man can keep his seat.

> Now don't let Satan, my dear girl, in this chapter, take advantage of any one spot of rising-ground to get astride of your imagination, if you can any ways help it; or if he is so nimble as to slip on,— —let me beg of you, like an unback'd filly, *to frisk it, to squirt it, to jump it, to rear it, to bound it,—and to kick it, with long kicks and short kicks*, till like *Tickletoby's mare*, you break a strap or a crupper, and throw his worship into the dirt. [III. xxxvi. 168]

Women must resist the temptation to read as sexual *double entendres* what narrator Tristram insists are but literal, quite innocent, references. In extending his caution, however, Tristram draws a comparison which is itself a gross sexual *double entendre*, woman as an "unback'd filly" whose energetic exertions throws any man "so nimble as to slip on" from the saddle into the dirt, thus preserving the chastity of her imagination from the assault of any impure thought as she would her virginity from any more physical assault. The reference, in effect, only encourages identification of women with horses that can be sexually ridden, thus inspiring the very kind of "imaginative conversation" which on the surface level Tristram insists he is trying to discourage.

It is the very ambivalence of biblical Dinah's relation to Shechem, I believe, that attracts Sterne—that is, the possibilities offered by the episode of suggesting without directly stating a comic sexual situation. The ambiguities of the biblical narrative allow Sterne to engage the reader in the very lascivious thoughts which he seems to adamantly discourage. The pious reader of the Bible, incapable of imagining a biblical matriarch as sexual aggressor, may quickly assume that Dinah had to have been sexually violated; thus Bruce Vawter summarizes the incident as "the local squire, used to taking what he wants and where he finds it, oppresses a comely peasant maiden."[16] For such a reader, it is poetically just that the sexually oppressive male suffers first phallic diminishment and then the ultimate oppression of being violently murdered by Dinah's kinsmen. But, as we have just seen, the biblical text allows the possibility, assumed by many of the text's earliest male readers, that Dinah was a willing partner, if not actually the sexual aggressor, and that the "defilement" she suffers is the religious one of having intercourse with an uncircumcised male rather than the physical and emotional one of rape. In Sterne's retelling, appropriately enough, it is the daughter of the local squire who is pursuing her social and economically vulnerable inferior; the woman is the sexual "oppressor" and the man the "oppressed." As Samuel Richardson's sentimental *Pamela* and Henry Fielding's satiric *Joseph Andrews* suggest, to the eighteenth-century mind a woman, while ennobled by marriage to her social superior, is discredited by any liaison with a man who is her social inferior; the latter situation, it was assumed, could only be the result of the woman's inability to control her sexual appetite. Indeed, by offering recurring images of women who—like the trumpeter's and the innkeeper's wives of "Slawkenbergius's Tale"— desire to touch the male member in order to reassure themselves of its real size and of men incapable of or unwilling to satisfy their partners' desires, Sterne comically reverses gender expectations, depicting women as far less timid and men as far less aggressive than sexual stereotyping would allow them to be.

Sterne's importing the biblical Dinah story into *Tristram Shandy* makes this point in two ways. First, it implies a comic reading of the biblical episode, coyly suggesting a more deliberate intention on Dinah's part than the biblical narrative states, one which is inevitably resisted by the pious reader whom Sterne hopes to unsettle. Then, through the character of Dinah Shandy, Sterne satirizes the masked—and celebrates the occasionally unmasked— sexual appetites of all women, thus freeing women from hiding their desire behind such facades as the velvet mask that Aunt Dinah was forced to wear during her assignations with the coachman (VIII. iii. 416-17). Sterne's sexual comedy is compounded by the fact that, like biblical Shechem, most of the men in *Tristram Shandy* suffer from some genital "wound" or sexual inadequacy that leaves them incapable of satisfying any woman's appetite, much less that of a Sternean virago. The redactor of Genesis and/or the author of Genesis 34 never reveals what happens to Dinah after she is "rescued" by her brothers and returned to her father's camp. Sterne, we shall now see, delights in painting the comic frustration of the Shandy women whose lovers or spouses have been phallically diminished, or of whose services they are deprived entirely. It is the comedy of the Shandy women's frustration and the Shandy men's embarrassment that we now consider.[17]

The Book of Genesis is concerned not simply with the events which occurred "in the beginning" but with questions of biological generation or sexual propagation as well. A single problem is addressed again and again throughout the Book's fifty chapters, namely how the Lord's promise to man of fruition will be realized in a world where of all the forces hostile to man, none is more destructive than man's own sinful impulses. Thus, at the same time as they are cursed with the inevitability of death, Adam and Eve are commanded to be fruitful and to multiply; the command is the more urgent in light of their now inevitable deaths. The succeeding generation, however, sees one brother kill another, dramatically halving the family's seeming chances of survival. Again and again the issue of generation is raised: barren women are feverishly determined to produce progeny, enlisting both surrogates and miracles in the cause, as they compete with more fruitful rivals; daughters seduce their father while sons fear to catch sight of their father's inadvertently exposed genitals lest they be cursed for looking upon that powerful source of life. Again and again the race is faced with near extermination, but again and again regeneration takes place. From Noah and his wife, as from the carefully chosen pairs of animals that accompany them, the earth will be replenished after the flood; out of the aged, exhausted loins of Abraham will come countless descendents; eleven sons of Jacob, threatened with starvation, are saved by the brother they thought they had eliminated many years before. Again and again survival hangs precariously by a single thread, yet repeatedly that thread proves strong. The drama of Isaac's sacrifice is typical: an aged couple is promised a son long after they are capable of siring and conceiving a child, *if* they remain faithful to God; their faith is tested, however, when Abraham is ordered to sacrifice the very child that his unwavering loyalty to God has procured. Sarah laughs when told that she will bear a child very late in life, yet all the Book of Genesis is a comedy of generation. The race *does* survive, against unlikely—even impossible—odds. God provides, making the potential tragedy of human existence into a comedy, a black one at times but a comedy nonetheless.

Tristram Shandy may in this regard be more closely related to Genesis than Sterne himself consciously understood or tried to suggest through his Dinah allusion. Beginning at the disrupted moment of the hero's conception and concluding with the revelation of the family bull's impotence, *Tristram Shandy* chronicles a family's frustrated yet comic attempts at generation. Walter is as beleaguered a patriarch as Abraham ever was, forced to see his hopes for the renewal of his line defeated first by the sudden death of his older son, Bobby, and then by the triple misfortune of Tristram's crushed nose, misnaming, and accidental circumcision; as Tristram himself observes, "any man in the world, who was at so much pains in begetting a child, as my father was" would be sorely vexed by the misfortunes he meets in the process (III. xxx. 161). Even his attempts at breeding livestock miscarry: Obadiah may be at fault with the breeding of the mare, but the parish bull is exposed as impotent or sterile. Infamous great-aunt Dinah ironically proves the most fruitful member of the family. (She is survived by at least one child she conceived by the coachman, we know, inasmuch as Walter inherited only £1000 upon her death rather than a larger estate. But her offspring would take their coachman-father's name, which the novel does not even record.) The last male to carry the Shandy name, childless Tristram, is in dangerously poor health even as he writes his *Life and Opinions*. Yet, as with the Book of Genesis, the reader cannot doubt but that the Shandys will survive; the inexhaustible spirit of life sounds from the depths of the novel. The Shandy family comedy, in fact, is all the richer because the threats against it are so great.

The threat to human continuity is particularly represented in the novel by the Shandy men's phallic inadequacy. Like biblical Dinah, all three generations of Shandy women find themselves paired with men with obvious shortcomings. Tristram's great-grand-mother protests that her spouse's "nose" is but "an ace of clubs" (III.xxxiii. 164), signalling the decline of Shandy male "noses" from which the family never recovers. The novel hints that Elizabeth, Tristram's mother, may have sought satisfaction with another man— possibly Parson Yorick—since Tristram's calendrical calculations of his conception are obviously in error, and a pattern of cuckoldry images surrounds mention of his parentage.[18] And Jenny must excuse the sad sight of Tristram standing, limp garters in hand, apologizing for his manhood and for "what had *not* pass'd" (VIII.xxix. 395). But the woman in the novel who seems destined to be most disappointed in this regard is Toby's neighbor, Widow Wadman. "A daughter of *Eve*, for such was Widow *Wadman*, and 'tis all the character I intend to give of her," says Tristram in introducing her to the reader (VIII. viii. 420). "[N]ever did . . . eyes behold, or . . . concupiscence covet any thing in this world, more concupiscible than widow *Wadman*," he says in explaining her allure (VI. xxxvii. 356). But as one tradition of interpretation holds regarding biblical Dinah and mother Eve, the widow is not merely alluring; she sets out deliberately to allure. If biblical Dinah "went out" to see the "daughters of the land" in an ambiguous action that led to her affair with Shechem, Widow Wadman "silently sallied forth from her arbour" to besiege Toby's fortifications on the bowling green (VIII. xxiii. 443), where like some comic Medusa her chief weapon in overcoming Toby's amorous resistance is her eye. "[O]f all the eyes, which ever were created," Tristram courteously explains to his most inquisitive reader, Madam, "from your own . . . up to those of *Venus* herself, which certainly were as venereal a pair of eyes as ever stood in a head—there never was an eye of them all, so fitted to rob my uncle *Toby* of his repose" as that of Widow Wadman (VIII. xxv. 445).

Rhapsodizing about the "eye full of gentle salutations—and soft responses," Tristram finds himself almost done in by it and must draw himself quickly back: "It was an eye————But I shall be in love with it myself, if I say another word about it."

For Toby, in short, Widow Wadman is woman at her seductive best and sexually most desirous. In deciding his character's social status, Sterne surely had in mind the age-old comic association of widowhood with sexual appetite that runs from Petronius' tale of the Widow of Ephesus, through the Lady Wishforts of Restoration comedy, down to the eager "widder wimmin" who pursue Jed Clampett on television's *Beverly Hillbillies*, for Widow Wadman is similarly eager to pursue the sexual pleasures which marriage introduced her to but which widowhood has deprived her of. The unbridling of her heretofore restrained desires after romantic thoughts of Toby enter her head is outrageously suggested by her kicking open the nightshirt which her maidservant Bridget tries decorously to pin closed at the feet as Mrs. Wadman prepares for a night of what will prove very uneasy sleep (VIII. ix. 422)—as uneasy as that of the nuns of Strasburg in "Slawkenbergius's Tale" when thoughts of Don Diego's "nose" dance through their heads, or of the court ladies of Navarre when left to themselves to consider the importance of a man's whiskers in the "Fragment upon Whiskers."

That opposites attract is the principle of both magnetics and comedy. The impossible pairing of the venereal, concupiscent Widow Wadman and modest, asexual Toby Shandy is, as Tristram says, the actual subject of his book. The novel's principal themes culminate in the final volumes' description of the pursuit of the man who presumably does not know the right end of a woman by the woman who anxiously wants to be as fully "known" by him as possible. Like the women of Strasburg whose determination to touch Don Diego's nose and "feel it to the bottom" only alienates him, causing him to retreat into haughty disdain, Widow Wadman's concern with verifying the nature and extent of Toby's groin wound, when finally understood by Toby, so injures his pride and offends his modesty that he has nothing to do with Widow Wadman or with the female sex for the rest of his life. Her motives, she may convince herself, are pure—indeed, are seemingly as sensitive and compassionate as sentimental Toby's own. But Tristram/Sterne's coy use of *double entendres* in narrating the scene in which she first expresses her concern suggests that her interest masks sexual selfishness.

> I am terribly afraid, said widow *Wadman*, in case I should marry him, *Bridget*—that the poor captain will not enjoy his health, with the monstrous wound upon the groin——
> It may not, Madam, be so very large, replied *Bridget*, as you think——and I believe besides, added she,—that 'tis dried up—
> ——I could like to know—merely for his sake, said Mrs. *Wadman*——
> ——We'll know the long and the broad of it, in ten days—answered Mrs. *Bridget*, for whilst the captain is paying his addresses to you—I'm confident Mr. *Trim* will be for making love to me—and I'll let him as much as he will—added *Bridget*—to get it all out of him—— [VIII. xxviii. 448]

"I could like to know—merely for his sake," Mrs. Wadman adds as a hurried, self-justifying afterthought, just as Bridget will let Corporal Trim make as much love to her as *he* will, not because she will presumably receive pleasure from his attention, but solely, more nobly, to serve her mistress' interests and "get it all out of him," *it* presumably being the requisite information. No doubt they will know—or at least hope they will know—"the long and the broad" of another ambiguous *it* in another ten days.

The mask that Mrs. Wadman wears to veil her sexual thoughts, however, is dropped and her actual concern exposed to the reader when, in a scene of richly comic linguistic confusion, she inwardly debates on what terms she might accept Captain Shandy's offer to show her the spot where he received his wound.

> —You shall see the very place, Madam; said my uncle *Toby*.
> Mrs. *Wadman* blush'd——look'd towards the door——turn'd pale——blush'd slightly again——recovered her natural colour——blush'd worse than ever; which for the sake of the

unlearned reader, I translate thus——
    "L—d! I cannot look at it——
What would the world say if I look'd at it?
I should drop down, if I look'd at it—
I wish I could look at it——
There can be no sin in looking at it.
——I will look at it."
    . . . .
    ——You shall lay your finger upon the place—said my uncle
Toby.
    ——I will not touch it, quoth Mrs. *Wadman* to herself.
    [IX. xx. 479]

Here is Tristram himself engaging in an imaginative "conversation"
with his own characters in an unverbalized scene, "translating" for
the reader Mrs. Wadman's physiological responses into the unspoken thoughts which inspired them—the very kind of narrative "conversation" that he encourages his reader to engage in. Her concern
with possible scandal ("What would the world say if I look'd at it?"),
for example, causes her to look involuntarily to the door to see if
any possible witness is about to come in, whereas a naive or "unlearned" reader might think that hurried glance, following her first
blush, indicates rather her intention to flee the room because her
matronly modesty has been offended.

But more significantly the scene is perhaps the novel's finest
instance of comic confusion caused by the ambivalence of referents
and by conflicting private associations. Toby, of course, is referring
to the spot on the map of Namur which indicates his location during the siege when he was originally wounded; all his years of struggling to be able to locate the spot as precisely as possible are
undermined by Mrs. Wadman's assumption that he will actually
expose his groin to her. Toby's inability to conceive of a woman's
interest in his genital adequacy is matched by the ease with which
Widow Wadman assumes she is being offered the chance to view
his private parts. Mrs. Wadman's resolution of her ambivalent feelings—her conclusion that no harm would be done if she looked

without touching "it"—recalls the Abbess of Andouillets' causistry in resolving another embarrassing and potentially sinful dilemma.

The amours of Uncle Toby, which Tristram reports only in the final two volumes of his story, are actually the first incident chronologically in the Shandy family history to be narrated. The novel, thus, moves backwards, like Joseph Heller's *Catch-22*, to the scene which explains so much of what has already been reported. Engaging Tristram in narrative conversation, as he has been invited to do, the serious or "learned" reader must wonder if Tristram's uncertainty at the opening of the novel as to "whether this modesty of his [Uncle Toby's] was natural or acquir'd" (I. xxi. 50) is not actually resolved by these chronologically prior events which are reported in the narrative only at the very end. Several details in the novel suggest that the shock of learning that Widow Wadman's seemingly generous good-nature and compassion concerning his wound were actually motivated by sexual self-interest caused Toby to retreat into self-willed sexual innocence—that is, into a determination never to know the right end of a woman from the wrong. First, there is Tristram's final revelation, after all his hints to the contrary, that Toby was perfectly "fit" for marriage. Nature, Tristram protests,

> had formed him of the best and kindliest clay——had temper'd it with her own milk, and breathed into it the sweetest spirit— —she had made him all gentle, generous and humane—she had fill'd his heart with trust and confidence, and disposed every passage which led to it, for the communication of the tenderest offices——she had moreover considered the other causes for which matrimony was ordained——
> And accordingly * * * * * * * * * * * * * * * * *
> * * * * * * * * * * * * * *
> The DONATION was not defeated by my uncle *Toby's wound*. [IX. xxii. 481]

Toby, then, is not only undamaged genitally, but presumably very well-formed. After revealing this, Tristram protests feeling the same shock that his kinsman must have felt upon learning from Corporal Trim and brother Walter that "the Devil, who is the great disturber of our faiths in this world, had raised scruples in Mrs. *Wadman*'s brain about it [i.e., Nature's 'donation' to Toby's marital fitness]; and like a true devil as he was, had done his own work at the same time, by turning my uncle *Toby*'s Virtue thereupon into nothing but *empty bottles, tripes, trunk-hose,* and *pantofles*" (481). Toby's great "Virtue," presumably a larger-than-average genital en-dowment, has been reduced in Mrs. Wadman's mind to one of the stock props of the impotent old man in *commedia dell'arte* comedy— a list of props, by the way, as visually suggestive as Tristram's own limp garters when he stands apologetically before Jenny. Ah, the evils of a woman's sexual imagination, which can associate whiskers with genitals, become obsessed with the size of a man's nose, and emasculate him entirely once a devilish suggestion takes root in her brain!

But the suggestion, of course, is Tristram/Sterne's own, and one that he himself has planted in the reader's mind. The reader has been lured into making a sexual association here just as he was in the two cases of Tristram's presumed castration, and as the ladies of the court of Navarre are by Mme. de la Fosseuse's deliberately curi-ous emphasis on the word "whiskers." Toby's sexual healthiness should have been suggested to any reader attending to such a hint (as Madam should have been attending to the reference to Eliza-beth Shandy's religion in I. xx) by Walter's having been so con-cerned with Toby's erotic enthrallment with the widow that he resorted to the ruse of substituting camphorated cerecloth for buck-ram when Toby went to have a new pair of trousers made for court-ing, camphor having been supposed to act as an anti-aphrodisiac (VI. xxxvi. 355). How many readers, instead, view the scene as an indication of Walter's own battle with his "ass," the flesh, rather than a suggestion of Toby's potential for innocent randiness? Rather, what is wounded during Toby's amours with Widow Wadman is that sense of "trust and confidence" which Nature endowed him with, his "tenderest feelings" having been betrayed by her sexual self-in-terest masked as a sentimental profession of regard for his suffering. Toby's "wound" is finally as much psychosexual as it is physical. In-timidated by the widow's sexual forwardness, he has "acquired" a modesty that conveniently allows him to remain safely oblivious to any further sexual threat. Toby himself associates military defeat with the battle of the sexes waged against him by Mrs. Wadman, dating the "shock" he received from her as occurring "the year after the demolition of *Dunkirk*" (II. vii. 77). That shock, he says both proudly and complacently years later, "has given me just cause to say, That I neither know, nor do pretend to know, any thing about 'em [women], or their concerns."

And possibly with just cause, for Tristram makes another curious association with that same military defeat at Dunkirk.

> The *French* were so backwards all that summer in setting about that affair, and Monsieur *Tugghe*, the deputy from the magistrates of *Dunkirk*, presented so many affecting petitions to the queen,— beseeching her majesty to cause only her thunderbolts to fall upon the martial works, which might have incurred her displeasure,— but to spare—to spare the mole, for the mole's sake; which, in its naked situation, could be no more than an object of pity——and the queen (who was but a woman) being of a pitiful disposition,— and her ministers also, they not wishing in their hearts to have the town dismantled, for these reasons. . . . [VI. xxxiv. 352]

Tristram's lapsing into ellipses leaves the reader to uphold his end of the narrative conversation yet again and to imagine the state secrets which the narrator supposedly cannot reveal. On one level, obviously, the passage continues the novel's description of Toby's interest in the military operations conducted earlier in the century, reporting the plea of a defeated city that the victorious sovereign preserve some of the municipal works vital to the city's economy. But on another level, the incident may suggest something of the nature of Toby's trauma, especially as it has been associated by Toby himself with the "shock" he received that same summer from the Widow Wadman. The sovereign in question is, significantly, a woman and, as Watt notes, "mole" in Sterne's day was a slang term for penis; the plea, suggestively, is to be spared castration. The queen, like Mrs. Wadman, is a daughter of Dinah and granddaughter of Eve, possessing the power to destroy or to preserve any Shechem's "mole."

The psychic wound that Toby received from Mrs. Wadman is associated with just such an operation, for as Tristram reports,

> My uncle *Toby* knew little of the world; and therefore when he felt he was in love with Widow *Wadman*, he had no conception that the thing was any more to be made a mystery of, than if Mrs. *Wadman*, had given him a cut with a gap'd knife across his finger. . . . [VIII. xxvii. 447]

When Widow Wadman debates inwardly whether to put her finger on the very spot where Toby received his groin wound during the siege of Namur, she comes as close as any woman in the novel to performing that biblical symbolic act of castration, for when he finally understands the nature of her consideration Toby is "wounded" for life.

Little wonder, then, why any mention of happily voracious Aunt Dinah should upset Uncle Toby. To be made to recall the significance of her name is to be reminded of the genital wound and eventual loss of life experienced by biblical Shechem when he fell in love, and thus of his own close call with Widow Wadman. Significantly, the novel's first mention of Toby's "modesty" and the first hint of his asexuality occur in I. xxi, the very chapter in which that disturbing first reference to the significance of Aunt Dinah's name also occurs!

The Comedy of Castration

"What a jovial and a merry world would this be, may it please your worships, but for that inextricable labyrinth of debts, cares, woes, want, grief, discontent, melancholy, large jointures, impositions, and lies!" sighs Tristram (VI. xiv. 329) midway through the narration of what he earlier calls the "train of vexatious disappointments" that has followed him all his life (I. xv. 32). For Freud, notes Maurice Charney, "the essential purpose of comedy is to teach us how to live in an irrational and possibly meaningless world."[19] Paradoxically, the most heroic way of mastering adversity may be simply by laughing at it: Tristram's genius is that he is able to enjoy the comic confusion that results when he is lost in that "inextricable labyrinth," rather than bemoan the confusions and disappointments that plague him so. His world, consequently, is all the more jovial *because* of those vexations, not in spite of them. The joy that infuses *Tristram Shandy*, even when narrating the worst disappointments under the most pathetic circumstances which characterize "this scurvy and disastrous world of ours" (I. v. 7), derives from the success of Tristram/Sterne's attempt to exaggerate every threat presented in the world of the novel until it is so horribly grotesque that it is actually ludicrous.[20]

It is within this particular context, I believe, that Sterne's use of the biblical Dinah and Shechem story can finally best be understood. The world of the biblical *récit* is undeniably tragic. Whether she was sexually violated or had been religiously defiled by her liaison with the uncircumcised Shechem, Dinah ultimately experiences only deprivation and unhappiness, not renewal. Likewise, it finally does not matter whether Shechem fell in love with Dinah only after initially raping her or was engaged from the beginning in a mutually gratifying love affair with her, if the consequences of his action are to suffer first a symbolic sexual maiming and then the ultimate destruction of his creative powers, death. No one in the immediate story is satisfied with what transpires for, as at the conclusion of Shakespeare's *Romeo and Juliet*, the fairest flowers of both families have been blasted; both tribes' hopes of renewal through the most promising members of the younger generation have been destroyed. Even within the larger biblical history, renewal for the Jews comes only generations later when land once belonging to Shechem's people is finally settled and securely held by them. The death of Shechem, the sacrifice of Dinah's happiness, and the alienation of their future neighbors must force the Jews to question the value of the final accomplishment; the Promised Land may be finally theirs, but at what a cost!

In Sterne's retelling, however, Dinah is far from the tragic cause or symbol of inter-tribal strife and religious warfare. She has, in fact, been transformed into the opposite of the "violated womb"—the comic woman of enormous sexual appetite. Sexual intercourse is not a violation which pollutes or defiles a woman in *Tristram Shandy*, as it does in the biblical *récit*, and so is not something that she must fear. Rather, a woman's problem in the world of Sterne's novel is that a good man is so hard to find—or, as Mae West might have it, a hard man, always good to find, is disappointingly nowhere in sight. Consequently, in a parody of biblical Dinah's leaving the protection of her father's camp to explore the larger world, Dinah Shandy is forced to seek sexual gratification outside her class because the men within it, as we have seen, are impotent or otherwise inadequate. Because her sex drive is stronger than the social taboos that forbid sex outside of marriage or with a man of an inferior social class, Miss Shandy is free to good-naturedly pursue her heart's desire, unlike biblical Dinah whose personal happiness is destroyed by just such codes and desires. The reader is given no indication that Aunt Dinah ever suffers regret for having so exhuberantly sought sexual happiness. In fact, far from condemning her, the narrative seems to celebrate her in much the same way as Chaucer celebrates the Wife of Bath: as the woman who was not shy about warming her hands before the fire of life and who can contentedly say years later, "I have had my world as in my time."

Dinah Shandy's character effectively eliminates from the novel the first of those psychosexual threats offered by the biblical *récit*, her amorous good will and her uninhibited desire for physical gratification being so exaggerated that they obscure the possibility that her liaison with the coachman is in any way destructive of her happiness or of any one else's. Her comedy is compounded by the fact that, unlike biblical Dinah whose two brothers enact a violent revenge to redeem their family's honor, Dinah Shandy is "defended" only by two nephews so emotionally removed through time from the original incident that, whatever shame or embarrassment the more contemporary members of Dinah's family might have felt, Walter's and Toby's response to her "defilement" are socially inconsequential, even impotent. This must be a deliberate maneuver on Sterne's part since Dinah must have had at least one brother, the father of Walter and Toby, yet every other member of Aunt Dinah's generation is mysteriously absent from the novel despite the fact that Tristram intends to tell the Shandy family history from as far back as the generation of his great-grandparents, Dinah's parents. One generation removed, however, Walter's primary interest in her history is linguistic, insofar as it exemplifies his theory of names and may be affectionately used to tease his brother about the latter's unfortunate relationship with Widow Wadman. Likewise, even though Toby's response to any mention made of his aunt's history is more physically demonstrative than Walter's, it is limited to violently whistling "Lillabullero." The potential tragedy of a woman's defilement and of a family's violent revenge is reduced by Sterne in the spirit of "true Shandeism" to a comedy of manners in which a female's sexual voracity only intensifies her collateral male descendents' consciousness of their own sexual inadequacy. Far from being a daughter of Jacob in an eighteenth-century powdered wig, or another Clarissa, Dinah Shandy is a female Tom Jones, the source of irrepressible sexual good feeling in a world where decorum insists that people at least pretend they are superior to their supposedly "baser" desires.

The threat to the male member which figures prominently in the biblical story is likewise deflected through comedy in *Tristram Shandy*. As both John Stedmond and William V. Holtz have shown, the great theme of *Tristram Shandy* is man's inability to accomplish what he sets out to do, "whether he aims to make love, to write a book, or simply to communicate a thought."[21] Story telling is just as difficult an act for Tristram to complete as the act of his conception was for his father, Madam's question interrupting his concentration just as surely as Mrs. Shandy's did Walter's (I. i. 4). It is questionable whether Tristram's weakening health will not abruptly abort his narrative of his earlier years; his death, it goes without saying, will inevitably prevent him from completing the story of his entire life. Thus, it is not surprising to find as regular features of style dashes that leave sentences incomplete; asterisks that signify the deletion of words; interruptions that prevent communication acts from being completed; and digressions that keep the story from ever being finally told. Endemically, texts within the text are never finished:

Diego abandons his ode to Julia in mid-creation when informed that his mules are saddled and his servant is ready to leave (IV. "ST." 202); Julia's letter to him breaks off not simply in mid-sentence but in mid-word (idem.); and Trim never completes "The Story of the King of *Bohemia* and his seven castles," no matter how many times he returns to it (VIII. xix). Even words, the most basic units of meaning and communication, are regularly "castrated": Julia, of course, dies "un————"; the Abbess of Andouilletts halves words with her novice; and Tristram is left to protest the habit of successive generations simplifying or modifying a complicated or archaically spelled ancestral name, complaining that "in a course of years" the very best surnames in the kingdom "have generally undergone as many chops and changes as their owners" (I. xi. 18). Appropriately, passages about Tristram's possible castration are themselves castrated. Dashes and asterisks replace the words that Tristram doesn't dare repeat in his father's fulminations against Dr. Slop and Susannah (VI. xiv. 329), and the very information about Tristram's condition that the reader most desires is denied him when Dr. Slop's lowering his voice in professional confidence is likewise rendered by asterisks (III. xvii. 139).

Yet, by the curious alchemical process of Sterne's comedy and art, the further Tristram's narrative is castrated, the larger it grows. The more unmanageable his story is made by associative digressions, the more it actually expands. Likewise, sentence ideas are free to go in a dozen different directions when their original syntax is not completed, and meanings proliferate when a word is not finished. Interruption is a death of sorts, causing a halt in the natural rythmn of the organism. But Sterne seizes upon the fact that by following a straight narrative line, a story moves intransigently to an irrevocable conclusion or "death." Tristram intuitively indulges and even exaggerates his own and his family's tendency to digress because when it has been so "castrated," his narrative cannot end; its thwarting is, paradoxically, a seemingly infinite expansion. "Castration" is stylistically exaggerated and transformed through comic exaggeration from something to be feared to something that must be celebrated.

Thus, the Shandy family, like Jacob's, will somehow go on, despite threats to its continuance and despite its own fears. Walter's woefully inadequate and disrupted sexual performance *does* produce a child, one as zany and incomplete as the act of conception itself. Tristram's frustrated attempt to write a book *does* succeed when he makes the digressions that interrupt the story he is telling into the stuff of the story itself. ("*Non enim excursus hic ejus, sed opus ipsum est,*" he gives as the epigraph to Volume VII.) And Aunt Dinah continues as the Shandy matriarch despite the fact that she's been "cut" from the family, her courage in refusing to obey the social conventions that would deny her gratification, no matter how seemingly eccentric, anticipating the spirit of her great-nephew's book which likewise cannot be bound by convention. In fact, great aunt-Dinah may be the spirit that presides over *Tristram Shandy*, not Muddle, for her story—with its biblical background—is generationally the first to illustrate how incipient tragedy may be averted and raised to the level of life-enhancing comedy.

Notes

[1]Laurence Sterne, *The Life and Opinions of Tristram Shandy, Gentleman*, ed. Ian Watt (Boston: Houghton Mifflin, 1965), V. xxxii. 297. References to this edition of the novel will be cited parenthetically in my text and, following the convention of Sterne criticism, will offer the volume and chapter numbers to aid readers using editions with differing paginations. A modern spelling edition of the King James Version of the Bible is used for scriptural citations.

[2]Editors Watt and Ian Ross, for example, assume that Walter's reference is evidence of the Shandy family's class consciousness. Watt: "Presumably because it was rather a commonplace name" (50, note 5). Ross: "Dinah had been a popular name among servants and labourers since the mid-seventeenth century" (Oxford: Clarendon P, 1983, 548, note 4). James Work quietly passes over the significance of her name in his influential Odyssey P edition (1940).

[3]Melvyn New et al., eds., *The Florida Edition of the Works of Laurence Sterne*, vol. III (Gainesville: UP of Florida, 1984), 110, note 73. 15-16.

Howard Anderson, ed., *Tristram Shandy: A Norton Critical Edition* (New York: Norton, 1980), 47, note 6.

[4]John Traugott, quoted in "Sternian Realities: Excerpts from Seminars Chaired by John Traugott," in *The Winged Skull: Papers from the Laurence Sterne Bicentenary Conference*, ed. Arthur H. Cash and John M. Stedmond (Kent, OH: Kent State UP, 1971), 86-87.

[5]Gerhard von Rad, *Genesis: A Commentary*, rev. ed. (Philadelphia: Westminster P, 1972), 334-35. The finest literary reading of the *récit* is Meir Sternberg, *Poetics of Biblical Narrative* (Bloomington: Indiana UP, 1985), 445-75, although I have difficulty with his characterization of Jacob as a "do-nothing" who is oddly unable to act or even react.

[6]In *The Redaction of Genesis* (Winona Lake, IN: Eisenbrauns P, 1986), 56-59, Gary A. Rendsburg analyzes the story in these terms, comparing the "anomalous design" of Dinah's rape which results in Jacob's pact with foreigners, with that of Rebekah's association with a foreign ruler in Genesis 26, which similarly results in Isaac's prospering in Abimelech's land. Cf. Samuel Sandmel, *The Hebrew Scriptures* (New York: Oxford UP, 1978), 365-66, which hypothesizes that verses 2, 5, 13, 27, and 31 dealing with rape were later introduced into the earlier account involving the love story of Shechem and Dinah in order to justify the massacre and land transaction.

[7]Nehama Aschkenasy, *Eve's Journey: Feminine Images in Hebraic Literary Tradition* (Philadelphia: U of Pennsylvania P, 1986), 124-25, 128. Aschkenasy demonstrates more sympathy for Dinah than von Rad does, although she does not make clear if she feels the narrative asks the reader to feel such sympathy as well.

[8]H. Freedman, trans., *Midrash Rabbah: Genesis* (London and New York: Soncino P, 1983), 735-36. Aschkenasy, *Eve's Journey*, 129, makes passing reference to this tradition. For von Rad's comments, see *Genesis: A Commentary*, 331.

[9]Michael Payne summarizes the "central biblical motifs of sexuality and the land" in "The Song of Songs as Lyric Drama," *The CEA Critic* 12 (1985): 12-19; esp. 18.

[10]I say this fully recognizing the irony that, outraged by his sons's excessive zeal, Jacob orders his family to undergo rites of purification and to decamp to Bethel. Inspired with a fear of Jacob's gods by the violence of the Jews' actions, the local tribesmen refrain from pursuing them. After their purification at Bethel, however, the Lord renews his covenant with Jacob (Gen. 35). Thus, as a self-contained story, the affair of Dinah

and Shechem is a dark tale about the human price of a manifest destiny. Within the larger cycle of Israelite history, however, the incident establishes the Jews' claim to land which Abraham's covenant recognized belonged to another people ("the land wherein thou art a stranger"—Gen. 17:9). "Readers" among later generations may thus feel justified in ownership of land not originally theirs; his people's later loss of Canaan is the steep price paid by Shechem for having "defiled" the Jews' kinswoman.

[11]*The Standard Edition of the Complete Psychological Works of Sigmund Freud*, gen. ed. and trans. James Strachey, 24 vols. (London: Hogarth P, 1966-74), 18: 273-74; cf. 5: 366-67. Freud's equation has proven a provocative one and has been used widely in literary and art criticism. See, for example, Laurie Schneider, "Donatello and Caravaggio: The Iconography of Decapitation," *American Imago* 33 (Spring 1976): 76-91; and Richard P. Wheeler, *Shakespeare's Development and the Problem Comedies: Turn and Counter-Turn* (Berkeley and Los Angeles: U of California P, 1981), 112, note 8.

[12]Madlyn Kahn discusses the association of hair with physical power in her survey of Western representations of Delilah. Her conclusion is that "whatever else may vary in the representations of Delilah's treachery, one undeviating factor remains: Delilah is the embodiment of men's deep-rooted fear of the danger threatened by erotic involvement with a woman." See her "Delilah," *Art Bulletin* 54 (1972): 282-99. This is reinforced by a paper that Natasha Korda of Johns Hopkins U read at the 1988 Modern Language Association meeting in New Orleans entitled "Unlocking Samson," which equates Delilah's destruction of Samson's strength with feminist attempts to unlock phallocentrism's "secret."

[13]See Mieke Bal, *Murder and Difference: Gender, Genre, and Scholarship on Sisera's Death*, trans. Matthew Gumpert (Bloomington: Indiana UP, 1988), chap. 5, for an astute analysis of the sexual theme of the narrative, and particularly of how readers uncomfortable with Jael's aggressiveness have censored the episode in an attempt to protect her "honor" and consequently that of Yahweh.

[14]Katharine M. Rogers, *The Troublesome Helpmate: A History of Misogyny in Literature* (Seattle: U of Washington P, 1966), 276, 71.

[15]At the heart of Medusa iconography, thought Freud, was the male's subliminal fear of castration when, in coitus, he sees his phallus swallowed by the female's mouth-like vagina; see note 15 above. In *Lethal Love: Feminist Readings of Biblical Love Stories* (Bloomington: Indiana UP, 1987), 54-55, Mike Bal analyzes woman's hair as "the *vagina dentata*,

that phantasmagoric horror for men who fear to lose the penis and, syn-
ecdochically, the self." Psychosexually, a woman's hair represents her
sexual attractiveness in which a man is entangled and weakened. Likewise, male castration anxiety is often represented through hair loss, a re-
ceding hairline in middle age suggesting parallel loss of virility. Cf.
Marjorie Garber, *Shakespeare's Ghost Writers: Literature as Uncanny Cau-
sality* (New York: Methuen, 1987), chap. 5, on Medusa-like women.

I am grateful to the students of my comedy seminar at the Tennessee Governor's School for the Humanities (1988) for discussions in which
we pursued the comic aspects of this theme; in particular to the group
which analyzed *Sir Gawain and the Green Knight* with me in these terms.
As in the biblical Dinah story, agricultural fertility depends upon a symbolic sexual encounter after which, in the Middle English comic epic, the
man is saved from beheading or death. Sir Gawain's power to spiritually
renew Arthur's court is related to the Green Knight's power to annually
revive the sterile, wintry countryside. But Sir Gawain's power derives from
his resisting the sexual temptation offered by Lady Bercilak. Presumably,
had he given in to her seductions, he would have been deprived of his
virile powers like the biblical heroes Adam, Samson, David, and Solomon
who "one and all fell prey/To women that they had used" (lines 2411-
28), and subsequently been beheaded by the Green Knight. Refraining
from coitus, in this case, results in the male's being spared beheading; the
hero is renewed rather than emasculated or castrated.

[16]Bruce Vawter, *On Genesis: A New Reading* (Garden City, NY:
Doubleday, 1977), 357.

[17]Readers familiar with Sterne criticism will recognize my general
indebtedness to the discussion of the novel's sexual elements in these
important essays: A. R. Towers, "Sterne's Cock and Bull Story," *English
Literary History* 24 (1957): 12-29; William B. Piper, *Laurence Sterne* (Boston: Twayne, 1965), 66-84; Robert Alter, "*Tristram Shandy* and the Game
of Love," *American Scholar* 37 (1968): 316-23; Frank Brady, "*Tristram
Shandy*: Sexuality, Morality, and Sensibility," *Eighteenth-Century Studies*
4 (1970): 41-56; Dennis W. Allen, "Sexuality/Textuality in *Tristram
Shandy*," *Studies in English Literature* 25 (1985): 651-70; and Max Byrd,
Tristram Shandy (London: George Allen and Unwin, 1985), 31-34, 40-
41.

[18]See John A. Hay, "Rhetoric and Historiography: Tristram
Shandy's First Nine Kalendar Months," in *Studies in the Eighteenth Century*, ed. R. F. Brissenden (Tronoto: U of Toronto P, 1973), 73-91. Hay's

essay, needless to say, is ignored by Leigh A. Ehlers in "Mrs. Shandy's 'Lint and Basilicon': The Importance of Women in *Tristram Shandy*," *South Atlantic Review* 46 (1981): 61-75. Determined to see the women in the novel, particularly Elizabeth Shandy, as being "invested with considerable, though untapped, restorative powers" (61), Ehlers extends the field of Tristram's suggestions to include Trismegistus and, by extension, Osiris and Isis (69), in order to provide a model for the venerable woman. Ehlers likewise ignores the novel's recurring images of female sexual appetite.

[19]Maurice Charney, *Hamlet's Fictions* (New York: Routledge, 1988), 147-48. Charney applies Freud's theory in analyzing *Hamlet* as comedy, specifically the Graveyard Scene, which of course is the scene that provides Sterne with the prototype for his own Yorick. See as well Michael D. Bristol, *Carnival as Theater* (New York: Routledge, 1985), 185-93. I have analyzed Sterne's comic deflection of psychic threats in a related context in "'Madame, Spare That Mole!': Comic Responses to Psychosexual Threats in Sterne's *Tristram Shandy*," *Publications of the Arkansas Philological Association* 16 (Spring 1990): 15-30.

[20]As Richard Lanham notes, it is the same "hobby-horsical" maneuvers that render the Shandy men absurd that allow Walter, Toby, and Tristram to survive the most serious threats to their emotional and mental well-being; see, for example, his analysis of Walter's psychologically redemptive use of language in *Tristram Shandy: The Games of Pleasure* (Berkeley and Los Angeles: U of California P, 1972), 54-56. Likewise, Patricia Meyer Spacks' analysis of Walter's use of language in her *Imagining a Self: Autobiography and Novel in Eighteenth-Century England* (Cambridge: Harvard UP, 1976), 144. Such a maneuver, as Arnold Weinstein points out, allows the individual "to recoup, mentally, what we lose, materially"; see his *Fictions of the Self: 1500-1800* (Princeton: UP, 1981), 230.

[21]William V. Holtz, *Image and Immortality: A Study of Tristram Shandy* (Providence: Brown UP, 1970), 85. Cf. John M. Stedmond, *The Comic Art of Laurence Sterne* (Toronto: U of Toronto P, 1967), esp. 131.

Nine:

A Genealogy of Ruths: From Female Harvester to Fallen Woman in Nineteenth-Century England

Eve Walsh Stoddard

The early nineteenth century was a period of intense economic upheaval as England changed from a traditional agricultural economy to an industrial one. Small landholders and cottagers were displaced as farming became a modern, technological business. The story of Ruth was associated with the harvest, not only because of her work as a gleaner but perhaps also because she and Naomi exemplify the same cycle of emptiness and fullness that agrarian nature does. Nineteenth-century British literature appropriates the biblical character of Ruth and transforms it into two different traditions, both shaped by socio-historical preoccupations. The predominant Romantic figuration of Ruth is as a female agricultural laborer, common yet ideal, as in Keats's "Ode to a Nightingale." The Victorian tradition appears to have a more problematic relationship to the biblical story. From William Wordsworth's "Ruth" to George Crabbe's and Elizabeth Gaskell's, the issue of the "fallen" and abandoned woman becomes associated with the name "Ruth" and by extension, with the biblical story. In this tradition the writers see their Ruths as innocent victims ostracized by a harsh and unforgiving patriarchal society. Two later novels, George Eliot's *Adam Bede* and Thomas Hardy's *Tess of the D'Urbervilles*, which use Ruth as a subtext without naming her explicitly, reinvest the issue of the "fallen woman" with the image of the female farm worker. All the nineteenth-century British Ruth figures are lower class laborers.

Because the term "patriarchy" is central to my analysis, both of the original Ruth story and of its recent descendents in England, I would like to clarify its meaning. In her book *The Creation of Patriarchy*, historian Gerda Lerner points out that the term has both a narrow and a broad meaning. The narrower, more technical one refers to a legal system deriving from ancient Greece and Rome in

which the "male head of the household had absolute legal and economic power over his dependent female and male family members."[1]
This system of family authority persisted until the end of the nineteenth century and fully applies to the literary works I examine here.
However, the broader definition of patriarchy subsumes the narrower one as it extends the power of the father and his metaphorical representatives (priests, uncles, judges, bosses, kings, God, etc.)
into all areas of life, material and ideological. Lerner defines it as

> the manifestation and institutionalization of male dominance
> over women and children in the family and the extension of male
> dominance over women in society in general. It implies that men
> hold power in all the important institutions of society and that
> women are deprived of access to such power.[2]

The Victorian texts that allude to Ruth in varying degrees criticize
the patriarchal system by exposing its inhumane treatment of the
females it keeps dependent.

Female gleaners such as Keats alludes to in "To Autumn"
formed the subject of many engravings and paintings during the
early nineteenth century. Constable's "The Gleaners—Brighton
1817" is a well-known example. The poets and artists who allude
to Ruth, directly or as subtext, in these representations do not use
biblical authority to coerce contemporary females into submission
and "filial piety." Rather, they use the Ruth story to confer respect
on female harvesters. These women have a dignity that servants and
factory hands lose, and they connote a romantic connection between the female and the agricultural cycles of nature.

The association between the female and nature as opposed to
the male and culture is one of a series of hierarchical binary oppo-
sitions used to subordinate women in patriarchal societies. Thus one
might interpret the representations of Ruth figures as condescend-
ing and oppressive. However, in the Romantic period, most poets
and artists valorize nature over culture, and images of peasants signify revolutionary sympathy with the lower classes. In the 1800 Preface to the *Lyrical Ballads*, Wordsworth explicitly states that to give
a "systematic defense of the theory" behind his poems could not be

done "without retracing the revolutions not of literature alone but likewise of society itself."[3] He declines such an undertaking, but he does justify in detail his privileging both of the rural lower classes and of nature itself:

> Low and rustic life was generally chosen because in that situation the essential passions of the heart find a better soil in which they can attain their maturity, are less under restraint, and speak a plainer and more emphatic language; because in that situation our elementary feelings exist in a state of greater simplicity and consequently may be more accurately contemplated and more forcibly communicated; because the manners of rural life germinate from those elementary feelings.[4]

This rationale for the *Lyrical Ballads* could apply as well to the biblical story of Ruth. Part of its appeal for English readers would be its agricultural setting and activity, fairly rare in the Bible, but capable of bringing the ancient story into the familiar world of England's "green and pleasant land."

With the exception of John Keats, all the writers I discuss in this genealogy of nineteenth-century English Ruth characters are social critics and reformers. While several of the narratives explicitly discuss religious sects and values, the texts emphasize religious and moral toleration. In alluding to the biblical tale of Ruth, the writers have chosen one of the least overtly "religious" stories, one in which God plays no direct role. Yet the story provides its heroine with acceptable credentials for a Christian audience since she is alleged to be an ancestress of David and hence of Jesus. Linking a "fallen" woman to the biblical Ruth confers authority on the modern writer's vision of her innocence. At first glance the nineteenth-century appropriation of Ruth to portray the "fallen woman" seems extremely peculiar. However, when we divest ourselves of stereotypically pious readings of the biblical story, we find textual evidence that her behavior with Boaz would not meet some accepted nineteenth-century Christian standards of female behavior. First of all, middle and upper class women would not go out and work in a field. Secondly, no respectable woman would go in the middle of the night and lie down beside a man who had been drinking at a harvest feast, even if he was related by marriage. A nineteenth-century mother-in-law who told a young woman to do such a thing would be judged at best a fool and at worst a madame. I am not suggesting that we apply anachronistic standards to Ruth, but rather that "interpretive communities" will tend to compare behavior in stories to their own and respond accordingly. In Ruth's case, this would leave them somewhat puzzled.

In the commentary to the Anchor Bible *Ruth*, Edward F. Campbell Jr. notes the ambiguity of the Hebrew words for "uncover his legs" (Ruth 3:4, 3:7, 3:8, 3:14): "The question is whether the story-teller meant to be ambiguous and hence provocative. It seems to me that he did; therefore the intentional ambiguity of the translation 'legs' which leaves open the question of how much of his legs?"[5] Campbell delineates a series of double entendres and innuendoes in the episode on the threshing floor: "Together with the air of mystery there is built up a carefully contrived ambiguity; it revolves around whether Ruth's act in approaching Boaz under such compromising circumstances will result immediately in sexual intercourse. The story-teller clearly means to have his audience reckon with this possibility."[6] Campbell's interpretation is that Ruth lays herself open to being taken advantage of, but that Boaz's response demonstrates his righteousness. The verb he uses in telling her "to lodge" there for the night "is never used in the Hebrew Bible with any sexual undertone."[7]

Nonetheless the moment of choice for Boaz suggests why more recent writers might appropriate the Ruth figure to characterize the innocence of a class of "fallen women," victims blamed and ostracized by society. Virginity is a reified state, really an absence, that is commodified in the interests of exogamous exchange of women. Male society consolidates its wealth and power through buying and selling undamaged women in marriage. The Book of Ruth is interesting precisely because she is not a virgin, though neither is she a whore. The ambiguity of her status outside this binary opposition is recapitulated in the ambiguity of her encounter with Boaz on the threshing floor. She comes within a hair's breadth of being a whore, leaving Boaz to make the choice. Her status and perhaps her survival are entirely dependent on his behavior. But unlike the nineteenth-century visions of patriarchal exploitation of women, the biblical tale shows patriarchy working in fecundity and charity.

What differentiates nineteenth-century English Ruths from their Moabite namesake is their lack of protection by the wings of the Lord, or Providence. In the Old Testament story, God's care for his people is enacted through the relationships of human society, particularly Israelite society. Crabbe, Gaskell, and Hardy expose a society that turns its back on the woman who transgresses the most stringent of patriarchal rules, by giving her body to a man outside the legitimate exchange system of marriage. While the biblical tale is an apparent celebration of patriarchy's enfolding care for the women at its mercy, the nineteenth-century narratives lay bare the devastating powerlessness and isolation of women who break the rules. According to Carol Lansbury, the "fallen woman" was such an issue in nineteenth-century England because there was a surplus of over half a million women throughout the first half of the century. This created intense competition for both husbands and jobs. Trade unions sought to exclude women from the employment pool. Thus most women could survive only through dependence on men, either in marriage or prostitution.[8] The social taboos against women who had forfeited their "purity" protected the marketability of middle and upper class daughters.

Esther Fuchs interprets Ruth's story as ideological "support of the patriarchal institution of the levirate, which insures the patrilineage of a deceased husband."[9] She quotes Robert Briffault's argument that "the levirate custom owes its origin to the assimilation of a wife to inheritable property."[10] Yet Ruth is not a passive piece of property. For unknown reasons, she actively and freely chooses to accompany Naomi to the land of Israel. And while being a handmaid or piece of property is dehumanizing, the alternatives of starvation, rape, or prostitution are worse. Within the context of a powerful patriarchy, Ruth behaves heroically and is accepted into the community. This is not to deny Fuchs's point that by projecting onto

woman what man desires most, the biblical narrative creates a
powerful role model for women. . . . It should be ascribed to the
imaginative and artistic ingenuity of the biblical narrator that one
of the most vital patriarchal concerns is repeatedly presented not
as an imposition on woman but as something she herself desires
more than anything else.[11]

Ironically, out of the five authors who create variations on the theme
of Ruth as fallen woman, the two who are women are the most
ambivalent about the lack of providence working through society.
One of Sandra Gilbert and Susan Gubar's main points in *The Madwoman in the Attic* is that "in publicly presenting acceptable facades
for private and dangerous visions, women writers have long used a
wide range of tactics to obscure but not obliterate their most subversive impulses."[12] A female writer in Victorian England simply
could not defend the innocence and virtue of a "fallen" woman as
openly as a man could. Such sympathizing would plunge the author
into the fallen category herself. The strategy Gaskell adopts is to
present the issue in terms of Christian teachings on forgiveness. She
works at reform within the patriarchal framework rather than casting shame on it, as the male writers do.

Before examining Romantic and Victorian re-visionings of
Ruth, it is useful to see how Milton uses her, not only because he
exerts such influence on his romantic "descendents," but also because his allusion to Ruth in Sonnet IX, written in 1645, demonstrates a patriarchal, manipulative use of biblical allusion. He uses
allusions to scripture as a preacher would, to hold up models of ideal
behavior to the audience. What is fascinating about the nineteenth-
century writers is the degree to which they do *not* do this, partly
because Romanticism moves literature away from direct instruction
and partly because the writers are at odds with received notions of
morality. Milton's sonnet addresses with praise a young lady, a "Virgin wise and pure,"[13] relying on a texture of biblical allusions for its
meaning. The apostrophized virgin is one of "those few" who "labor up the Hill of Heav'nly Truth" (1.4), despite the vexation of
those who luxuriate on "the broad way and the green" (1.2). While
the paucity of true believers might refer to both genders, the totally

female context of the poem suggests that particularly few women take the path of virtue. The sonnet's octave establishes the hill metaphor in the first quatrain, while the second quatrain elaborates on the listener's character through comparison with biblical women:

> The better part with *Mary* and with *Ruth*
> Chosen thou hast: and they that overween
> And at thy growing virtues fret their spleen,
> No anger find in thee, but pity and ruth.

Milton has chosen figures from both the Old and New Testaments to exemplify virtuous Christian womanhood. In this context the first virtue is clearly virginity. Yet Mary represents a somewhat paradoxical, if not miraculous, virginity and could be viewed as a "fallen" woman by the skeptic. Ruth is a widow rather than a virgin, but she is meant to exemplify loyalty and obedience.

The temperament of the apostrophized maiden harmonizes with the story of Ruth: "No anger find in thee, but pity and ruth" (1.8). Milton's somewhat redundant use of the homonym "ruth" as a rhyme with "Ruth" forges an association between the proper name and the quality that lingers in later English references to Ruth, especially Keats's. Yet if anyone exemplifies "ruth" in the biblical narrative it would seem to be Boaz, who treats Ruth so sympathetically. *Her* virtues seem to be loyalty, devotion, and obedience to her mother-in-law, as well as a charmingly quiet and humble heroism. Unlike the stereotypical maiden, Ruth is active; she insists on following Naomi, she goes out in the fields to glean and brings back food for Naomi, and she essentially invites Boaz to marry her. Yet we can infer ruth, or kindness and pity, in Ruth's devotion to her "empty" mother-in-law. Whatever traits can be ascribed to the Old Testament Ruth, modern readers and writers have appropriated elements of her character and story to serve their own artistic and political purposes. Milton probably has in mind Ruth's "conversion" to the God of Israel expressed in her oft-quoted expression of fidelity:

> Whither thou goest, I will go;
> and where thou lodgest, I will lodge:
> thy people *shall be* my people,
> and thy God my God. (Ruth 1:16)

Her emphasis is on loyalty to *Naomi,* one corollary being acceptance of Naomi's God. Nonetheless many pious readers tend to interpret this as a story about conversion from idolatry to true religion.

The sestet of Milton's sonnet is built entirely around a comparison between the lady of the poem and the parable of the virgins from the Gospel of Matthew (25:6). The first tercet's language carries on the allusion to Ruth within the context of the New Testament parable:

> Thy care is fixt and zealously attends
> To fill thy odorous Lamp with deeds of light,
> And Hope that reaps not shame.

"Fixt" and "zealously" hark back to Ruth's "steadfast" refusal to return home to Moab, instead taking the path to the true God of Israel. The personified "Hope" seems equated with Ruth by the metaphor "reaps." Ruth's agricultural work brought her to a wedding feast whose issue led eventually to the birth of Milton's symbolic "Bridegroom."

To summarize, Milton invokes the name of Ruth as a model of Judeo-Christian faith and steadfast devotion to the path of righteousness. If his female interlocutor can resist the path taken by Eve, she will be allowed to be a handmaiden at the marriage feast which will consummate this world's existence. A life of zealous virtue and virginity, avoidance of "shame," will be rewarded in the hereafter with an exalted form of servitude. The "Therefore be sure" gives the whole poem a tone of warning. The entire definition of female virtue is so bound up with avoidance of sexuality that the threat of falling is omnipresent. Somewhat peripheral to the thrust of the poem, but important for later images of Ruth, is the close association Milton makes between "Ruth" and "ruth." It is tempting to speculate that this association was in Milton's mind seven years earlier when he wrote in "Lycidas": "Look homeward Angel now and melt with ruth" (1.163). Lycidas is apotheosized as "Genius of the shore" (1.183) as his "large recompense" for virtue and early death. Moreover the latent association with Ruth inheres in the "look homeward," which implies the transplanting to another realm that Ruth undergoes.

The Romantic Harvester: Keats's Ruth

Despite its brevity, Keats's image of Ruth in Stanza VII of the "Ode to a Nightingale," written in 1819, is one of the best-known literary allusions to the book of Ruth. It seems to be part of a web of interconnected Romantic visions of female agricultural workers. These images are entirely secular and without the moral freight we saw carried by Milton's allusion to Ruth. They draw from the biblical story its tone and atmosphere of simple dignity within an agricultural setting. Stanza VII's allusion to Ruth is quite explicit, yet it has confounded critics by its apparent dissonance from the Old Testament story. The speaker asserts that the voice he hears in nineteenth-century Hampstead is the same one heard in ancient times and other lands:

> Perhaps the self-same song that found a path
> Through the sad heart of Ruth, when, sick for home,
> She stood in tears amid the alien corn.[14]

The only element of this portrait that harmonizes with the ancient narrative is Ruth standing amid alien corn. The biblical text gives no suggestion of homesickness or of tears, except when Naomi beseeches Ruth to return to Moab. Critics have sought to decipher this puzzle by assuming that Keats conflated Ruth with Shakespeare's Cordelia, Wordsworth's "Solitary Reaper," or Milton's "Lycidas." In a complex argument about Keats's rejection of Miltonic religion, Victor J. Lams, Jr. concludes:

His alteration of Ruth's situation and emotion helps Keats repudiate dramatically Milton's Christian consolation. The biblical Ruth had found a new home, happiness after grief, and the protection and help of the Lord God of Israel. . . . Keats's Ruth is a fatherless girl who knows no such comfort, an isolated soul.[15]

Lams' argument makes a reasonable case for the accretion of nightingale images in Milton and for Milton's role in Keats's mind as exemplar of the Judeo-Christian tradition Keats repudiated. However, a secularized reading of the book of Ruth makes sense without making Ruth into a tragic figure.

In a parenthetical aside, Earl Wasserman asks, "Is there not a strong suggestion that here the Biblical name serves also as a personification of 'ruth' and in this sense encompasses all mortality?"[16] If we accept Lams' contention that the entire nightingale experience is mediated through Milton's poetry, then the conflation of the proper name and homonym we saw in Milton's ninth sonnet, along with the line from "Lycidas," supports Wasserman's suggestion. Furthermore, Keats exists in relation to the nightingale's song, pure poetry itself, as Ruth does to Naomi. In stanza IV the speaker says "Away! away! for I will fly to thee/. . . on the viewless wings of Poesy." Using his "negative capability," or empathic imagination, Keats has left his "home" for the realm of the nightingale, not an easy journey. Just so he propels himself into the subjectivity of his imagined Ruth, a subjectivity not revealed to us in the Bible. Thus, the imaginary homesickness of Ruth is an unconscious turning point in the fancied flight of the poet out of himself that is the poem. Keats projects the sadness that he feels at being tugged back down to earth and death, even though the return "homeward" does not become explicit until the repetition of "forlorn" at the beginning of the eighth and final stanza.

Fifty years ago H.W. Garrod suggested that "the image of Ruth amid the corn came to Keats by some obscure process of association, from Wordsworth's 'Solitary Reaper.'"[17] Subsequent critics have accepted the suggestion. Wordsworth's poem compares the song of the "solitary Highland Lass" to that of the nightingale. Both poems are about a song of surpassing beauty that becomes a metaphor for pure poetry. Both songs draw out the poet-listener's imagination to remote times and places because the songs are without determinate meaning; they are pure sound. Wordsworth asks in the third stanza, "Will no one tell me what she sings?"[18] Keats would have had to make the association between the Highland reaper and Ruth, but female harvesters were easily associated with the biblical character. Once Keats made that connection, Wordsworth supplied the note of sadness: "Alone she cuts and binds the grain,/And sings a melancholy strain" ("Solitary Reaper," 11.5-6). The sadness is reiterated in stanza 3:

> Or is it some more humble lay,
> Familiar matter of to-day?
> Some natural sorrow, loss, or pain,
> That has been, and may be again? (11.18-24)

It is precisely the tragic nature of "natural sorrow, loss, or pain" which Keats seeks to escape in "Ode to a Nightingale," but later embraces fully through the personified figure of Autumn in one of his last poems. Although "To Autumn" has no explicit connection with Ruth, the female manifestations of harvest labor in stanza 2, as winnower, reaper, and gleaner, especially "sitting careless on a granary floor," may evoke her story. "To Autumn" celebrates the process of temporality to which Keats was bitterly recalled in stanza VIII of the earlier poem.

Keats's image of Ruth amid the alien corn thus synthesizes Milton's conflation of "Ruth" with "ruth" and his line from "Lycidas": "Look homeward Angel now and melt with ruth." It also seems to rely on Wordsworth's beautiful but plaintive vision of the Scottish reaper singing her undecipherable song, and to connect with Keats's own slightly later "To Autumn." All these poetic representations of female harvesters bespeak their dignity and beauty with no overt social or moral purpose. The readers of the Napoleonic era, however, would bring to the poems the sense that times were changing, that these women whose work had not changed since the time of the first Ruth were being replaced with new methods of large scale agriculture, as small scale farmers were driven off the land and into the growing towns.

The Abandoned Woman: Wordsworth's "Ruth"

The 1800 edition of *Lyrical Ballads* contains the first incarnation of Ruth as a woman deceived by an unfaithful man. Coleridge pronounced the poem "Ruth" to be "the finest poem in the collection."[19] Because she is legally married, she is not actually a "fallen woman" in the Victorian sense, but her story illustrates the same callousness of male society toward women as do the succeeding revisionary readings of Ruth as "fallen woman" by Crabbe, Gaskell, Eliot, and Hardy. Whereas the biblical tale ends with a return to plenitude, Wordsworth's poem ends with Ruth homeless and mad. The genealogy of Ruth figures who descend from this poem suggests that the issue of the fallen and abandoned woman became linked to Ruth from this point on, from Crabbe's "Ruth" to Gaskell's *Ruth* to Hardy's *Tess of the D'Urbervilles*.

Wordsworth's "Ruth" tells the story of a motherless girl, alienated from her father by his remarriage. Her loneliness allows her unusual freedom to wander "over dale and hill,/In thoughtless freedom, bold" (11.5-6). Like the solitary reaper, she creates music, "sounds of woods and floods" (1.9). She meets a youth who was a soldier for the crown, apparently in the French and Indian wars, and he paints a primitivist picture of the free life in nature they could lead in America. Ruth agrees tearfully to go back to America with her lover. They marry lawfully and prepare to board ship,

> But when they thither came, the youth
> Deserted his poor Bride, and Ruth
> Could never find him more. (11.190-92)

Ruth went mad and was imprisoned for almost a year. When released, she became a vagrant:

> The master-current of her brain
> Ran permanent and free;
> And, coming to the Banks of Tone,
> There did she rest; and dwell alone
> Under the greenwood tree. (11.211-16)

The tone of the poem is oddly neutral for Wordsworth. Whereas his earlier poems about abandoned women are critical of the social structure, this poem is more tragic than political. Ruth never taxed nature "with the ill/which had been done to her" (11.221-2). The poet comments that hers is "An innocent life, yet far astray!" (1.229). She cheers her loneliness with a home-made flute and begs for food. The conclusion says to Ruth that when she dies,

> Thy corpse shall buried be,
> For thee funeral bells shall ring,
> And all the congregation sing
> A Christian psalm for thee. (11.255-59)

The ending implies that this respectful treatment is somewhat un-usual given Ruth's wild and solitary life but that the poet wants to reconcile her apparent estrangement with Christian notions of pi-ety through the assertion of her innocence.

This modern Ruth lacks any protectors: her father slighted her, and her husband abandoned her. Although she wanted to follow her husband to an alien land as Ruth followed Naomi, she is not allowed to. Instead she experiences alienation in her own land. Such might have been the fate of the biblical Ruth had Naomi's kinsmen not rallied round her. The Christian affirmation at the end of the poem seems somehow at odds with the substance of the narrative. Both Ruth and her lover were children of nature. He learned "vices" from the human society of Indians and she experienced nothing but mistreatment and abandonment at the hands of those close to her. The book of Ruth is often read as a story about God's providence operating through humans. Wordsworth's reference to a Christian burial ceremony seems meant to suggest a social incorporation of Ruth into the fold, but it also reveals a kind of hypocrisy. Where was all this Christian piety when Ruth was living her lonely life in the woods? The connection, therefore, between Wordsworth's "Ruth" and the biblical tale is somewhat tenuous and ironic. Both Ruths marry men from another land, and both are "abandoned" by them, though in different senses. Although Wordsworth's poem can allude only negatively to the providence of the ancient tale, the attraction of the biblical story as a model of lower class dignity and beauty is obvious. It presents just such a model of the enduring qualities of human sympathy and emotion as Wordsworth sought to capture in the *Lyrical Ballads*.

A Critique of Patriarchy: Crabbe's "Ruth"

As we move from Wordsworth's "Ruth" to Crabbe's poem "Ruth," in *Tales of the Hall* (1819), we move not only to more direct consideration of the "fallen woman" but also to more explicit social criticism. Crabbe's poem narrates the seduction and abandonment of a Ruth figure as does Elizabeth Gaskell's novel *Ruth*, published in 1853. A.W. Ward speculates that the name of the novel was probably "suggested to Mrs. Gaskell by a masterpiece of tragic pathos which must in any case have been known to her as the production of a poet much read by her—Crabbe's story of 'Ruth,' in the *Tales of the Hall*—her familiarly with which is attested by special evidence."[20] It is puzzling that Ward mentions neither Wordsworth's "Ruth," which Gaskell surely knew, nor the biblical Ruth as possible precursors.

The subjects of Crabbe's narrative poems are similar to those of Wordsworth's *Lyrical Ballads*, lower class people marginalized by a changing and oppressive social structure. However, Crabbe was a clergyman of the Church of England, dependent on the patronage of the Duke of Rutland for much of his career. He was therefore not entirely free to express radical views, and when he did offer ugly realism in *The Borough* (1810), the reviewers attacked the "disgusting representations." Unlike Wordsworth, Crabbe remains within the stylistic constraints of eighteenth-century couplets, which militate against the simple presentation of character and tale that we find in both the biblical Ruth and Wordsworth's early poems. Despite the differences between Gaskell's radical Unitarianism and Crabbe's Anglicanism, both refract their sympathies for the "fallen woman" through a haze of religious sentiments while seeming to worry about appearing to sanction "vice." In his preface to "Ruth," Crabbe claims to eschew the "tone of a moralist,"[21] yet he carefully denies "confounding right and wrong" or excusing "the vices of man, by associating with them sentiments that demand our respect" (341). In this circumlocution he avoids identifying which actions narrated in the poem are vices. Is it the sexual relations of the engaged couple, the tyranny of Ruth's unfeeling father, the exploitation of the preacher, or Ruth's suicide? Or is it the forcible impressment which comes between Ruth and her lover? Ruth's loss of virginity seems the least evil action, from either a Christian or a secular point of view. It is an expression of love between committed lovers whereas the other actions all revolve around tyranny and oppression.

Crabbe's Ruth, like Gaskell's, runs amok in part because of her beauty and simplicity:

> Ruth—I may tell, too oft had she been told-
> Was tall and fair, and comely to behold;
> Gentle and simple, in her native place
> Not one compared with her in form or face. (361)

Ruth is a "quiet spirit," "apprehensive, mild, and sad" (361), even before anything goes wrong with her life. This correlates with Keats's attribution of tears to his Ruth, which might have stuck in Crabbe's mind. In Crabbe's tale the willing lover is prevented from marrying Ruth, first by her "worldly wise" parents, and then, after she becomes pregnant, by the intervention of war and a press gang. In fact one of Crabbe's major points in the tale seems to be political criticism of this method of military recruitment: "Where might is right, and violence is law" (362). Whereas the biblical Book of Ruth shows men *not* taking advantage of an unprotected woman, but rather coming together as a community to provide for her lawfully, this tale shows how thin the veneer of lawful protection is in early nineteenth-century England. When Ruth's fiance is killed, she loses her mind as Wordsworth's Ruth did upon the loss of her lover:

> Yet, though bewilder'd for a time, and prone
> To ramble much and speak aloud, alone;
> Yet did she all that duty ever ask'd
> . . . she wept upon her boy,
> Wish'd for his death, in fear that he might live
> New sorrow to a burden'd heart to give. (363)

This account is deeply ambiguous about Ruth's mental stability, seeking to present her as at once dutiful and despairing. As Gaskell's *Ruth* likewise makes clear, an illegitimate child faced the prospect of a life of ostracism and taunts.

Yet in Ruth's despondency, a protective male figure comes to her who might play the role of Boaz. He is a Methodist preacher who is by trade a weaver. But soon this kindly teacher joins together with Ruth's father in another manifestation of how "might makes right." Whereas the gentle caring celebrated in the biblical story of Ruth deflects our attention from the strictures of patriarchy, Crabbe's poem lays them quite bare. Ruth's father's sympathy is not for her but for his fellow male: "he grieved to have the man denied" (363). The preaching weaver uses his religion to distort his motives and to castigate Ruth. He claims to want her for spiritual reasons: "he would take her as the prophet took / One of the harlots in the holy book" (363). Not only does the preacher deny his own lust for Ruth, but he elevates himself to the stature of a prophet while degrading her to the level of a whore.

Crabbe's position as an Anglican cleric puts him in an awkward position vis-à-vis patriarchy. His vicious portrayal of the weaver-preacher may include an element of "professional jealousy" or scorn for ill-educated evangelical preachers. But his tale not only exposes the tyranny of patriarchy in his own day, it clearly connects it to the patriarchy of scriptural culture, suggesting that morality modeled on that culture is inadequate and unjust. When Ruth begged the preacher on her knees to give up his pursuit of her, he responded:

> What! did the holy men of Scripture design,
> To hear a woman when she said "refrain?"
> Of whom they chose they took them wives, and these
> Made it their study and their wish to please;
> The women then were faithful and afraid,
> As Sarah Abraham, they their lords obey'd
> And so she styled him. (364)

The very men who are designated protectors of the dependent female are those from whom she most needs protection. Through the preacher's speech, Crabbe highlights the scriptural message that women should be absolutely subject to men. Even more insidious is Ruth's mother's complicity with the male power structure. When Ruth refuses to marry her suitor, says her mother, "I gently blamed her." Her mother is a survivor because she respects male dominance.

Crabbe leaves us in no doubt of his sympathies. After Ruth cries: "Would there were no men," the narrator describes her as

> Doom'd to a parent's judgment, all unjust,
> Doom'd the chance mercy of the world to trust,
> Or to wed grossness and conceal disgust. (364)

Ruth is trapped. She will not "go harlot to a loathed bed" (364). Since her father has vowed to disown her, her only other option is the parish poorhouse. Given the surplus of women and the lack of jobs, the options tended to be marriage, prostitution, or starvation. An educated middle class *virgin* could be a governess, but a "fallen woman" tended to end in prostitution because all other doors were closed to her. Many might consider Crabbe's Ruth lucky that a man was willing to marry her despite her tainted state. Thus it is no surprise that Ruth drowns herself, leaving behind her child, "A creature doom'd to shame! in sorrow born" (365).

The *"Fallen Woman" Redeemed: Gaskell's Ruth*

Elizabeth Gaskell's novel *Ruth*, which was burned for its supposed indecency by many of her acquaintances, retains the plot elements sketched out in Crabbe's tale. However, the novel form allows for elaborate development of subtleties and subjective experiences that Crabbe merely gestures at. Although Gaskell's Ruth also must die in the end, she does so having redeemed herself in the eyes of her community, a minor miracle in Victorian society. The tyrannical patriarchy which rules Crabbe's Ruth represents only a part of Gaskell's vision of society. Against Mr. Bradshaw, the bourgeois domestic tyrant, she poses Thurston Benson, the dissenting minister who saves Ruth from probable suicide and shelters both her and her son Leonard in his modest home. Lansbury points out that the Benson home in no way fits the patriarchal family structure. Thurston and his sister Faith represent a gender role reversal, except that he is the intellectual and spiritual guide of the family (61). But he is delicate, sentimental, sympathetic, and impractical while Faith "had the power, which some people have, of carrying her wishes through to their fulfillment; her will was strong, her sense was excellent, and people yielded to her" (112). Their servant Sally lives on relatively equal terms with the Bensons as part of the family. Sally and Faith lack maternal instincts, both having "accepted single life with a great deal of satisfaction" (61). It is no accident that this non-hierarchal, non-patriarchal family is the one that adopts Ruth and cares for her, while the Bradshaws turn her out when they find she is "impure."

Gaskell's Ruth is fifteen when, as a lovely, ignorant, and beautiful orphan apprentice, she is seduced by the cavalier, self-centered Mr. Bellingham. None of the authority figures in Ruth's life has taken proper responsibility for her education—not her parents, her guardian, nor the dressmaker she works for. Ruth has no idea that she has "fallen" or that she has become a pariah in polite society until a little boy hits her in the face for trying to kiss his baby sister: "'She's a bad, naughty girl—mama said so, she did; and she shan't kiss our baby'" (71). Ruth "turned away, humbly and meekly, with bent head" (71). Her only care is to please those around her. As in Crabbe's tale, the male lover who has wrought his lady's destruction does not willingly abandon her. When Bellingham becomes ill, his mother arrives to nurse him, bringing with her the freezing standards of patriarchal society, and Ruth is abandoned in rural Wales. The Bensons perform the roles of Naomi and Boaz in the biblical story of Ruth, taking her back to their home in England, sheltering her under their wings. Yet their charity, unlike Boaz's, receives no ratification from the community at large. They are forced to lie that Ruth is a widowed relation. Otherwise she and her child would be ostracized.

Actually, Faith and Sally quickly undergo the transformation in values that the entire community, and by extension, Gaskell's entire reading audience, must go through before justice can be done to the "fallen woman" in Victorian society. When Faith first hears about Ruth, she says "It would be better for her to die at once" (111). But once she sees Ruth, she finds her "sweet and gentle" (114). However, Faith is thrown back again when Ruth responds to news of her pregnancy with joy and gratitude. Faith represents "Christian" society when she calls the expected "illegitimate" child "this disgrace—this badge of her shame!" (118). But Faith is quickly won over. Whereas the woman who should play Naomi to Ruth, Mrs. Bellingham, is responsible for her abandonment, Faith takes on the parental role willingly: "Thus she grew warm and happy in the idea of taking Ruth home" (126). Like Faith, the servant Sally has to overcome her initial socially ingrained attitude toward Ruth. Sally went in "to the beautiful, astonished Ruth, . . . with all her luxuriant brown hair hanging disheveled down her figure'" (143), and ordered Ruth to let her cut her hair:

> "Missus—or miss, as the case may be—I've my doubts as to you. . . . Widows wears these sort o'caps, and has their hair cut off. . . . I've lived with the family forty-nine year come Michaelmas, and I'll not see it disgraced by anyone's fine long curls." (143)

Ruth's "soft, yet dignified submission" wins Sally over immediately. The rest of Eccleston, particularly its chief dissenting family, the Bradshaws, all admire Ruth for her beauty and humility, until they find out that she is not a widow but an unwed mother. Mr. Bradshaw explodes when he finds that his model governess is an unwed mother: "If there be one sin I hate—I utterly loathe—more than all others, it is wantonness. It includes all other sins" (334). He concludes by expelling Ruth from his house, saying "between his teeth, 'if ever you, or your bastard, darken this door again, I will have you both turned out by the police!'" (337). Thus begins a long period of stigmatism for Ruth and Leonard.

Although Gaskell implicitly attacks patriarchy and stereotypical gender roles, the moral universe of Ruth is thoroughly Christian. We are not asked to condone, much less admire, Ruth's unlicensed love affair, but rather to excuse and forgive it because of her conversion to Christian righteousness and humility. This was cause for praise by contemporary readers. For example, *The Guardian* wrote of *Ruth*:

> her guilt is as little as can ever exist in such a case. Yet all through the book ... she is never suffered to forget her fall, nor are we either ... it is as the humble self-distrusting penitent ... that she wins our respect and love.[22]

The novel is problematically ambiguous about the degree to which social institutions are fundamentally flawed. The possibility remains that it is not Christian society but a misapplied and intolerant Christianity that is to blame for prostitution and suicide. Mr. Bellingham does not recognize Ruth when he sees her again because he can only assume she is lost:

> Poor Ruth! and, for the first time for several years, he wondered what had become of her; though, of course, there was but one thing that could have happened, and perhaps it was as well he did not know her end, for most likely it would have made him very uncomfortable. (285)

Even Bellingham comes around to Ruth by asking her to marry him, but she shows her new self-respect and integrity by refusing him as an unfit influence on Leonard. Gaskell probably felt it necessary to employ a kind of Christian rhetoric in order to reach her Victorian audience. As it was, she was daring in using words like "bastard" and in approaching the topic at all.

Ruth finally redeems herself and her son through nursing sick people, both poor and rich. She cannot get more pleasant work even though she is well-educated and a fine seamstress. She has to do what society considers debased and degrading work, but she transforms it into ministry. Before Florence Nightingale organized nursing into a fledgling profession, it was associated with immoral women: "It was *preferred*," wrote Miss Nightingale, "that nurses should be women who had lost their characters, i.e. should have had one child."[23] When a typhus epidemic strikes Eccleston, Ruth risks her life to nurse at the hospital. She is publicly apotheosized as a saint and her son is adopted by the town's doctor. But the once fallen woman cannot be allowed to live on as a revered member of society. She insists on nursing the man who ruined her, and through that final act of female self-abnegation, she brings about her own death. The community is reconciled through Ruth's work and death, yet Bellingham lives on after Ruth dies. There has been no real change. Charlotte Bronte asked "why should she die? Why are we to shut up the book weeping?" There are several answers to Bronte's question. First, although Ruth has personally redeemed herself, society has not changed. The upper class dandies live on unscathed while mistresses fall into ruin. Second, it might be too much for the Victorian audience to see Ruth live a long life of prosperity. Finally, the deaths and madness that recur in nineteenth-century inscriptions of women suggest also a failure of imagination on the parts of the authors. What could female life after rebellion possibly look like? George Bernard Shaw's *Mrs. Warren's Profession* (1893) is one of the first literary answers to this question, and it was suppressed for decades.

Ruth as Subtext: Adam Bede *and* Tess of the D'Urbervilles

The remainder of this essay will examine two novels which develop the issue of the fallen woman, which Gaskell's controversial book opened up. Neither George Eliot's *Adam Bede* (1859) nor Thomas Hardy's *Tess of the D'Urbervilles* (1891) alludes to Ruth by name, but Eliot and Hardy rework key plot elements of the scriptural tale as variations on a theme, creating a powerful subtext. Both novels situate the Ruth figure within the context of agricultural work at harvest time. As in the ancient story, the harvest forms not only the setting for sexual and marital encounters but also the metaphor for the outcome of a period of behavior or work. Eliot divides or doubles the Ruth figure into the saintly Dinah Morris and the shallow, worldly Hetty Sorrel who plays the "fallen woman" in the novel. Eliot thus undoes Gaskell's difficult effort to show that moral goodness and sexual experience can coexist in the same woman. While one might expect Dinah Morris to be associated with the Dinah of Genesis, there are no correspondences between the two characters. The biblical Dinah is sexually violated and as a result her brothers kill all the men of the nearby village. Dinah Morris, on the other hand, has no family; she is unusually independent for a woman, working in a factory and preaching to the workers. She is far too well respected to be violated by anyone. Hardy's novel doubles the Boaz figure into the villainous Alec D'Urberville and the noble-minded Angel Clare, while resurrecting Gaskell's argument about Ruth. Ironically from Tess's point of view the two contrasting men do not turn out to be so very different.

Adam Bede, written in the same decade as Gaskell's *Ruth*, takes a much less sympathetic look at the plight of the lower class girl seduced, impregnated, and abandoned by an aristocratic man. Like the Book of Ruth, the novel ends amid a celebration of the harvest, with the transfer of a loved woman from one brother to another. Early in the novel it is established that Dinah Morris, the beautiful and sympathetic Methodist preacher, comes like Ruth from a "foreign" land. When Seth Bede makes one of his many unsuccessful marriage proposals to her, he offers to "leave this country and go to live at Snowfield."[24] Dinah responds: "No, Seth; but I counsel you to wait patiently, and not lightly to leave your own country and kindred. Do nothing without the Lord's clear bidding. It's a bleak and barren country there, not like this land of Goshen you've been used to." (36) In the background to the biblical tale we know that Naomi has left Israel to live in Moab and her sons have married Moabite women. Just as Ruth moves to Israel, Dinah finally moves to the lush country of Hayslope to marry Adam. But by far the strongest echo of the biblical story is the emphasis Eliot places on the widowed mother-in-law's desire for Dinah to be her daughter-in-law. After the wedding we see "Lisbeth in a new gown and bonnet, too busy with her pride in her son, and her delight in possessing the one daughter she had desired, to devise a single pretext for complaint" (564). Furthermore, the novel concludes with an epilogue which parallels the genealogy most scholars believe to be appended to the book of Ruth. Just as Naomi has been made full again by the marriage of Ruth to Boaz and the birth of their child, so Lisbeth's name is carried on in the granddaughter we meet in the epilogue.

In the genealogy of nineteenth century texts about abandoned lovers named or represented as Ruth, Eliot's is the only one that is not primarily a work of social criticism. The splitting of the figure Ruth into an angel and a harlot, with the angel triumphant (i.e. married) and the harlot expelled at the end, suggests that the author ratifies the status quo of her oppressive society. Gilbert and Gubar suggest that the close relationship of Dinah and Hetty in fact shows their interdependence as social constructions in patriarchal society:

> Yet, even in books dedicated to dramatizing the discrepancy between the antithetical faces of Eve, Eliot seems to provide subversive evidence that the fallen murderess is unalterably linked to the angelic Madonna. In *Adam Bede*, for example, the two Poyser nieces are orphans, occupying neighboring rooms, and Hetty actually dresses up as Dinah, even as Dinah seems to haunt Hetty.[25]

Eliot has relatively little sympathy for Hetty. If Adam is, as the title suggests, the hero of the novel, Hetty represents an illusion he must overcome in order to discover that Dinah is his true soul mate. This transition is accomplished first through Hetty's ruin, but secondly through the needs and perspicacity of Adam's mother, Lisbeth. The constant conjunction of Hetty and Dinah highlights their differences, which are extreme.

Hetty, like all the nineteenth-century Ruths, is exceedingly pretty, "a distractingly pretty girl of seventeen . . . a beauty with which you can never be angry" (85). Hetty has no feelings unrelated to her own vanity. We are constantly told that Hetty's beauty seduces everyone into admiring her, but as readers we are more objective about her shallow character and egotism. Dinah is the complete opposite of Hetty: utterly without vanity and completely self-abnegating. Dinah's character, except for its extreme religiosity, resembles that of the biblical Ruth. The cantankerous Lisbeth is immediately charmed by her: "a pure, pale face, with loving grey eyes . . . perhaps it *was* an angel" (112-13). Whereas Hetty's appearance wins everyone over, Dinah's voice and spirit impress those who admire her. But Dinah is no pure spirit; she works hard in a cotton mill. Dinah serves her lord through serving needy people, always through "that finest woman's tact which proceeds from acute and ready sympathy" (115). Lisbeth, who generally dislikes women, especially prospective daughters-in-law like Hetty, immediately says to Dinah: "I wouldna mind ha'in ye for a daughter" (116). When Hetty and Dinah are together, "it made strange contrast to see that sparkling self-engrossed loveliness looked at by Dinah's calm pitying face, with its open glance" (146). Dinah is full of "ruth," which Hetty lacks entirely. Thus, it is Dinah who plays the role of Ruth in *Adam Bede.* The "fallen woman" of the other Ruth stories provides a necessary counterpoint to Dinah's worthiness. When Hetty runs away to hide her pregnancy, she is a failed Ruth: "Her great dark eyes wander blankly over the fields like the eyes of one who is desolate, homeless, unloved, not the promised bride of a brave, tender man" (384). In her exile from Adam, she finally recognizes how she "felt a sense of protection in his presence" (386).

The Ruth subtext signals its presence in *Adam Bede* through images of the harvest. When Dinah and Mr. Poyser discuss the Bedes, Mr. Poyser says, "Adam's sure enough. . . . There's no fear but he'll yield well i' the threshing. He's not one o' them as is all straw and no grain" (149). This evokes the image of Boaz taking Ruth under his wing on the threshing floor. It also contrasts with the hollow Hetty, who turns out to be all straw and no substance. Book Four begins with a description of harvest time and the dangers of too much rain. The narrator comments, "If only the corn were not ripe enough to be blown out of the husk and scattered as untimely seed!" (309). This fear about the corn presages Hetty's fate. She is too young to handle the flirtation with Arthur Donnithorne. Her seed, the abandoned baby, is scattered, and she is left an empty husk. After redescribing the literal harvest, the narrator shifts to the metaphorical mode, foreshadowing Adam's discovery of Arthur and Hetty kissing. Although the day is sunny, it is "a day on which a blighting sorrow may fall upon a man" (309). The chapter which paves the way for Adam's proposal to Hetty opens with a mention of the harvest: "The barley was all carried at last, and the harvest suppers went by" (369). This emphasizes the parallel to and contrast with Adam's betrothal to Dinah, which also takes place in the chapter after a harvest supper. Just as Hetty must be expelled from the community for her sins, Dinah must become a wife and mother. Dinah does everything under the guise of absolute submission to God's will, but she nonetheless stands out as a heroic actor. The same is true of Ruth, who submits and follows, yet takes destiny into her own hands by going out into the fields and offering herself to Boaz.

Hardy's *Tess of the D'Urbervilles* is set almost half a century after *Adam Bede* and presents a much harsher vision of rural life. As the last nineteenth-century reworking of the of the Ruth story, *Tess* shows what happens to an unprotected female in a society that retains patriarchal power without its concomitant protectiveness. While *Adam Bede* takes place in a village with a resident squire and vicar, *Tess* shows the breakdown of the old village organization. No paternalistic responsibility is taken by anyone in *Tess*; even the nice farmer at Talbothays turns out his dairy workers when they are not needed. Hardy paints a picture of migrant workers who change jobs at least once a year. Similarly Alec d'Urberville's "manor house" is built purely for its owner's pleasure; it has no farms or village attached to it. The fact that "Tess" means "gleaner" suggests that *Tess* is a modern revision of the Book of Ruth. Hardy spent considerable effort on choosing a name for his heroine; the name, like the vision of the entire novel, is bitterly ironic. Whereas Ruth's agricultural labors brought her a rich harvest, Tess's brought her a life of hardship, despair, and public execution.

Just as Eliot splits the Ruth figure into saintly virgin and foolish whore, Hardy splits the Boaz figure into "Angel" Clare and villainous Alec d'Urberville. Moreover, as the virgin and the whore are dialectically interdependent in patriarchal society, so are the male seducer and the husband. The categories we use to define these "opposites" actually define each other. While Eliot shares with Milton the vision of two fundamentally different types of female nature, Hardy argues for the essential innocence of his "fallen" protagonist. The highly controversial subtitle makes his view explicit: "A Pure Woman Faithfully Presented." Unlike the other Ruth figures, Tess is actually raped rather than seduced, though this makes little difference to Victorian society. Even as Angel Clare rejects Tess, he admits she was "more sinned against than sinning." Hardy's point seems to be that social taboos about sex are completely artificial and outmoded. Angel Clare has not taken holy orders because he has cast off what Carlyle regarded as the "old clothes" of Christian mythology. Angel thinks he is a secular humanist, yet he retains an almost superstitious reverence for female "purity." He cannot explain or defend this, nor can he overcome it. Hardy seems to suggest that the fetish of female virginity is the cornerstone of patriarchal society.

Tess reenacts the role of Ruth twice with Alex and once with Angel, replaying different versions of it in multiple circumstances. Tess's father is a drunk and her mother a fool. In the first enactment of her role as Ruth, Tess's mother, like Naomi, leads her to an alien "land" in search of protection and perhaps marriage. Yet while

Naomi encourages Ruth *not* to follow her, Mrs. Durbeyfield pressures Tess to seek help from her rich pseudo-relations, the Stoked'Urbervilles. Tess is uncomfortable with the manipulative Alec, but her mother pushes her within his control. Like all the Ruth figures, Tess is obedient, saying "Do what you like with me, mother."[26] As soon as Tess leaves her home to become fowl tender at the d'Urbervilles, Alec shows his true colors. He terrifies Tess into submitting to his "kiss of mastery" (45) by driving recklessly. The subtext of Ruth appears in Tess's cry, "But I thought you would be kind to me, and protect me, as my Kinsman!" (45). Unlike Boaz, Alec responds "kinsman be hanged!" (45). By September, he has conquered her. Tess lies sleeping as the narrator asks "where was Tess's guardian angel? Where was the providence of her simple faith?" (63).

A month after the rape, as Tess travels home to her parents, the narrator emphasizes that her birthplace and Alec's home are in two very different locales, "Even the character and accent of the two peoples had shades of difference" (65). After her "ruin," Tess hides herself away for a while. A year after her rape, she emerges clearly in her role as Ruth to work in the fields at harvest time. Hardy represents the harvest in a dual light. On the one hand, the machinery carries a note of doom. Like Tess later in the novel, the small animals of the field retreated away from the mechanical reaper "till the last few yards of upright wheat fell also under the teeth of the unerring reaper, and they were every one put to death by the sticks and stones of the harvesters" (p.76). Yet, on the other hand, the narrator admires the female harvesters, "by reason of the charm which is acquired by woman when she becomes part and parcel of outdoor nature" (77). Hardy seems to have Keats's image of Ruth in mind when he describes Tess at work:

> It is Tess Durbeyfield, otherwise d'Urberville, somewhat changed— the same, but not the same; at the present stage of her existence living as a stranger and alien here, though it was no strange land that she was in. (pp. 77-78)

Her sisters bring her baby to be nursed, and the fellow laborers seem fairly accepting of Tess's position. Yet after her baby's death, in May again, she decides with a resurgence of youthful hope to leave home to be a dairy maid at Talbothays.

In her second enactment of the journey of Ruth, Tess seems to meet the guardian "angel" whose absence allowed her ostensible protector and kinsman, Alec, to rape her. One might expect Angel Clare, with his sensible agnosticism and his experience of argicultural life at Talbothays, to be able to accept Tess's past. His name and his actions recall the imagery of protection in the Book of Ruth, signified by the covering wings of the Lord and the covering robe of Boaz. When Angel first distinguishes Tess from the other dairy maids, it is as "a fresh and virginal daughter of nature" (106). He is surprised by her depth of questioning, considering her youth and class. But the narrator comments that "Tess's passing corporeal blight had been her mental harvest" (110), perhaps another allusion to Ruth. On the wagon ride, when she finally acquiesces to his proposals of marriage, Angel "wrapped round them both a large piece of sail cloth" (164) to keep off the rain. Here finally is the man who appears to live up to the providential role of Boaz in the Book of Ruth. Preparing for the wedding, Tess was "carried along upon the wings of the hours, without the sense of a will" (179). On their wedding night both Angel and Tess confess to having had sex previously. But because of an irrelevant "sentiment" about purity, Angel can no longer see Tess as the woman he fell in love with. His dissipation was a minor slip, easily forgiven, but Tess's is beyond all forgiveness: "You were one person; now you are another. My God— how can forgiveness meet such a grotesque—prestidigitation as that!" (202). Thus Angel sends Tess back to her hapless parents, not knowing or caring to what dangers he exposes her.

Cast adrift by Angel, Tess enters on her third reworking of the Ruth plot, forced to take an extremely difficult job as a farm laborer at a place where the owner resents her. Having realized the dangers to which her youthful female beauty lays her open, Tess at one point cuts off her eyebrows and covers her head with a kerchief as if she had a toothache. A year after her marriage, Tess sets out to meet

Angel's parents. Her Ruth-like role is reflected in the narrator's comment that "her dream at starting was to win the heart of her mother-in-law, tell her whole history to the lady, enlist her on her side, and so gain back the truant" (263). But she loses her nerve, and on the return journey Tess meets Alec again. He pursues her relentlessly, appearing on the threshing floor where Tess is performing strenuous work.

This threshing scene is a far cry from that of Ruth or Keats's "To Autumn." The barn has been transformed by machinery into a hellish scene.

> Close under the eaves of the stack, and as yet barely visible, was the red tyrant that the women had come to serve—a timber-framed construction, with straps and wheels appertaining—the threshing-machine which whilst it was going, kept up a despotic demand upon the endurance of their muscle and nerves. (289)

The engine-man appears to be "a creature from Tophet. . . . He served fire and smoke" (289). Tess in particular is subject to the tyrannical thresher as her job is to feed corn to the machine. When Alec appears in the barn, Tess's friends suggest the parallel with Ruth, calling her "in a sense, a widow" (292). D'Urberville mockingly invokes their "kinship" again by calling her "coz." He blames her for luring him away from preaching, but then admits: "of course you have done nothing except retain your pretty face and shapely figure" (293). Tess, who has come through painful experience to understand the vulnerability of an unprotected woman in the world, cries out bitterly, "Once victim, always victim—that's the law!" (295). Alec's parting words reinforce Tess's despair: "Remember, my lady, I was your master once! I will be your master again" (296). In light of Tess's class and "impurity," the title "lady" is viciously ironic. Added to the insuperable tyranny of the threshing machine, the threat of Alec is compounded by the patriarchal assistance of Tess's boss, always unkind to her, who suddenly offers to let her go to join Alec. This is in marked contrast to Boaz' command to the male workers not to bother Ruth.

By the time Angel comes to "redeem" Tess, she has truly sold herself into slavery. She murders Alec and follows Angel who is finally able to love her unconditionally. But he is too late: she is arrested as she lies on an ancient Druid altar at Stonehenge. The final twist on the Ruth story comes in Tess's wish that Angel might marry her sister, Liza-lu. This is a reversal of the levirate law that a man should marry his brother's widow in order to "give him" a child to perpetuate his name. The reversal is, of course, not trivial, because it challenges the priority of patrilineage in our society. The novel ends as Angel and Liza-lu observe the site of Tess's execution: "As soon as they had strength they arose, joined hands again, and went on" (355).

Conclusion

While all these narratives of fallen Ruth figures, Eliot's excepted, attack the social constructions that damn women for not being virgins, all of them also kill off the victimized females at an early age. Only Wordsworth's Ruth, the earliest, is able to live out a natural life span, and she is a social outcast. It is Wordsworth's myth of a saving relationship to nature that allows his Ruth to survive without a place in human society. One of Hardy's messages in *Tess* is that Wordsworth's vision of nature is false: "Some people would like to know whence the poet whose philosophy is in these days deemed as profound and trustworthy as his song is breezy and pure gets his authority for speaking of Nature's holy plan." Wordsworth's is the nature of the Stoics and the Enlightenment, a visible incarnation of order and harmony. Hardy's, however, is the nature of Tennyson and Darwin, "red in tooth and claw." Yet Hardy is ambivalent on this point, emphasizing how various are the landscapes Tess lives in at different times. It is not nature, but patriarchy that executes Tess.

The Book of Ruth was an attractive book of the Bible for English readers because of its agricultural setting and deeply human cast. In the years we have surveyed, from 1800 to 1891, English society became fully industrialized. Rural life became a subject for nostalgia, as in the "Solitary Reaper," "To Autumn," and *Adam Bede*. Among the middle classes women were ideologically trained to inhabit a limited private sphere, to guard the morals of their families, and by extension, the nation and the empire. Yet the majority of women were not middle class wives and mothers. The working poor, spinsters, and prostitutes were victimized by society and then viciously repudiated for their victimization. They could not possibly attain to the ideal of the "angel of the hearth." In the same way that T.S. Eliot's *The Waste Land* alludes negatively to such earlier texts of purity and plenitude as Spenser's "Prothalamion," these narratives by Wordsworth, Crabbe, Gaskell, and Hardy invoke the story of Ruth to show how the kinship ties and community protectiveness it exemplifies have broken down in England. Uncovering the vulnerability of a pretty girl to the depredations of powerful men, they reveal the hypocrisy and double standards inherent in patriarchy.

Notes

[1]Gerda Lerner, *The Creation of Patriarchy* (New York: Oxford UP, 1987), 238.

[2]Lerner, 238-9.

[3]William Wordsworth, *The Lyrical Ballads 1800*, ed. R.L. Brett and A.R. Jones (London: Methuen, 1965), 154-55.

[4]Wordsworth, 156.

[5]E.F. Campbell, Jr., *Ruth*, Anchor Bible (New York: Doubleday, 1975), 121.

[6]Campbell, 131.

[7]Campbell, 138.

[8]Carol Lansbury, *Elizabeth Gaskell: The Novel of Social Crisis* (New York: Barnes and Noble, 1975), 52.

[9]Esther Fuchs, "The Literary Characterization of Mother and Sexual Politics in the Hebrew Bible," in A.Y. Collins, ed., *Feminist Perspectives on Biblical Scholarship* (Chico, CA: Scholars P, 1985), 130.

[10]Fuchs, 30n.

[11]Fuchs, 130.

[12]Sandra Gilbert and Susan Gubar, *The Madwoman in the Attic* (New Haven: Yale UP, 1979), 74.

[13]John Milton, *Complete Poems and Major Prose*, ed. Merritt Y. Hughes (New York: Odyssey P, 1957). All further references to Milton will be from this source and the line numbers will be cited parenthetically.

[14]John Keats, *Poetical Works*, ed. J. Stillinger (Cambridge, MA: Harvard UP, 1974), 281.

[15]V.J. Lams, Jr., "Ruth, Milton, and Keats's 'Ode to a Nightingale,'" *MLQ* 34 (1973): 432.

[16]Earl Wasserman, *The Finer Tone* (Baltimore: Johns Hopkins UP, 1953), 217.

[17]H.W. Garrod, *Keats* (Oxford: Oxford UP, 1939), 115.

[18]William Wordsworth, *Poems in Two Volumes and Other Poems, 1800-1807*, ed. Jared Curtis (Ithaca: Cornell UP, 1983); all further references to "The Solitary Reaper" will be from this text and line numbers will be indicated in parentheses.

[19]Coleridge, *The Collected Letters*, vol. 1., ed. E.L. Griggs (Princeton: Princeton UP, 1956), 623. [20]Elizabeth Gaskell, *Ruth*, rpt. ed. (New York: G.P. Putnam's Sons, 1906), ix. All further references will be from this source and the page numbers will be indicated in parentheses.

[21]George Crabbe, *The Poetical Works of George Crabbe*, ed. A.J. Carlyle and R.M. Carlyle (New York: Oxford UP, 1914), 340. All further references will be from this source and the page numbers will be indicated in parentheses.

[22]*Manchester Guardian*, 2 February 1853.

[23]Lansbury, 77.

[24]George Eliot, *Adam Bede* (New York: Washington Square P, 1964), 36. All further references will be from this source and the page numbers will be indicated by parentheses.

[25]Gilbert and Gubar, 496.

[26]Thomas Hardy, *Tess of the D'Urbervilles*, ed. W.E. Buckley (Cambridge, MA: Riverside P, 1960), 39. All further references will be from this source and the page numbers will be indicated by parentheses.

Ten:

God's Women: Victorian American Readings of Old Testament Heroines

Mary De Jong

Zilpah P. Grant, principal of Ipswich Female Seminary in Ipswich, Massachusetts, from 1828 to 1839, "proclaim[ed] the eternal duty of woman's obedience to man." She reminded students that Old Testament matriarch Sarah was honored for her faith and wifely obedience. That, according to contemporary biographer Gail Hamilton, was Grant's "orthodoxy" speaking. The pious educator also advised young women to marry men worthy of obedience; and, with "feminine common sense," she told her own fiancé, "'I know that you have a right to command, but I mean to be so on the alert that you will have no occasion.'" Hamilton reported with unconcealed delight that Zilpah Grant Banister (1794-1874) made her ideas appear to be her husband's, and therefore "ruled her home just as graciously and completely as she had ruled her school."[1]

In paying tribute to Grant's strength of character, Hamilton satirized the ideology of female subordination—still orthodox when she wrote in 1886, and still legitimized by ideologues with biblical references. Many Victorians indeed regarded Sarah as a model wife. The Rev. Charles Adams, for instance, called her "the most distinguished of her sex, and in most respects a fit companion of one of the greatest men of this world's history."[2] It was this assumption that women should be evaluated in relation to men that provoked Hamilton and more radical critics of nineteenth-century patriarchy.

Anna Howard Shaw, the first woman ordained by the Methodist Protestant Church, ridiculed orthodoxy's idealization of subordinate biblical women and devaluation of assertive ones. In 1891 she delivered an address rebutting Methodist Episcopal bishop John H. Vincent's statement that "God's women are not the Deborahs and Miriams, but the Ruths, Rachels, and Marys." Praising the heroic public careers of Deborah and Miriam, she inquired why Vincent considered the other biblical women exemplary. He had not specified which of the Marys in the New Testament he approved. Rachel was known only for her beauty, bereavement, and "high sense of the subserviency of woman to man." As for Ruth, the two things for which she was "remarkable" did not justify apotheosis as "a type of God's woman": loyalty to her mother-in-law (Shaw joked with her female audience on that point) and "a peculiar method of obtaining a husband." Shaw then argued seriously that forceful, loving, self-respecting women who do God's work should be called "God's women."[3]

Gail Hamilton (1833-1896) and Anna Howard Shaw (1847-1919) were neither typical nor fully like-minded women. Hamilton, a professional author who wrote *Woman's Wrongs* (1868) to protest a clergyman's belittlement of her sex, did not favor woman suffrage; Shaw devoted thirty years to working for it. But both discredited androcentric definitions of women. Their irony at the expense of male presumption of authority, female subservience, and mothers-in-law was a response to a barrage of prescriptive statements about their sex.

Propositions about the nature and place of women—frequently designated as Woman and "the sex"—were debated in America as early as the 1790s and posited with increasing urgency after the formal beginning of the woman suffrage movement in 1848.[4] In addition to conduct books, novels, and essays about actual and fictitious women, there were countless sermons, funeral addresses, and lectures about the female "sphere," defined by Margaret Fuller in *Woman in the Nineteenth Century* (1845) as "[Woman's] duties, responsibilities, rights, and immunities *as* Woman."[5] The numerous biographies of and references to biblical women in nineteenth-century popular literature are best understood as contributions to the age's project of assigning Woman her proper place in American society.

Historical and biographical writings were considered enjoyable yet powerful means of character formation. "Every one," asserted the clerical author of "Christian Biography" (1853), "can successfully study *models* and follow *examples*"; eminent Christians "become types or standards of goodness and greatness, after which others measure themselves, and up to which they aspire."[6] Many biographical sketches of pious women—biblical heroines along with modern missionaries and "mothers in Israel" (Judges 5:7) like Susannah Wesley—appeared in gift books (elaborately bound annuals with engravings and miscellaneous literary contents). Popular as gifts for girls and women, these anthologies flourished in America from 1825 to 1860. Periodicals intended for religious and specifically female audiences also portrayed Bible women as exemplars of women's virtues and follies. Articles and poems about biblical heroines regularly appeared in the *Ladies' Companion* (a popular New York women's magazine), *Sartain's Union Magazine* (a semi-literary Philadelphia monthly), *Ladies' Repository* (a widely-circulated Methodist family magazine published in Cincinnati and New York), and *Christian Union* (a New York religious weekly).

By mid-century, book publishers had recognized public interest in "Female Scripture Biography," a clergyman's name for the genre he helped to popularize.[7] Harriet Beecher Stowe included her sketches for the *Christian Union* in an anthology called *Woman in Sacred History* (1873); her sketches alone were issued as *Bible Heroines* (1878). Comparable anthologies and collections include *The Women of the Old and New Testaments* (1848), ed. the Rev. H. Hastings Weld; Grace Aguilar, *The Women of Israel* (1851, 1883); and the Rev. Morton Bryan Wharton, *Famous Women of the Old Testament* (1889). Sarah Josepha Hale, best known for her influential forty-year editorship of the highly successful monthly *Godey's Lady's Book*, included scriptural heroines in her *Woman's Record* (1853), a biographical encyclopedia. Some books and articles on biblical women specifically addressed female readers; many professed an intention to promote religion and morality.[8]

In various ways writers and editors acknowledged readers' preference for literature that was diverting as well as instructive. The Rev. George C. Baldwin defensively stated that his sketches of biblical women were not meant "to tickle your ears with curious novelties, but simply to excite your interest in the Bible, and practically to do you good, by depicting the biographies God has left on record, and evolving the practical instructions they embody."[9] But most writers elaborated on their scriptural sources. Poets were more interested in passion and sentiment than in lessons. Prose-writers, borrowing techniques from novelists, described clothing, customs, and physical settings, invented dialogue, and ascribed motives to persons whose behavior is not interpreted by the biblical narrators. They usually presented their subjects as "heroines": not as heroic figures but as women involved in delicate and distressing situations; observed in relation to others, often parents, suitors, husbands, and sons; and described as attractive, if not beautiful.

Poets and prose writers recreated emotionally charged moments in the Bible heroines' lives—for example, Hannah's offering her son Samuel to the Lord. Most authors highlighted physical details and emotional states that they saw as expressions of femaleness—"graceful limbs," "small white hands," "dove-like eyes," dark "tresses," "rich lips," "snowy breast [that] heaves with joy," "maiden pride," "maternal wo."[10] Unlike most poets, the prose writers devoted space to moralizing on female character and conduct. The Rev. S. D. Burchard spoke for many contemporaries when he stated, "we see" in the stories of Bible women "much to admire, much to condemn, much that is profitable for doctrine and instruction."[11]

This article, based on examination of over 325 poems, stories, and essays about Bible women published in nineteenth-century American books and periodicals, focuses on sixty-one prose portrayals of four Old Testament heroines: Hagar, Jephthah's daughter, Ruth, and Esther. Prose rather than verse writings have been stressed because the former reveal more about the writers' interpretation of their material. Their evaluation of the heroines' admirable and repellent qualities is particularly remarkable because, despite their evident and often stated assumption that Woman's nature is always and everywhere the same, they recognized that certain situations, beliefs, and behaviors of Old Testament figures were largely determined by their "oriental," pre-Christian environment. These four heroines were chosen for two reasons: they were favorite subjects with nineteenth-century writers, and they represent a range of female social roles from daughter to widow and from slave to queen.[12]

The scripture biographers treated their primary source, the Bible, as an indisputably authoritative document. Some drew upon historical and theological scholarship (often without identifying their sources), yet all took for granted their own qualifications to elucidate the primary text. Contrasting their enterprise with fiction on the one hand and "profane history" on the other, they presented themselves as historians relating chapters of the grand story of God's love for humankind. Enjoying without embarrassment the privilege of hindsight, and unaware that the biblical canon was established by men who determined "What Shall Be Remembered," they assumed that the Bible records "What Really Happened,"[13] that it is divinely inspired, and that one can know God's will by reading the book. To such readers, God's will was revealed in olden times by divine intervention (as when an angel of the Lord told Hagar to "submit" to her mistress, Sarah [Gen. 16:9]); it was expressed in the outcomes of particular conflicts (God must have approved Sarah's expulsion of Hagar, for the divine covenant was established with Sarah's son). To such readers, God's will was also enunciated for all time in the Ten Commandments, the Sermon on the Mount, the apostolic epistles, and other non-narrative passages of scripture. Humankind had only to follow pious precepts and examples.

Yet the popular historians sometimes differed in their interpretations of Old Testament stories. A few writers were troubled, for instance, by Queen Vashti's losing her crown for refusing the Persian tyrant's summons to display herself for his male guests, but most were content because she was replaced by Esther, an apparently docile wife who influenced the king on behalf of God's people. Since providence was the theme of many scripture biographies, writers confronted with human tragedy either passed quickly over the suffering of pawns like Hagar, victims like Jephthah's daughter, and high-principled pagans like Vashti, or traced that suffering to individual wrongdoing or "Eastern" ignorance. God's disposal of individuals was not questioned. Human beings were held accountable for their deeds, even those traceable to God's purposes. In short, it was taken for granted that Old Testament stories have two major uses: (1) to demonstrate divine power and purpose in human history, and (2) to illuminate the standards of behavior that define God's people. One scripture biographer verbalized a prevalent view: "The Bible is a book of facts, developing all the great principles of moral obligation which concern man."[14]

These writers reveal no consciousness that historical and interpretative texts are not based simply on facts, that such works are culturally constructed, ideologically motivated, and "always rhetorical."[15] The popular historians themselves produced value-laden texts, appropriating biblical authority to make prescriptive statements about gender roles in Victorian America. Like Anglo-American writers generally, they reiterated that the nineteenth century was an enlightened age; it followed that their contemporaries—especially women, as the greater beneficiaries of the gospel—"ought to be Christians."[16] Scripture biographers praised virtues conducive to piety, patriotism, and the patriarchal social order. They condemned any form of self-interest; for females, selfishness was the cardinal sin.

Their reading and social experience led most people to believe that God and nature had designated Woman as wife and mother. Her special mission, as delimited by the Rev. Daniel Wise, was "to mould character—to fashion herself and others after the model character of Christ."[17] Not all commentators would have endorsed Wise's identification of Woman's sphere with the home and "social circle"—Evangelicals advocated involvement in churchly, charitable, and certain social reformist activities—but the quoted definition of Woman's mission as moral guide and exemplar was representative of mainstream thought. Nineteenth-century scripture biographers assessed Hagar, Jephthah's daughter, Ruth, and Esther according to the orthodox construction of "God's women": as women who married heroes, bore heroes, or otherwise served purposes larger than themselves. The following discussion notes what poets identified as the emotional center of each life-story, then examines the prose writers' interpretations of the heroines' behavior.

Hagar, the "Dark-Browed" Daughter of Egypt

Hagar, the bondmaid of Sarah, was an especially popular sub-ject with poets, who usually evoked her maternal grief at the pros-pect of Ishmael's death in the wilderness of Beersheba. She was occasionally allowed to reprove Sarah or Abraham, but most po-ets showed no interest in assigning responsibility for her plight.

The prose historians treated Hagar differently. Certain that Sarah's son, Isaac, was chosen by God, they found little basis for sympathy and less for approval in this bondservant whose Egyptian origin they reiterated. Her insolence toward Sarah and ambition for her son, Ishmael, were variously attributed to human vanity, "woman's fallen nature," "ardent tropical blood," "vain and merce-nary expectations," and the ignorance of a "poor simple woman" or "girl" who was elevated beyond her proper level.[18] But the popular historians almost unanimously faulted Hagar for not knowing her place and criticized Sarah for proposing that Abraham acquire an heir through Hagar. When Sarah condoned polygamy—which was legal in her society but not, the story-tellers insisted, pleasing to God—she betrayed the weakness of her faith in God's promise to make Abraham the father of a great nation. According to one typi-cally androcentric commentator, Sarah thus embroiled an otherwise harmonious household in "guilt and discord that almost broke [Abraham's] heart."[19] Nevertheless she was generally praised as an admirably unselfish and obedient wife and an excellent mother.

As if uneasy about Sarah's demand that Hagar and Ishmael be banished, some writers affirmed that Abraham's subordinate fam-ily had behaved intolerably. One called Ishmael "wicked," and sev-eral suggested that his mockery of Isaac was instigated by a jealous Hagar. Most writers assumed or argued that since God evidently supported Sarah's actions, they must be understood as just. Despite all the differences of status, piety, and temperament that Victorians found in these two women, they perceived both as mothers whose interests were threatened by polygamy. The agony of the elevated and then debased slave as she wandered in the desert was inter-preted as maternal anxiety—exacerbated, according to some writers, by self-reproach. Love for one's own son was natural and not necessarily deserving of praise. For commentators who knew how a story was meant to turn out, not all mother-loves were equal: while Sarah was commended for protecting Isaac and his inheritance, Hagar was rebuked for comparable endeavors and declared presumptuous for supposing that she and Ishmael were the instruments of God's promise. (No matter that Sarah, Abraham, and possibly the angel of the Lord had given her that idea.)

To nineteenth-century writers, as to the narrator of the Hagar-and-Sarah portions of Genesis, these two mothers were representatives of unequal peoples. Gender-, class-, and race-conscious Victorians saw Hagar the "dark-browed child of Egypt"[20] as a properly subordinated wife and servant. None explored the likenesses between Hagar, born in Africa but carried away by members of a privileged nation, and slaves in nineteenth-century America. Her story, inevitably intertwined with Sarah's, was read as a fable about domestic relations. It was retold because it defined who the chosen people are (they descend from and are nurtured by godly parents); it demonstrated that godly mothers, like good servants, know their place. Seeking nothing for themselves, God's women consult the will of husband/master and patiently await God's time. Several writers professed to find comfort in Hagar's story as an illustration of benign providence. Much was made of God's mercy in responding to her cry of despair (Gen. 21:16)—sometimes interpreted as a prayer, though her outburst is not designated as such in the King James Bible, the version most people knew. Cheerful commentators passed over a point that *is* clear in the King James text: that the Lord responded to Ishmael's voice, not hers.

Jephthah's Daughter, Human Sacrifice

Poets portrayed the daughter of Jephthah as beautiful, affectionate, and doomed by her warrior father's vow to sacrifice to God the first that emerged from his household upon his return from defeating the Ammonites. Nearly two-thirds of these poets indicated that she was put to death in fulfillment of the oath. Although the vow was sometimes attributed to heathen influence, few poets suggested that the story could have ended in any other way. Apparently they assumed that God accepted Jephthah's terms. Rather than hold God or Jephthah responsible, however, most poets romanticized her as a willing martyr. American magazines and anthologies reprinted Lord Byron's "Jephtha's Daughter" (1815), in which the heroine tells Jephthah, "I have won the great battle for thee, / And my father and country are free!" Set to music in *Godey's Lady's Book* in 1831 and thus widely available as a parlor song, Byron's lyric reinforced the ideal of daughterly devotion.[21] One American woman poet called Jephthah's daughter the "fair prototype" of "filial love and patriotic virtue."[22]

Prose writers found the same bases for pious inspiration and moral reflection in her story, but they also acknowledged or inadvertently revealed that it made them uncomfortable. In this case, the popular historians were uniquely concerned with hermeneutics. They conceded problems in interpreting Jephthah's vow to make a "burnt offering" to the Lord of "whatsoever cometh forth of the doors of my house to meet me," should he defeat Ammon (Judges 11:31). Still more controversial was the proper reading of this portion of Judges 11:39: Jephthah "did with her [his daughter] *according* to his vow which he had vowed" (italics in King James Version). Most of the popular historians asserted that God did not approve such oaths, noted that Mosaic law expressly forbade human sacrifice, or made both points. One writer called the biblical text indeterminate.[23] Two maintained that the daughter was put to death, one of them suggesting that this reading would never be doubted, "were it not for the fearful result it involves."[24]

Yet two-thirds of the popular historians did challenge the widely-held view that she was killed. They argued that she was devoted to a celibate life, probably serving in the tabernacle. This was no "popish abuse," hastily explained one writer with an eye on mainline Protestant readers: there was a Hebrew tradition of vestal virgins. Another linked Jephthah's daughter with the "consecrated women"—foreign missionaries and pastors' assistants—of nineteenth-century Protestantism.[25] One Victorian rescued the innocent

daughter by arguing that Jewish law provided for the bloodless redemption of oaths.[26] But the intention and wording of the fatal vow
remained troublesome. A clergyman unable to tolerate uncertainty
claimed that a knowledge of Hebrew conjunctions "removes all difficulty": the original text revealed to him that Jephthah committed himself to giving *or* burning an offering to God.[27] All the others
either maintained that Jephthah had pledged a human burnt offering or conceded that the key verses are unclear both in Hebrew and
in King James English.

For most writers, the story was tragic because Jephthah's daughter was childless. His grief on meeting her was usually attributed to
the realization that his line would end with her. Some writers of
Jephthah-dominated narratives digressed to condole with the
daughter who relinquished hopes of becoming a "mother in Israel"
and a foremother of the Messiah. Just one popular historian pointed
out that God had excused Abraham from sacrificing his son Isaac
(Gen. 22:11-13), whereas Jephthah actually gave up his only daughter; that writer stressed that Jephthah, unlike Abraham, himself proposed the offering.[28] A few poets who dramatized the sacrifice as
presently taking place suggested that God might intervene to save
the daughter, but no prose historian questioned the silence of
heaven when she was sacrificed. A small minority evidently perceived that silence as problematic, however, for they read an
unstated meaning into the text: that God had justly determined to
punish Jephthah for his impious oath.

It was tacitly assumed that the daughter was Jephthah's and
Jevohah's to dispose of. No writer commented directly on the father's
self-centered response when she joyfully came forward to celebrate
his homecoming: "Alas, my daughter! thou hast brought me very
low, and thou art one of them that trouble me" (Judges 11:35). Yet
one-third of the popular historians were sufficiently bothered by this
accusatory speech to omit or alter it. After "thou hast brought me
very low," one inserted "little as thou thoughtest to do so." Another
invented this outburst for the moment when Jephthah realized what
his vow meant: "O God, forgive me! my child, forgive me!"[29]

Victorian writers praised the daughter's filial loyalty, piety, and quiet submission to duty. To some she exemplified "female heroism," also called "moral heroism" but defined in terms of the excellences of "female character": "meek endurance," "patient suffering," and "ever active and unwearied sympathies in the domestic and social sphere of life."[30] The majority saw no reason to call her "heroic." One who evoked her father's heartbreak wondered "which we should most admire, whether the *heroic distress* of the father, or the *graceful submission* of the daughter to the will of Heaven."[31] Some popular historians did not bother to relate that the "daughters of Israel" yearly mourned her sacrifice (Judges 11:39-40), and none called it ironic that the name of an ideally pious, loving, submissive woman is not recorded.[32]

Ruth, "Ancestress" of Christ

Poets and prose historians alike focused on the "filial" love, loyalty, and dutifulness of this "Moabitess" who left her natural parents to live with her widowed Israelite mother-in-law. Ruth stood by Naomi despite the latter's foreignness, lack of wealth and male protection, and urgent advice to return to her own family as Naomi's other Moabite daughter-in-law, Orpah, had done. Ruth's "self-forgetful love" and "clinging affection" were contrasted with Orpah's self-interest.[33] "Selfishness is a mean, low quality in any one," remarked one clergyman, "but in woman it is especially to be deprecated" because it makes her "unfit for the [domestic] relations in life she was created to sustain."[34] For Ruth's unconscious generosity in resolving to accompany Naomi to Judea, the popular historians pronounced her "a model of the noblest self-devotion," an "artless heroine" whom readers could only want to "bless."[35]

But, as Anna Howard Shaw realized, Ruth's manner of acquiring a second husband needed some justification for a Victorian audience. After Ruth had begun to glean—apparently by chance, in the fields of Boaz, Naomi's kinsman—Naomi decided to invoke the Hebrew custom that entitled a childless widow to the protection of her husband's nearest male relative. As instructed by Naomi, Ruth went to the threshing floor where Boaz had been "eating and drinking" and was now reclining, and lay at his feet. When he started at noticing her presence, she identified herself and said, "[S]pread . . . thy skirt over thine handmaid; for thou art a near kinsman" (Ruth 3:3, 9). In this way she proposed marriage. One clergyman, calling her interaction with Boaz that midnight "too beautiful, delicate, dangerous, and sublimely virtuous, to be recited here," referred readers to the Book of Ruth.[36] Other scripture biographers hurried to explain that this apparently bold request was proper in Ruth's time, place, and situation. The Rev. Baldwin affirmed that although she did what no nineteenth-century lady would do, she was a "pure woman" who faithfully obeyed her mother-in-law; trusted Boaz as a "pure, good man" who "loved her"; and had already begun to love him.[37] Some apologists deflected charges of immodesty by saying that for a person of Ruth's refinement, presenting herself to Boaz must have been extremely difficult.[38] Sarah Hale, a leading proponent of a predominantly conservative model of female virtue, managed to misread Ruth's story as an illustration of "what woman can do, if she is true to the best impulses of her nature, and faithfully works in her mission, and *waits* the appointed time."[39] Ruth waited only for Boaz's response to her initiative.

Her piety could be taken for granted, however, even by authors who noted her heathen upbringing, for the Bible quotes her as telling Naomi, "thy God [shall be] my God" (Ruth 1:16). A few writers discounted her love for Naomi by saying she accompanied her mother-in-law largely because of "*religious faith*" and a "bright hope of a future life."[40] More affirmed the women's bond by saying that Ruth discovered the true God through interaction with Naomi.

Characterized, then, as dutiful, affectionate, selfless, obedient, modest, and pious, Ruth met nineteenth-century middle-class criteria for the True Woman.[41] Scripture biographers praised her as a model of female excellence, especially for the young; several exalted Naomi beside her, the two embodying ideal qualities of young and old women.[42] They also insisted that female virtue is rewarded; the Rev. John P. Durbin unabashedly asserted that it pays. For embracing Naomi and her God, Ruth was rewarded with marriage and motherhood. As Durbin put it, Heaven satisfied the dearest desire of the "female heart": "'rest, *each in the house of her husband.*'"[43] Another clergyman urged young readers to consider it "a privilege to yield, to sacrifice, to minister," anticipating a "rich harvest" on earth and in heaven.[44] Ruth's pious biographers further noted that she was privileged to be the grandmother of David and an "ancestress" of Jesus. Hence "her name is recorded for ever" in the Bible.[45]

The Book of Ruth was read as a love story: the deep affection of Ruth and Naomi, the mutual regard of Boaz and Ruth, and a gracious God's purpose that Christianity encompass Gentile as well as Jew. Ruth's relationship with Boaz, an older man who calls her "my daughter" (Ruth 2:8; 3:10, 11, 18), was sometimes romanticized. Some writers said that her exotic beauty and modesty attracted his attention.[46] Almost as charmed by his chivalry as by Ruth's beauty of form and character, writers commended his honorable treatment of an unprotected woman and stated matter-of-factly that he purchased her along with Naomi's property. Although several speculated about legal aspects of Naomi's claim on Boaz, no one raised the possibility that in accepting his support she and Ruth were primarily interested in financial security.[47]

Authors who perceived the Book of Ruth as a story about women did not view it as an extraordinary friendship but as a mother-daughter relationship with relevance for nineteenth-century social roles. Assuming that husbands are more important than female intimates, authors consistently praised Naomi for releasing Ruth and Orpah from any obligation to her, since they could have little hope of marrying in Judea.[48] The biblical narrator reports that Naomi herself deprecated female bonding by telling the people of Bethlehem to call her "Mara" (which means "bitter"): for "I went out full, and the Lord hath brought me home again empty" (Ruth 1:21). It was perhaps in reaction to that statement so inconsiderate of Ruth's feelings that the women of Bethlehem would congratulate Naomi for two priceless blessings: the kinsman who gave her a grandson, and "thy daughter-in-law, which loveth thee, which is better to thee than seven sons" (Ruth 4:15). This tribute by Naomi's female neighbors was summarized or quoted by half the popular historians, but one-third of these omitted the sentence valuing Ruth above seven sons.

Esther the Queen, "a Very Woman"

Most poets portrayed Esther as a lovely patriot who overcame timidity and "selfish" or "womanly" fear to plead her people's cause with her husband, Ahasuerus, King of Persia.[49] Likewise fascinated by her beauty and resolution, prose writers further praised her modesty, dutifulness, and capacity for self-conquest. These virtues were usually traced to her "filial" love for and loyalty to her cousin Mordecai, who had adopted her as a child and—the authors insisted, though the Book of Esther does not—instructed her in the religion and history of Israel. After Esther became queen, Mordecai's enemy, Haman, persuaded Ahasuerus to issue an irrevocable decree for the slaughter of all Jews under Persian rule. Disobeying the king's order that none should approach his throne unbidden, Esther successfully interceded for her people—strengthened, some writers argued, by the "faith of her fathers."[50]

The popular historians differed on how patriotic and pious she was. Since she kept her nationality secret at the palace, some reasoned that she could not have been zealous in worshiping God or observing the ceremonial aspects of Judaism. Others pointed out that Mordecai had told her to conceal her race and religion. The Rev. Daniel Wise deliberately countered allegations that she was "purposeless" and indifferent to religion.[51] But most writers saw no need for persuasion. Half asserted or assumed that she prayed during her ordeal, though the canonized Book of Esther does not say so. God is not mentioned at all in this book, a fact pointed out by just two writers. Several drew upon, but did not name, the apocryphal account of Esther's prayer affirming her devoutness and identity as a Jew.

Esther was sometimes held up as a model woman. Wise urged female readers to "imitate her virtues," modesty, docility, piety, and heroism (defined as "self-devotion"). Raised from poverty to luxury, "she remained as humble and teachable on her throne as when she sat on an orphan's couch."[52] Though intent on "elevat[ing] our sex," Sarah Hale (1788-1879) praised the same virtues. She called on "every daughter of America" to emulate Esther's piety, patriotism, and "self-sacrificing devotion": elements in the early nineteenth-century ideal of Republican Womanhood which restricted female participation in politics to whatever influence they could exercise on males.[53]

More writers portrayed Esther as representative of her sex. While praising her virtues, they placed equal or greater stress on her "feminine" weakness, tact, and wiles. The Book of Esther does show her sense of peril in confronting the king, but the popular historians greatly emphasized it. Stressing her timidity, several writers altered or collapsed the Old Testament chronology. In the Book of Esther, she asks favors of the king at 5:4, 5:7-8, 7:3-6, and 8:3—weeping only in the last instance, when she asks him to countermand his decree for the Jews' destruction. Some writers placed tears in her eyes when she first approaches Ahasuerus; others quietly appropriated a detail from the apocryphal narrative: her fainting from fear. While agreeing that a woman in Esther's position must have been terrified, writers disagreed on whether she was "heroic." One-fourth said that she was, over half did not even raise the issue, and two solved the problem and affirmed her femininity by styling her *"no bold heroine"* but "a very woman."[54] To most writers, this Jewish Queen of ancient Persia was after all a typical female who found courage in fervent prayer.

The nineteenth-century True Woman was home-loving and affectionate as well as meek and devout. Several of Esther's Victorian biographers stated that she would have preferred a humble life with Mordecai to the luxury of the royal palace. A few even convinced themselves that she was fond of Ahasuerus: Hale called that dangerous despot her "lover and friend," and the Rev. Burchard imagined her "pleading, dewy eyes beaming [on Ahasuerus] with deep emotions of love and gratitude."[55]

Not proud and imprudent like Vashti, Esther showed a peculiarly female "tact" in determining to "soften and charm" her husband before pleading her people's cause. Two popular historians suggested that she let Ahasuerus flatter himself with the idea that she desired his company enough to risk her life for it.[56] One called her "politic" in delaying her petitions until the time was right. Like all women, wrote another, she "shrewdly" waited "until *her influence over her husband ha[d] reached its highest pitch*."[57] Most writers noted that she dressed in gorgeous array before facing Ahasuerus, but only two (both men) observed that she used her sexuality. According to the Rev. Wise, she "inflamed the love of her lord, the king, until he panted with desire to bestow upon her the costliest proofs of his attachment."[58]

Yet the main point of these sketches was neither feminine influence nor female power. Read as an edifying story about "filial" love as well as pious and patriotic duty, the Book of Esther was characterized by twelve out of sixteen popular historians as an illustration of the mysterious but unerring ways of providence. Vashti's pride, Mordecai's racial loyalty, Haman's malice, the king's impressionability—all were interpreted as threads in the tapestry of God's design for the chosen people. Though not a "mother in Israel," Esther was instrumental in preserving the line from which Jesus would spring. This woman who had the bodies of Haman's ten sons publicly hanged was remembered as gentle, pious, dutiful—and tactful when she resisted her heathen husband's decrees. Contemporary conduct books for women and popular pious novels like Susan Warner's *The Wide, Wide World* (1851) and Martha Finley's *Elsie Dinsmore* (1868) likewise reinforced female subordination, but permitted daughters and wives to disobey orders to commit immoral or impious acts.

* * *

The popular historians generally accepted the social hierarchy and its ideologies of gender as ordained of God. Ideals of nineteenth-century American middle-class (Protestant) female behavior were reified as universally definitive of Woman. Born before Christ or after 1800, Gentile or Jew, slave or free, virgin or not, Woman was naturally timid but capable of piety and filial and maternal love that empowered her to transcend weakness and selfishness.

But Old Testament women were not popular as heroines because they were heroic. Authorial commentary on Hagar, Jephthah's daughter, Ruth, and Esther is consistent with the prevalent view that heroism takes different forms in women than in men. Male heroism, called simply "heroism," meant aggressive, courageous, life-endangering public action.[59] Writers who granted the existence of female heroism placed it in the private sphere and defined it as endurance, fortitude, and, most significantly, self-forgetfulness—what the Rev. Daniel Wise, a specialist in advice literature for women, called "woman's self-devotion."[60]

To valorize self-sacrifice is not necessarily to prescribe passivity and dependency. Scripture biographers reinforced actions motivated by duty and devotion, and some of them approved nineteenth-century women's religious and charitable activities beyond the home. A few endorsed economic self-reliance: two clergymen praising Ruth's effort to earn a living also complimented nineteenth-century women who supported themselves. Nor was wifely obedience always insisted upon. Several commentators noted that Sarah, twice praised in the New Testament as a model wife, sometimes told Abraham what to do. And though many criticized Vashti's pride, a few admired her self-respect. Stowe and Hale perceived two issues in Vashti's story, women's rights and men's use of law to limit those rights.[61]

Still, the heroines in this study were commended when they submitted to God or to relatives and spouses whose claims were justifiable by nineteenth-century patriarchal standards. To Victorians claiming that filial loyalty and patriotism are rewarded in this world, the fate of Jephthah's daughter only proved her sex's debt to Christianity. Patriotism informed by piety was the only "public" virtue consistently applauded in women—and, as Shaw and other suffragists learned, many Americans believed that direct involvement in politics was beyond Woman's sphere.

Re-told tales about Old Testament heroines were orthodoxy's answers to "the Woman Question." Confident that they knew how the stories were meant to turn out, scripture biographers repeated familiar "facts," embellished with sensory description and dialogue; then they interpreted biblical stories in nineteenth-century terms. Female scripture biography does not reflect unanimity in every detail. But writers and readers who agreed that the Bible is a historical record, that God is just and purposeful, and that God's women are selfless constituted an "interpretive community," a group defined by shared reading strategies that yielded common interpretations.[62] Pious Americans' reading of Old Testament narratives confirmed their community and identity as "the world's modern Palestine"[63] and their doctrine that a favored nation needs True Women.

Notes

[1]Gail Hamilton [pseudonym of Mary Abigail Dodge], "An American Queen," *North American Review* 143 (1886): 340-41.

[2]Adams, "Character of Sarah," *Ladies' Repository* 9 (October 1849): 305.

[3]Vincent is paraphrased in Shaw's "God's Women," *Woman's Journal* (7 March 1891), 73. The other quoted phrases are Shaw's, 74.

[4]Elizabeth K. Helsinger, Robin Lauterbach Sheets, and William Veeder, *The Woman Question: Society and Literature in Britain and America, 1837-1883*, 3 vols. (New York: Garland, 1983).

[5]Fuller, *Woman in the Nineteenth Century*, ed. Arthur B. Fuller (Boston: John P. Jewett, 1855), [11]. On male and female "spheres" see Ann D. Gordon and Mari Jo Buhle, "Sex and Class in Colonial and Nineteenth-Century America," in *Liberating Women's History: Theoretical and Critical Essays*, ed. Berenice A. Carroll (Urbana: U of Illinois P, 1976), 278-300.

[6]Charles Collins, "Christian Biography," *Ladies' Repository* 13 (August 1853): 361, 363.

[7]P.C. Headley, *Historical and Descriptive Sketches of the Women of the Bible* (Auburn, NY: Derby and Miller, 1853), [vii].

[8]Hale, *Woman's Record* (New York: Harper and Brothers, 1853), vii, viii; Grace Aguilar, *The Women of Israel*, 2 vols. (New York: D. Appleton, 1883), 1:[7] and 16; J. M. Wainwright, ed., *The Women of the Bible* (New York: D. Appleton, 1849), [viii].

⁹Baldwin, *Representative Women* (New York: Sheldon and Co., 1860), 134.

¹⁰"Hagar," *Southern Literary Messenger* 6 (April 1840): 303; Sarah Hale, "Queen Esther: Or Woman's Patriotism," in *The Women of the Old and New Testaments*, ed. H. Hastings Weld (Philadelphia: Lindsay and Blakiston, 1848), 172; Caroline May, "Esther," *Sartain's Magazine* 7 (November 1850): [267]; Thomas Hood, "Ruth," *Home Journal*, (21 February 1846); Miss G——, "The Moabitess," *Godey's Lady's Book* 14 (February 1837): 69; John Hewitt, "Jeptha's [sic] Daughter," in his *Miscellaneous Poems* (Baltimore: N. Hickman, 1838), 16; W. W. Marsh, "Jephtha's [sic] Daughter," in *Werner's Readings and Recitations No. 7*, comp. Elsie M. Wilbor (Belmar, NJ: Edgar S. Werner and Co., 1892), 84; Agnes Strickland, "Hagar and Ishmael," *The Christian's Annual* (Philadelphia: Henry F. Anners, 1846), 47.

¹¹Burchard, *Daughters of Zion* (New York: John S. Taylor, 1853), 223.

¹²The 325 texts used for this paper were collected from nineteenth-century magazines (I looked through full or partial runs of over 40 titles and examined five or more volumes of 29 titles), over 200 gift books, 18 collections of scripture biography, and several dozen books of poetry.

¹³ The quoted expressions are from Paul Hernadi, "Clio's Cousins: Historiography As Translation, Fiction, and Criticism," *New Literary History* 7 (1975-76): 248. Elizabeth Schüssler Fiorenza brings these terms into her discussion of sacred historiography in *Bread Not Stone: The Challenge of Feminist Biblical Interpretation* (Boston: Beacon P, 1984), 145.

¹⁴Headley, *Historical and Descriptive Sketches*, [vii].

¹⁵Fiorenza, *Bread Not Stone*, 144.

¹⁶Baldwin, *Representative Women*, 45. The writer of "Woman in the Gospels" declared that "the woman who is not a Christian is a traitor to her own sex" (*Church Review* 60 [1891]: 77).

¹⁷Wise, *The Young Lady's Counsellor* (New York: Carlton and Phillips, 1854), 88. See also Hale, *Woman's Record*, xxxvii.

¹⁸Quotations from Aguilar, *Women of Israel*, 1:53; Harriet Beecher Stowe, "Hagar the Slave," in *Woman in Sacred History* (New York: John B. Alden, 1888), not paginated; C. C. Van Arsdale, "The Life, Character and Death of Sarah," in *Women of the Old and New Testaments*, ed. Weld, 69; John Cunningham Geikie, *Old Testament Characters* (New York: James Pott, 1897), 33.

¹⁹Headley, *Historical and Descriptive Sketches*, 35.

[20]Anne C. L. Botta, "Hagar," *Poems* (New York: G.P. Putnam's Sons, 1881), 95.

[21]*Godey's Lady's Book* 2 (May 1831): [277].

[22]Jane W. Fraser, "Jephthah's Daughter," in *Christian Keepsake*, ed. John A. Clark (Philadelphia: William Marshall and Co., 1840), 223. I have preserved the authors' various spellings of the father's name.

[23]Thomas DeWitt, "Jephthah's Daughter," in *Women of the Bible*, ed. Wainwright, 59.

[24]Headley, *Historical and Descriptive Sketches*, 113n.

[25]Asahel Abbot, "Jephtha's Daughter," *Ladies' Wreath* 4 (April 1850): 424; Wharton, *Famous Women of the Old Testament* (New York: E.B. Treat and Co., 1889), 152-53.

[26]DeWitt, "Jephthah's Daughter," 65.

[27]Burchard, *Daughters of Zion*, 153.

[28]DeWitt, "Jephthah's Daughter," 73. Charles Adams argued that God abominated human sacrifice by saying "it was [never] intended" that Abraham kill Isaac (*Women of the Bible*, 5th ed. [New York: Carlton and Porter, 1851], 54).

[29]Geikie, *Old Testament Characters*, 165; "Heroism of Jephtha's Daughter," *The Family Treasury of Western Literature, Science, and Art*, ed. Jethro Jackson (Cincinnati: Applegate and Co., 1854), 11.

[30]Burchard uses the expression "female heroism," *Daughters of Zion*, 151; see also "Heroism of Jephtha's Daughter," 12. The other quoted phrases are from DeWitt, "Jephthah's Daughter," 71.

[31]Abbot, "Jephtha's Daughter," 423-24, emphasis added.

[32]Wilbur Sypherd, *Jephthah and His Daughter: A Study in Comparative Literature* (Newark: U of Delaware P, 1948), surveys Western treatments of the story and lists forty-five names that have been given to this woman (10 n. 1).

[33]Geikie, *Old Testament Characters*, 180; Clement M. Butler, "Naomi, Orpah, and Ruth," in *Women of the Old and New Testaments*, ed. Weld, 122.

[34]Baldwin, *Representative Women*, 150.

[35]E.Y. Higbee, "Ruth," in *Women of the Bible*, ed. Wainwright, 98; Burchard, *Daughters of Zion*, 159; Butler, "Naomi, Orpah, and Ruth," 122.

[36]John P. Durbin, "Ruth: Or the Reward of the Daughter-in-Law," in *The Opal*, ed. Sarah J. Hale (New York: J. C. Riker, 1848), 98.

[37]Baldwin, *Representative Women*, 142, 143, 144.

[38]See, for example, Aguilar, *Women of Israel*, 1:245; Headley, *His-*

torical and Descriptive Sketches, 137.

[39]Hale, *Woman's Record,* 56.

[40]"Family of Naomi," *Family Pictures from the Bible,* ed. Elizabeth Ellet (New York: G.P. Putnam, 1849), 99, 100.

[41]In "The Cult of True Womanhood: 1820-1860," Barbara Welter finds four "cardinal virtues" in the dominant cultural ideal of womanhood: "purity, piety, submissiveness, and domesticity" (*American Quarterly* 18 [Summer 1966]: 152). Ronald W. Hogeland's more comprehensive "'The Female Appendage': Feminine Life-Styles in America, 1820-1860" (*Civil War History* 17 [1971]: 101-14) examines four models of womanhood—"Ornamental," "Romanticized" (Welter's "True Womanhood"), "Evangelical," and "Radical."

[42]E.g., Durbin; Andrew P. Peabody, "Ruth and Naomi," *The Christian's Gift,* ed. Rufus W. Clark (Boston: Albert Colby, 1860), 9-24.

[43]Durbin, "Ruth," 95, drawing upon Naomi's words in Ruth 1:9. Geikie, Higbee, and Aguilar also spoke of Ruth's "reward."

[44]Peabody, "Ruth and Naomi," 23, 24.

[45]Higbee, "Ruth," 108.

[46]See, for example, Headley, *Historical and Descriptive Sketches,* 135-36; Burchard, *Daughters of Zion,* 169.

[47]On the book's "inconsistent treatment of legal matters," especially levirate marriage, see Jan Wojcik, "Improvising Rules in the Book of Ruth," *PMLA* 100 (March 1985): 145-53.

[48]E.g., Durbin, "Ruth," 93. Only one writer expressly stated that the women were friends, not mother and daughter: R.G. Moulton, "Ruth, the Gleaner," *Women of the Bible,* by Eminent Divines (New York: Harper and Bros., 1900), 90-92.

[49]Quotations from Marie Roseau, "Esther," in *Women of the Old and New Testaments,* ed. Weld, 85, 86.

[50]Aguilar, *Women of Israel,* 2:90.

[51]Wise, "Piety on a Throne—Queen Esther," *Ladies' Repository* 18 (January 1858): 17-20.

[52]Wise, "Piety on a Throne," 20. Burchard's view of Esther's "model of excellence" is similar (*Daughters of Zion,* 223). In *The Young Lady's Counsellor,* 146-50, Wise had portrayed her as a model of female "self-reliance."

[53]Hale, "Queen Esther," in *Women of the Old and New Testaments,* ed. Weld, 172. On Republican Womanhood, see Linda K. Kerber, *Women of the Republic: Intellect and Ideology in Revolutionary America*

(Chapel Hill: U of North Carolina P, 1980), 228-31, 269-88.

[54]Baldwin, *Representative Women*, 255; Aguilar, *Women of Israel*, 2:95.

[55]Hale, "Queen Esther," 161. Cf. Burchard, *Daughters of Zion*, 210, apparently plagiarized from Hale. The Esther of the Apocrypha declares that she "abhor[s] the bed of the uncircumcised."

[56]Hale, "Queen Esther," 166, 167. See also Burchard, *Daughters of Zion*, 210-11, again copying Hale or a common source.

[57]"Queen Esther," *The Literary Emporium* (New York: J.K. Willman, 1845), 373; Baldwin, *Representative Women*, 262.

[58]Wise, *Young Lady's Counsellor*, 147-48. See also Headley, *Historical and Descriptive Sketches*, 225.

[59]Ayrault, "Heroes and Heroism," *The Knickerbocker* 45 (June 1855): 551-59.

[60]Wise, "Piety on a Throne," 19. The other attributes of female heroism listed above are found, with little variation, in many sources—including Wise's "Womanly Heroism—Mrs. Sarah B. Judson," *Ladies' Repository* 14 (March 1854): 97-100.

[61]Hale, *Woman's Record*, 62; Stowe, "Queen Esther," *Woman in Sacred History*, not paginated.

[62]Stanley E. Fish, "Interpreting the *Variorum*," *Critical Inquiry* 2 (Spring 1976): 465-85.

[63]Headley, *Historical and Descriptive Sketches*, viii.

Eleven:

"Unique and Irreplaceable": Margaret Laurence's Hagar

Rosalie Murphy Baum

Margaret Laurence's special interest in the Old Testament and especially in the story of Israel began with her years in Somaliland. There, as she explains in *The Prophet's Camel Bell*, she saw the Somalis, like the Children of Israel, as "people of the Desert," and she herself experienced the life of "a stranger in a strange land."[1] She was also profoundly affected by the concept and experience of bondage. She saw Somaliland as "the end of a bitter journey at the beginning of a lifetime of bondage, for there the Arab slave routes had emerged at the sea, and from there the dhow-loads of slaves had been shipped across the gulf of Aden to be sold in the flesh markets of Arabia."[2]

Laurence's experiences in Somaliland between 1950 and 1952 clearly affected her 1964 novel, *The Stone Angel*.[3] Geographically, Laurence set the work in the Canadian prairies, an area which her protagonist, Hagar, thinks of as a desert compared to the colorful and exciting Scotland where her family, the Curries, were once a sept of the Clanranald MacDonalds. As a girl in the late 1800's, Hagar listens to her father's tales of her Highlander family and thinks of them as "the most fortunate of all men on earth, spending their days in flailing about them with claymores, and their nights in eightsome reels. They lived in castles, too, every man jack of them, and all were gentlemen."[4] She bitterly regrets that she lives in Manawaka, with "the bald-headed prairie stretching out west of us with nothing to speak of except couchgrass or clans of chittering gophers or the gray-green polar bluffs" (12). And, during the drought of the 1930's, the prairie virtually becomes a desert, with "rippled dust . . . across the fields," the wind "everywhere, shuffling through the dust, wading and stirring until the air was thickly gray with grit" (149-50).

But it is in Laurence's characterization and thematic development that she shows most clearly the effects of her experiences in
Somaliland and of her reading of the Old Testament. Hagar's desert,
the reader eventually realizes, encompasses her whole life, not simply
the geographical prairie of her childhood and young adulthood. The
desert is within her. The novel is clearly the story of one woman's
sense of being a stranger (or outsider) throughout most of her life
and of being in bondage, less to outside forces (although such forces
certainly are significant) than to herself. Such bondage prevents her
ever leading an emotionally healthy or satisfying life.

It is clear that in *The Stone Angel*, as in her other fiction,
Laurence is performing a "political act"[5] in her sense of the phrase.
By describing the dilemma of one particular twentieth-century
woman as "truthfully" as she can, Laurence is taking the political
step of "increasing awareness"[6] in her readers—of increasing their
awareness of one woman's experience of alienation and bondage.
She is also describing the society which contributed to the formation of her alienated and subject fictional character, a society which
her character helped to form. As response to the novel has indicated, of course, Hagar's dilemma and struggles have turned out to
be the dilemma and struggles of many women.

Increasing the complexity of the character of Hagar and of
reader reaction is also the fact that Laurence demonstrates love for
Hagar—as she does for all of her protagonists—even though she
judges Hagar to have "really damaged her children."[7] This love
stems from Laurence's profound political belief that "each individual
human being has great value. Each person is unique and irreplace-
able."[8] Critic Stephanie Demetrakopoulos would probably also suggest that this love comes from Laurence's "response as a woman and
a mother" to a particular adult feminine archetype; she would emphasize that Laurence's accomplishment shows "her depth as a
human being and as a woman,"[9] with the more "permeable-ego-
membrane"[10] that Nancy Chodorow identifies.

In naming her protagonist "Hagar," Laurence, of course, un-
leashes the historical imagination of many of her readers and creates endless potential reverberations within the concepts of

alienation and bondage. Few would wish to argue that the relationship between literature and myth is simply that of transcription; but *The Stone Angel* is a particularly brilliant example of a lesser known biblical figure, in this instance, Hagar, becoming the stimulus for "original conceptions and formulations."[11] The novel joins the company of "literary classics . . . [which] have been variously interpreted as legitimating religious values and commitments, reconceptualizing them, repossessing them, relativizing them, defamiliarizing them, confounding them, and even, whether intentionally or not, undermining or supplanting them."[12] One of its functions is to explore "some of the latent as well as the manifest dimensions"[13] of paradigms established by the quest myth and the stories of Israel and of Hagar.

Thus, the biblical Hagar, about whom little is known, becomes Laurence's incredibly complex and morally ambiguous Hagar. Insofar as both women are outsiders and in bondage for cultural reasons, they are similar—even though the conditions of their bondage, apparently, vary greatly. But Laurence's Hagar is very much an outsider and a woman in bondage because of her own character and temperament. This point is most persuasively made through the point of view of the novel: Hagar tells her own story, as first-person narrator. It is *her own* account of her thoughts and actions and of the actions and speeches of others (as she sees or hears them), as well as her account of her memories that reveals the essentially imprisoned nature of her life. One can only speculate, of course, whether the biblical Hagar may also have felt and reacted as Laurence's modern Hagar does: the third-person narration of the biblical story does not allow Hagar to speak for herself. In terms of individual character and temperament Laurence offers us only one possible Hagar—among innumerable other possible (archetypal) Hagars.

To understand Laurence's use of the biblical story, in Genesis (16;21;25:12) and in Paul to the Galatians (4:22-30),[14] we will first examine both the parallels between the details of the two stories and the changes which Laurence has made in the biblical story. Then we will examine the way in which Laurence has fleshed out the little-known biblical Hagar, giving her motivations and drives which a modern reader readily identifies with. Thus, we will be examining a unique fictional human being within what Northrop Frye identifies as one of the universal structural principles (or myths) of literature. Frye identifies the Israel story as one of the "falls and rises" of biblical history: "Israel . . . passes through a sea and a wilderness, and under Moses and Joshua reaches its promised land again."[15] *The Stone Angel,* as we shall see, parallels only the falling curve— or wilderness phase—of the cycle. Leonard Thompson also speaks of the biblical exodus, or wilderness, pattern, in which the wilderness is often a place of drought and famine, a place where the struggle for life takes place on an elemental level, and a place of refuge.[16] All of these senses of wilderness appear in *The Stone Angel.* Thompson also notes one of the paradigmatic features of biblical sibling stories: that of the younger son's ruling the elder, a feature found in the relationship between the biblical Jacob and Esau and between *The Stone Angel's* John and Marvin. That this "theme of favoritism producing conflict runs throughout the book of Genesis" has been noted by many writers, including James S. Ackerman, who describes the "ever-increasing alienation within the human community" in Genesis, an alienation which is not, interestingly enough, later overcome by "the covenant community of Israel."[17] That this pattern of alienation continues into the modern period is, of course, ably attested to by Laurence's novel, in which the unique Hagar adds one more figure to the Hagar paradigm.

We know very little about the biblical Hagar, who was Sarai's handmaiden and bore Abram his son Ishmael. We do know that she was a bondwoman, an Egyptian; thus, her bondage, on the obvious level at least, is that of external circumstances. We know nothing of her thoughts and feelings about her position in her society. We think it probable that she was a spirited woman. Sarai reports to Abram that, after Hagar has conceived, she "has despised me" (Gen. 16:5). And Hagar earns her name, which means "one who fled," by fleeing into the "wilderness" (Gen. 16:7, 21:14) twice: once before the birth of Ishmael when Sarai "ill-treated her" (Gen. 16:6) and once after Sarah refuses to allow Ishmael to be heir with her own son Isaac (Gen. 21:10).

Laurence's Hagar is twice referred to as the Egyptian (34, 84) and flees three times in the novel: the first time from her father and the strictures of her proper upbringing; the second time from her husband Brampton, usually called Bram (a name clearly derived from Abram); the third time from her son Marvin and his wife. Her first and second flights clearly parallel those of the biblical Hagar: the first into the "wilderness" of the uncouth life of Bram; the second to establish a safe and decent home for her son John. Laurence's Hagar is also a second wife, although Bram's previous wife, Clara, is dead. And she is an incredibly strong and spirited woman—her son Marvin refers to her as a "holy terror" (272). In fact, it is primarily Hagar's strength that causes great anguish in the novel, largely because of the many ways in which she is a bondwoman. On one level, Laurence's Hagar is culturally a bondwoman: to her father, then to her husband, and finally, as a housekeeper, to Mr. Oatley.[18] On another level, she is bondwoman to herself, not realizing until she is near death that her pride and fear have been "chains" within her, which have "shackled" everything she has touched (261).

That Laurence does not want Hagar to be a bondwoman because of *simple* external circumstances, such as the physical captivity of the biblical Hagar, is made clear in the novel by the fact that Hagar's family background is good, her father is a respected leader in Manawaka, and her upbringing is that of a lady, much courted by the eligible young men of Manawaka. Thus, the fictional, twentieth-century Hagar is apparently as respectable and free as the biblical Sarah; and Hagar's father and husband, like Abraham, expect to establish dynasties.[19] There is *apparently* nothing in Hagar's external circumstances to prevent her from living the life of a free woman—at least as that role is defined in twentieth-century Manawaka. (An additional small detail which suggests the physical identification of the fictional Hagar with the biblical Sarah is the fact that Sarah is 90 when Isaac is born, and Hagar is 90 as she begins to tell the story of her life in *The Stone Angel*.)

In addition to the dissimilarity between the cultural positions of the two Hagars, Laurence creates one additional major difference in their stories—one that again, in part, identifies Hagar and Sarah. In *The Stone Angel*, Hagar has two sons; and although both sons are conceived in passion,[20] as was the son of the biblical Hagar (Galatians 4:23), the sons have as their models the grandsons of Sarah.[21] There are unmistakable parallels between Marvin and John, in *The Stone Angel*, and Esau and Jacob, in the Bible. Like Jacob, John, the younger, is the beloved of his mother; like Esau, Marvin is loved by his father. Physically Jacob would probably have been more like John, slight "thin and wiry" (108); Esau, more like Marvin, "solid" (27), "thickly built" (108), "serious and plodding" (99), probably hairy like Bram (60). Like Jacob, John is a boy of guile. Hagar often finds him unfathomable. When she tells John that the two of them are leaving Bram and Manawaka, John's face "was still as stagnant water, and his eyes, those live eyes bright and watchful as a bird's, were shrouded against my [Hagar's] glance" (125). As John gets older, Hagar realizes that he lies and hedges; she says he spins "spiderwebs" (139) of lies to suit his purposes and "could charm the birds off the trees when he wanted to" (138). Marvin, on the other hand, is a steady, reliable individual, incapable of guile; he is not a quick thinker, and words do not easily "come to his bidding" (114). A man of "monolithic calm" (27), according to Hagar, he is as open and straightforward as Esau and cannot bear any kind of bickering or recrimination.

Hagar herself, who never can quite feel that Marvin is her son (53), thinks of John in terms of Jacob until the very end of her life. At his mother's request, John (nearly 30) struggles to straighten the stone angel over Hagar's mother's grave in the cemetery in Manawaka. As he slips and strains, Hagar wishes he "could have looked like Jacob, . . . wrestling with the angel [Gen. 32:23-29] and besting it, wringing a blessing from it with his might" (159). But John knows early in his life that Marvin is actually the son who could realize Hagar's hopes and ambitions; he himself can never be her Jacob. In fact, the significance of the scene with Hagar, John, and the statue is that John is almost certainly the person who has not only toppled the statue but also painted "the pouting marble mouth and the full cheeks" with "vulgar pink" lipstick (159). He finds the toppling humorous—"The old lady's taken quite a header" (158)—and insists that the statue looks "a damn sight better" (159) with the lipstick. Hagar, however, who admits to herself that she could never bear the statue, makes a predictable decision. The two of them *must* right and clean the angel for appearance's sake; it would be "impossible" (159) to leave it in that condition since Lottie Simmons comes to the cemetery every Sunday. The gap between her concern with respectability and John's desire to be genuine could not be greater.

One of the significant discoveries of Hagar's last days is that Marvin, now close to 65, has cast himself in the role of Jacob. Hagar realizes that he is "truly Jacob, gripping with all his strength and bargaining"—*with her*. On one of his visits to the hospital, Marvin clutches her hand as though he is saying, "*I will not let thee go, except thou bless me*" (271; Gen. 32:26). Marvin, the rejected son, the unloved and unappreciated son—who, with his wife, has cared for Hagar for 17 years in her old age and now in her final illness—is fighting for her blessing. Hagar thinks of asking his forgiveness for her treatment of him in the past—essentially for her not having loved him—but knows that Marvin does not want an apology; and she decides to give him what he wants, even though she knows she will be lying to him. As Marvin grasps her hand, she says to him, "You've been good to me always. A better son than John." Marvin's "anxious elderly eyes" (272) believe her; it could not occur to him that a dying person would lie. Thus, the identity of Jacob in Hagar's life umbrellas the entire novel. She may have wished John to be a Jacob, with a life blessed by the divine, but he dies in early manhood, after trying for most of his life to escape the strictures she has placed upon him. Marvin tries to become a kind of Jacob—in that he craves her blessing and in that he happens to be with her at the weakest point in her life, when she expresses her fear of death to him. (This cry of fear is the most revealing emotional statement Hagar ever makes to another human being.) But Marvin has never really had her love. With the dead John, of course, there has been no possibility of a blessed dynasty for many years. With Marvin, at least his son Steven and daughter Christina—both of whom Hagar cares about—can carry on the family line.

Thus, Laurence has taken a minor—albeit important—character from the Bible and, by emphasizing certain parallels but including important differences, created a novel which sheds light on the nature of bondage and on the female identity. Hagar's primary condition in the Bible is that of cultural bondage in the physical sense; Hagar's, in *The Stone Angel*, of cultural bondage in a more psychological sense. Hagar's primary identity in the biblical story is as child-bearer and mother, that is, in what has been traditionally seen as the essentially *female* role. Child-bearing for Laurence's Hagar is a much less significant event; to the end of her life she is still struggling to define and realize her identity, both as a woman and as an individual. In other words, the biblical Hagar is portrayed as a bondwoman of national politics, not of gender politics. The modern Hagar is not a bondwoman of national politics in this respect: she is as free as Sarah is free. She is, however, a bondwoman of gender politics, reflected in the culture around her and in the development of her own character and temperament. Thus, Laurence's novel speaks most eloquently to the modern woman and to any modern reader trapped in his or her own temperament and character. (This last sentence can surely be translated as *every* reader.)

Hagar's lifetime of bondage stems from several sources. In many ways this bondage is cultural. She is brought up as a lady of good family and never really loses her excessive respect for respectability and appearances. As a girl, she is particularly anxious to be "neat and orderly," imagining that life has been created "only to celebrate tidiness" (2-3). After her marriage, she acknowledges that her husband is a "good-looking man," "a big-built man," and that she could be proud of him if he "never opened his mouth" (61) to reveal his accent, bad grammar, or vulgar manners. She thinks of love as something connected with "words and deeds delicate as lavender sachets" (70) and thus never realizes until long after Bram is dead that they have shared a love. She finds life with Mr. Oatley, the man for whom she later keeps house, "orderly" and "proper," despite the fact that Mr. Oatley's respectability has been made possible by his smuggling of immigrants. In old age Hagar surrounds herself with the trappings of proper and elegant living: "the needle-point fire bench, the heavy oak chair from the Shipley place, the china cabinet and walnut sideboard from her father's house" (31), "the knobbed jug of blue milky glass" that was her mother's, "the gilt-edged mirror . . . from the Currie house" (51). At the same time she carps at her son and daughter-in-law, who care for her, and despises what she sees as her daughter-in-law's cheap taste. She insists, for example, that the fabric of Doris's dresses is "artificial," unlike her own "real silk . . . spun by worms in China, feeding upon the mulberry leaves" (24). (Doris says Hagar's dresses are actually acetate.)

Hagar's father clearly has the most formative effect on her early years. (Her mother died in giving birth to her.) Hagar is sent to a young ladies' academy in Toronto for two years to learn "embroidery, and French, and menu-planning for a five-course meal, and poetry, and how to take a firm hand with servants, and the most becoming way of dressing my hair" (36). When she returns to Manawaka, she thinks of herself as "Pharaoh's daughter reluctantly returning to his roof . . . in the wilderness" (37). Her father's comment to her on her return is that "It was worth every penny for the two years. . . . You're a credit to me. Everyone will be saying that by tomorrow" (37). Hagar quickly begins fighting with her father, who refuses to let her teach and treats her as though she "were a thing and his" (37); but she remains at home for three years, keeping her father's accounts, playing "hostess for him," and chatting "diplomatically to guests" (38). Thus, the twenty-four year-old Hagar, who meets the uncouth, rebellious Bram and decides to marry him, has little if any knowledge of who she is and does not know the difference between appearances and real human order or decency.

The degree to which Hagar is not allowed an individual identity within her family as she grows up never becomes clear to Hagar until years after she has married Bram. She realizes that in growing up, she was "sister" to Dan and Matt, "miss" to her father when he was angry, or "daughter" (11) when he was pleased. No one called her by her name.²² Later, of course, she is "Mother" to John and Marvin. As Hagar realizes in her old age, when she begins to understand her love for Bram, the only person close to her who ever called her by her name was her husband; but she was incapable during the marriage of realizing the significance of the fact.

Obviously the emphasis on respectability and the de-emphasis on any kind of individual identity create a kind of bondage for Hagar. But other values which she learns from her father are even more significant in creating her life of bondage. Hagar grows up in a house with three men—her father and two older brothers—and her dutiful Auntie Doll, a widow who acts as housekeeper. Early on Hagar picks up the notion that her mother was "a flimsy, gutless creature, bland as egg custard" (2) and that her two brothers take after her mother in being "graceful unspirited boys" (5). *She* is the strong one of the family; she is "sturdy" like her father and bears "his hawkish nose and stare that could meet anyone's without blinking an eyelash" (5). But strength, for Hagar, becomes identified with the repression of emotion.

In becoming the strong one of the family, she loses the ability to express or demonstrate feeling. Once, as a child, when her father spanks her hands with a foot ruler and she refuses to cry, her father hugs her, saying "You take after me. . . . You've got backbone" (7). Later in life, when Hagar's son John is dying, he cries out to his mother in pain and asks for her help. Then he utters "a low harsh laugh that increased his pain" (215) and says that, of course, she can do nothing. In this scene, her favorite son, the son she wishes were Jacob, describes the emotional desert of her life. She cannot convey love, compassion, concern—the only small help anyone can give a person in physical agony.

Hagar recalls instances from even her early childhood when she had been unable to forget appearances and express emotion. When their eighteen-year-old brother Dan is delirious and dying, Matt begs her to place their deceased mother's old plaid shawl around her and hold Dan when he cries out for his mother. Hagar refuses; she is "unable to bend enough" (21). Her detestation of her mother's and Dan's frailty is too great, so Matt takes on the role instead and, wearing the shawl, comforts his dying brother. When Hagar, "tall and sturdy and dark" (23), and Lottie, tiny and fair, discover a group of hatching chicks in the garbage, "feeble, foodless, bloodied and mutilated" (22), it is Lottie who crushes the suffering chicks. Hagar refuses. Even when Hagar marries Bram and is sexually aroused—feeling "my blood and vitals rise to meet his" (70)—she never lets him know. He lives and dies thinking that she is repelled by him and simply doing what he demands. Often Bram apologizes for his sexual advances, saying he is sorry to "bother" her, "as though it were an affliction with him, something that set him apart" (102) from educated, cultured, fine people like her. In her last days, Hagar realizes that with Bram, as with everyone close to her, she has "prided" herself "upon keeping my pride intact, like some maidenhead" (71). She has simply never been able to express weakness or affection. Clearly she is an incredibly strong human being (51), but that strength has become a "stubborn" (1) strength, unable often even to experience human emotion and, until her very last days, unable to express it to others.

The great tragedy of Hagar's bondage is, of course, the degree to which it is psychological as well as cultural. Again, her cultural position is closer to Sarah's than to her prototype's. She does experience a cultural bondage—that of gender politics—but national politics have not given her the physical bondage of the biblical Hagar. The greatest irony of her situation is that the strength of her character and temperament is such that she takes forceful steps to end stages of her life which *she* sees as bondage; and in doing so, she places herself more and more in a state akin to physical bondage. She flees—only to become an outcast of society in her life with Bram, a servant in her life with Mr. Oatley, and a homeless wanderer in her flight from Marvin and Doris.

The novel, then, is also a story of flights, flights from what Hagar sees as unbearable conditions of bondage. The biblical Hagar's first flight, when she is pregnant with Ishmael, occurs because she feels that Sarai "ill-treated her." The first flight of Laurence's Hagar is from the suffocating strictures of her father and immediate cultural heritage. When she meets Bram Shipley and decides to marry him, she thinks of her spirited Highlander ancestors. She fancies that she hears in Bram's "laughter the bravery of battalions" (40). She is also awakened sexually by him and becomes "drunk with exhilaration" at her "daring" to keep company with someone so "common" (42) and to defy her father's commands. Thus, both women's first flights involve sexual realization and attempts to assert themselves against what they find to be unbearable conditions. The results of the modern Hagar's flight, however, are that she is disowned by her father and treated as an outcast by the people she regards as respectable in Manawaka. She finds herself scrubbing floors, something she had never done before in her life, and at harvest time serving meals to "a bunch of [half] breeds and ne'er-do-wells and Galicians" (101).

The biblical Hagar's second flight occurs because Sarah will not allow Ishmael to be heir with her own son, Isaac; and this flight results in Ishmael's securing his eventual destiny as ancestor of 12 Arab tribes. The second flight of Laurence's Hagar occurs because she can no longer endure what she experiences as the shame and wretchedness of her life with the man John's schoolmates call "bramble Shitley" (116). The flight enables John to live what Hagar thinks of as a respectable life. She serves as housekeeper to Mr. Oatley, a man who has made a fortune smuggling Oriental wives into the country, while John tells his friends that her employer is his uncle. Given the source of Mr. Oatley's wealth and John's lie, there is irony in Hagar's thinking of her new life as "orderly, and conducted in a proper house" (139); and her attempts to give John a new life fail. John is never able to establish himself in a respectable community, keeps bad company, and engages in daredevil behavior. At the one point in his twenties when he is beginning to get a grip on his life and plans to settle down with Arlene, his mother's meddling leads to his death. Thus, although both women's second flights are motivated by the debased positions of their sons' lives, the second flight of Laurence's Hagar does not safeguard her younger son's destiny as does the biblical Hagar's. Further, Hagar Shipley—by her own decision and act—becomes a servant, like her biblical prototype. This is the same Hagar who, as a child watching her Auntie Doll cooking, thinks "how sad" it is "to spend one's life in caring for the houses of others" (29).

Hagar Shipley's third flight occurs as the novel opens and involves only her own destiny. Ill with cancer, Hagar flees her home with her son Marvin and his wife, Doris, because she fears that they plan to place her in a retirement home. This physical flight—from her home—offers parallels to the biblical Hagar's flight in the Beersheba desert. Hagar and Ishmael are supplied with bread and water by Abraham before they leave. After the water is used up, Hagar wanders in the desert with her son, despairing that they will die, until an angel of God tells her not to fear. She soon finds a well of water nearby. Laurence's Hagar buys soda biscuits, jam, cheese, and chocolate bars for nourishment—a more modern repast—but soon realizes she has forgotten to get anything to drink. Wandering in a deserted cannery, she suffers great thirst: her throat becomes "blocked and shut" (166), and she finds it painful to swallow. As she steps out after a morning rain, however, she notices "a raucous gang of sparrows" (166), whirling and settling. She discovers a "rusty and dinted bucket," which has gathered rain for the swallows, and thinks to herself that the sparrows have led her to the water. She explicitly calls the bucket of water her "well in the wilderness" (166). The clear implication is that the sparrows have served Hagar as the angel served her prototype, with both women then discovering the water which saves their lives.

Laurence has carefully structured *The Stone Angel* in such a way that the episodes of Hagar's third flight are interspersed with Hagar's memories of her past life. This structure flows naturally from the nature of Hagar as narrator: a ninety-year-old woman, whose mind had already begun to wander even before her present illness. "Rampant with memory" (3), Hagar physically flees while her mind, through memory, actually returns to review the past. In this return—through memory—the complex nature of Hagar's lifetime of bondage is clarified. In a sense too her recollections form a kind of flight—in that she recalls incident after incident of her earlier life and attempts, until the very end of the novel, to deny the kind of desert her life has been, the kind of bondage in which she has lived for 90 years. Only after she has been found by Marvin and faces the universal bondage of all human beings—the last hours before death—does the pattern of her memories finally dawn on her. She realizes that she can recall only two "truly free" (274) acts in her life; and they are acts of her last days in the hospital.

As the novel progresses, it becomes increasingly clear that Hagar is to be identified with the stone angel of the title. The novel opens with Hagar's recalling the stone angel which marks her mother's grave and noting that her mother "relinquished her feeble ghost" at the moment that Hagar gained her "stubborn one." Hagar then describes the blindness of the monument—not simply "sightless" (1) because made of stone but also because the eyeballs had been left blank by the carver—before she begins her account of her own life, an account in which she gradually begins to realize the blindness of her own life. The angel motif recurs frequently in the novel, with Laurence blending observations that Hagar makes in the present with realizations that she is finally experiencing, too late, about the past. For example, in one scene the elderly, enfeebled Hagar—weak, shaky, and flatulent—is being guided through the dining room by her daughter-in-law; she feels humiliated and thinks that Doris is guiding her as though she were "stone blind" (50). Scenes later, however, in recalling Bram's last illness and recognizing her inability to have a caring relationship with Bram, she becomes angry—"not at anyone, at God, perhaps, for giving us eyes but almost never sight" (153).

Hagar herself is identified with an angel in three significant scenes. Once she recalls that John calls her "angel"—bitterly, ironically—when, having deserted Bram years before, she returns to Manawaka for her husband's dying days. Once, in her last days, she feels cold in bed and envisions herself lying in the snow as children do, spreading their arms and sweeping them down to their sides to create "the outline of an angel with spread wings." She feels the "icy whiteness" (71) cover her; her sense of being physically frozen obviously suggests her frozen emotional state. And once she is cast in the role of the angel by Marvin, when he struggles for her blessing. This latter image suggests most of Hagar's adult life, a life in which three men—her husband and two sons—struggle unsuccessfully for her approval, with only John giving up and rebelling.

Of even greater significance than her identification with the figure of the angel, however, is the growing awareness of a Hagar, "rampant with memory," that in her life she has been "stone blind" to the meaning of life. She becomes angry at the God who gives eyes but not sight; she wonders "why one discovers so many things too late. The jokes of God" (52). In her life, she has most often been "transformed to stone." On the most emotional day of her life, the day her beloved son John died, she had been "transformed to stone and never wept at all" (216). Several years before, she had not cried when Bram died either. Now, in old age, she realizes that she had had so much to say to her two loved men, Bram and John, her two "lost men" (4). But she had told them nothing. She re-thinks her old judgments and decisions and realizes that "How you see a thing—it depends which side of the fence you're on" (200). The strong, stubborn Hagar has had only one view throughout her life: that of pride, stubbornness, respectability, and fear of appearances.

The narrator, at 90—feeble, shaky, forgetful, constipated, farting, incontinent, not very "respectable"—suddenly realizes all that she and those close to her have missed. She recognizes that "pride" has been the "wilderness" of her life. She has lived a life of bondage; she has never been "free" because she carried her "chains" within herself and they spread out from her and "shackled" everything she touched. She realizes that all her life all she has really wanted was "simply to rejoice"; but she has never been able to because of her fear of "proper appearances." She has never spoken "the heart's truth" (261).

In her last days Hagar tries to change—but remains basically "unchangeable, unregenerate" (262). She dies feeling that she has committed two "free" acts in her whole life: she has lied to Marvin, who is "truly Jacob"; and she has painfully gotten out of bed, against the nurse's orders, to get a bedpan for a fellow patient. In both of these acts she has shown respect for another person's need—after a lifetime of associating need with disgusting weakness. She has even expressed weakness herself—for the only time in her life. With astonishment, she hears her own voice say, "I'm—frightened, Marvin. I'm so frightened—" (271). But Hagar's last words are complaints to the nurse, and her last act is in keeping with her true, unchangeable "nature." Wanting a drink, she stubbornly struggles with the nurse who is trying to help her by holding the glass: "I only defeat myself by not accepting her. I know this—I know it very well. But I can't help it—it's my nature. I'll drink from this glass, or spill it, just as I choose" (275). In a final movement, she wrests the glass from the nurse and holds it with her own hands—only to lose the ultimate struggle and die.

Hagar may not be able to change as an individual and thus may never significantly realize her human potential; but she has had, before her death, a moment of profound and positive revelation about the nature of bondage and freedom. B. W. Powe has commented that Laurence's women "live as full, flawed, often floundering beings; they live humanly, skeptically, without an irritable reaching after abstract faiths and comforting falsehoods; they live with life as they find it: harsh, painful, comical, confounding, and ultimately opaque."[23] Hagar, at the end of The Stone Angel, is certainly still "floundering"; but life is no longer "opaque" to her. In her final realization, human worth and dignity and the value of life are affirmed; and the last weeks of her life, in which she traces the whole of her life, move her "toward a way of reconciling and being."[24]

Thus, Laurence's Hagar is a remarkably complex figure. She is as remote from Henry Wadsworth Longfellow's Hagar, in "The Jewish Cemetery at Newport," as a person can be. Longfellow's Hagar is a persecuted victim, as the biblical Hagar is usually characterized. Laurence's Hagar, however, enters the world of Herman Melville's Ishmael. In this world, according to Nathalia Wright, there is wilderness, but the wilderness is "a place of revelation. And if nothing more is revealed than that the nature of reality is like the nature of the desert—vast, voiceless, and fearful—that is itself a mature, a profound, and a positive discovery."[25] In addition, the fact that Hagar's search for meaning recalls several generic literary shapes gives the novel "an immense reverberating dimension of significance."[26] Hagar's search is a version of the quest-myth, which Frye regards as "the central myth of literature"[27]; in her role as wife and mother, she embodies characteristics of both the biblical Hagar and Sarah, two of the several kinds of maternal figures in the Bible; and her exoduses and returns, her bondage, more psychological than physical, and the very desert-wilderness of her life catch "the echoes" of all other literary works with similar patterns while sending "ripples out into the rest of literature and thence into life."[28] Thus, the shape of the novel derives from literary tradition and ultimately from myth.

Yet Laurence's immersion in the life of the Somalis and her own experience as woman, wife, and mother displace the mythic structures; they offer the material of plot which makes the story "credible, logically motivated or morally acceptable—lifelike, in short."[29] Laurence's turning to the Bible for the structures of her *tranche de vie* is usual in her work and is especially appropriate in *The Stone Angel*. Hagar is clearly a person with the values and authoritarianism, if not the religion, of Laurence's own Scots-Presbyterian grandparents. In fact, Laurence explained in 1969 that she felt "an enormous conviction of the authenticity of Hagar's voice, and . . . experienced a strange pleasure in rediscovering an idiom I hardly knew I knew, as phrases from my grandparents kept coming back to me."[30] Further, as Laurence once explained in an interview, understanding and accepting one's past is a process of "freeing oneself from the stultifying aspect of the past, while at the same time beginning to see its true value."[31] The oppression, then, of the biblical Hagar is to Laurence a potentially universal and eternal condition of human bondage, simply taking different forms in different people and at different times in history. Learning to recognize and deal with the nature of one's particular bondage, cultural or psychological, external or internal or both, is the only means of affirming human worth and dignity.

It has been noted many times that modern Canadian fiction by women, both English and French, frequently focuses on a mother figure and, even more significantly, that these works have not been marginalized as works about women by women but have struck "a responsive chord in the Canadian cultural context."[32] *The Stone*

Angel is obviously one of the finest examples of this development in Canadian fiction. It is about "women's problems—women's insights—women's very special adventures," but such a list presents simply the "raw material." As Joyce Carol Oates insists, "what matters in serious art is ultimately the skill of execution and the uniqueness of vision."[33] Laurence's portrayal of the universal human condition of bondage—entrapment in one's own temperament and character, perhaps in the pride and fear which shackles—is that of the "serious artistic voice," with its "sexless," "individual style."[34]

Notes

[1]Margaret Laurence, *The Prophet's Camel Bell* (Toronto: McClelland and Stewart, 1963), 9.

[2]Ibid., 5.

[3]*The Prophet's Camel Bell* was published one year earlier, in 1963.

[4]Margaret Laurence, *The Stone Angel* (Toronto: McClelland and Stewart-Bantam, 1979), 12. All page references are to this edition.

[5]Alan Twigg, *For Openers: Conversations with 24 Canadian Writers* (Madiera Park, BC: Harbour Publishing, 1981), 264.

[6]*Loc. cit.*

[7]*Loc. cit.*

[8]Ibid, 271.

[9]Stephanie A. Demetrakopoulos, "Laurence's Fiction: A Revisioning of Feminine Archetypes," *Canadian Literature* 93 (Summer 1982): 43, 44.

[10]Quoted in Demetrakopoulos, 44.

[11]John B. Vickery, "Literature and Myth," in *Interrelations of Literature*, ed. Jean-Pierre Barricelli and Joseph Gibaldi (New York: Modern Language Association, 1982), 69.

[12]Giles Gunn, *The Culture of Criticism and the Criticism of Culture* (New York: Oxford UP, 1987), 178.

[13]Ibid., 181.

[14]*The Revised English Bible* (Oxford: Oxford UP, and Cambridge: Cambridge UP, 1989). All references are to this edition. Changes in the spelling of the names Sarai/Sarah and Abram/Abraham correspond to the specific passage being cited.

[15]Northrop Frye, *The Great Code: The Bible and Literature* (New York: Harcourt Brace Jovanovich, 1981), 170. See also Frye's discussion in *The Anatomy of Criticism* (Princeton: Princeton UP, 1957), 56.

[16]Leonard L. Thompson, *Introducing Biblical Literature: a more fantastic country* (Englewood Cliffs, NJ: Prentice-Hall, 1978), 95.

[17]James S. Ackerman, "Joseph, Judah, and Jacob," in *Literary Interpretations of Biblical Narratives*, ed. Kenneth R. R. Gros Louis, with James S. Ackerman (Nashville: Abingdon, 1982), 97.

[18]For one feminist's reading of the novel, see Constance Rooke, "A Feminist Reading of 'The Stone Angel,'" *Canadian Literature* 93 (1982), 26-41.

[19]Jason Currie was disappointed in his two sons. He once said of Hagar, "Smart as a whip, she is, that one. If only she'd been—" (11). His son Dan died at 18; his son Matt inherited the Currie General Store, but he and his wife never had children.

After Hagar is married, she discovers that Brampton Shipley also wants to establish a dynasty. He hopes that his firstborn will be a son so that he has "somebody" (88) to leave his land to.

[20]Hagar reveals that her "blood and vitals rise to meet his [Bram's]" (70).

[21]Clara Thomas, *The Manawaka World of Margaret Laurence* (Toronto: McClelland and Stewart, 1976), does not identify Hagar's sons with Esau and Jacob. She writes that Hagar's son John grows up to be "an Ishmael, an outsider" (74).

[22]Hagar writes that her father called her by name only once—the day that she told him she intended to marry Bram.

[23]B. W. Powe, *A Climate Charged* (New York: Mosaic P, 1984), 140.

[24]Ibid., 141.

[25]Nathalia Wright, "Melville's Use of the Bible in *Moby-Dick*," in *Biblical Images in Literature*, ed. Roland Bartel (Nashville: Abingdon P, 1975), 37.

[26]Northrop Frye, *Fables of Identity: Studies in Poetic Mythology* (New York: Harcourt, Brace & World, 1963), 37.

[27]Ibid., 18.

[28]Ibid., 37.

[29]Ibid., 36.

[30]Margaret Laurence, "Gadgetry or Growing? Form and Voice in the Novel," Lecture at the University of Toronto, Fall, 1969, 4-5. Quoted in Patricia Morley, *Margaret Laurence* (Boston: Twayne, 1981), 77.

[31]"Sources" in *Margaret Laurence*, ed. William New (Toronto: McGraw Hill Ryerson, 1977), 15.

[32]Mary Jean Green, "Tradition as Mother: Women's Fiction and the Canadian Past," *The CEA Critic* 50 (Fall 1987): 42.

[33]Joyce Carol Oates, "Is There a Female Voice?" in *Feminist Literary Theory: A Reader*, ed. Mary Eagleton (New York: Basil Blackwell, 1986), 208.

[34]*Loc. cit.*

Epilogue:

The Recovery of Gender

Jan Wojcik

If the authors collected here go beyond excavation of intent to speculation on cultural significance, it is because the original texts, and every palimpsest inscribed upon them by artist or critic, have done the same. Their writing and rewriting are all efforts in the recovery of gender, a task as difficult and as vital in ancient Israel or Shakespeare's London as it is in modern Manawaka.

Biblical male characters such as Holophernes entertain what the anthropologist Ernestine Friedl calls "a natural concept of gender."[1] Its proponents usually begin with an observation that women have bodies appropriate for providing males pleasure and then for bearing and rearing children. As mothers they naturally spend considerable time sequestered away from public arenas. It seems only natural, then, that once men have had their pleasure and the women retire to the back rooms, the men assume leadership again. Refreshed after a good night's sleep at Judith's side, Holophernes can be the more fierce in the next day's siege of Judith's home city. He cannot see her beyond her seemingly natural role for him. Even more astonishingly, he cannot imagine that *she* can see herself beyond this role. If she *looks* good to him, she must *be* good for him.

In her indispensible study of *The Creation of Patriarchy*,[2] Gerda Lerner identifies this concept more or less as the assumption underlying the patriarchy pervading the Hebrew Bible. Her study is powerful and has been cited throughout this volume. Eve Stoddard, for example, basically accepts Lerner's claim about the Bible, arguing that several works of nineteenth-century English literature use biblical characters like Ruth and Boaz to criticize the tradition of patriarchy that continues undeterred from ancient times to the dawning of the industrial age. But our collection of essays as a whole takes Lerner's study to task for its partiality. Lerner correctly identifies the attitudes of biblical male characters, but by using the Bible as evidence for history she misses the complementary and contrasting attitudes of biblical female characters and biblical narrators. Consequently she would not be able to account for the rich tradition of western literature which responds to these different attitudes.

For example, the narrator of the Judith story, and Judith herself, entertain a wholly different concept of gender, what Friedl calls "an environmental concept of gender."[3] If the expectations that Holophernes has are of a piece with other male attitudes of his time and place, this does not mean that women are "naturally" subordinate. A million misconceptions do not withstand a single, true exception. Rather Judith understands profoundly that social environment determines sex roles. When she puts on her makeup she plays to the social expectations even of her own people. But when she prays to God for help in killing a man, she seeks divine sanction for acting as an unconventional woman just this once—at this time and place, in these historical circumstances. Of course, she points out, it is for God's good too. The existence of his own people hangs in the balance of the sword she will heft. She accepts the divine silence in response to her prayers as God's acquiescence.

Thus Friedl's distinction is useful, but indulgent. The two concepts do not have equal intellectual range. The natural concept begins with the readily available historical facts of sexual discrimination and the biological facts of sexual difference. But it soon circles back to its initial prejudice and can never be any more than a rationalization of a convenient but inequitable practice. That is why it is easy to find many male characters who still think as Holophernes once fatally did. In her essay on Du Bartas' *Judit*, Catharine Randell Coats has shown how Holophernes' attitude towards Judith represents what Calvin condemned as an irreligious imagination. In her essay on *Hamlet*, Nona Fienberg, in a nice phrase, has spoken of the "cultural resonances" (in Hamlet's mind) between Jephthah's sacrifice of his daughter and Polonius's political manipulation of Ophelia. Long after the biblical cautionary tale, many other male characters have come to life entertaining the illusions that women—even their own daughters—are the pawns of their pleasure and power.

This is a heady and dangerous thought. In her fascinating study, Mary De Jong has reviewed the extensive history of 19th century biblical critics who, using convoluted arguments, basically come around to sharing the concept of gender that gets Ahasuerus and Holophernes into trouble. The critics read books like Esther and Judith as divine sanction for sweet, submissive, religious females. With critics like these, no wonder the Bible has a hard time getting a clear-headed reading.

The environmental concept, on the other hand, spirals outward from the same facts into very difficult intellectual terrain. Just *what* is appropriate feminine behavior, every Judith, Joan of Arc, or Golda Meir must ask. What, indeed, are masculine and feminine? One finds that attributes such as gruffness and gentleness, leadership and submission, sensitivity and obtuseness are distributed in people regardless of their gender, often enough in the same person at different times of the day. One finds males who are kind to children and females who win olympic medals lifting enormous weights. Each exception disproves any rule.

Perhaps, by way of epilogue, we may propose the term "the recovery of gender" to describe the scope of this line of questioning. Recovery is used here in the sense of gaining back an understanding or becoming self-conscious of a phenomenon that it is all too easy to accept as a given. Today, for example, in many middle eastern countries heterosexual men stroll arm in arm on public streets and dance together in taverns. These same men consider it proper for their wives, sisters, and mothers to do hard work in the fields, often while they entertain themselves in cafes, or at most, drive the women to the fields in trucks. These behaviors reveal a different sense of the meaning of masculine and feminine than contemporaneously existed in many western counties. The men and women within each of these different cultures might think that their familiar behaviors are proper and beyond question: as much a part of the landscape as the hills. An enlightened traveler between the two cultures would be more likely to recover a sense of gender—to gain a sense of critical distance from the phenomenon.

This awareness could then proceed to circle around or spiral off but only the spiralists recover a sense of gender in the fullest sense of the term. For recovery also entails an effort to return to a prior place or understanding. Implicit in the environmental concept of gender is the belief that there was a prior time, an ur-time, before an arbitrary form of gender distinctions coalesced and was hardened by habit. At that fluid time, men and women both were aware of the change. Perhaps they welcomed the change as appropriate to their historical circumstances. When Judith made her plans, she lacked any pure, abstract principles to guide them. She understood that her success as a woman depended on how she manipulated the reigning myth of the ideal woman to escape a particular historical dilemma. When we read the biblical story of Jephthah's daughter, or see a performance of *Romeo and Juliet*, or read *Anna Karenina*, we find it easy to assume that the biblical writer, like Shakespeare and Tolstoy, scrutinized the societal restrictions on women that destroyed their female antagonists. When we encounter female characters who succeed—the biblical Judith, or the Greek theatrical characters of Medea and Clytaemnestra—we find that a beautiful widow, or a mother, or a wife often finds appropriate words and weapons to further her designs. Every narrative or dramatic presentation of a woman's place in history recovers such an ur-time . . . *if* that presentation is worthy of the term literature. Anything less is propaganda, usually for the naturalist party.

Logically then, the full recovery of gender never defines an ideal relationship between men and women. There are no principles to be worked back to upon which it can be predicated. Rather, to recover gender is to recognize the historically contingent nature of gender distinctions. This has been a constant theme among our authors. In my own essay, I show that the Samaritan Woman whom Jesus meets at the well evokes the image of Rebekah at the same well. She argues with Jesus that she had the right to the same freedom Rebekah once had to cultivate her own spirituality—different from both Rebekah's *and* Jesus's. Similarly Jayne Blankenship has written of Dante's refashioning of the character of Rachel. Dante goes beyond suggesting that she can be used as a type for either a model contemplative or an active woman; rather, her complex character is formed beyond "the binary need to choose." When choice is continual and creative, it is never definitive. Louise Simons has found Milton bound in an apparent contradiction. In one place he reads the story of the Levite's concubine with the "hermeneutics of intimacy," finding in her story a sound justification of a policy of divorce. In another place, he reads it as a justification for a holy war against the Irish. Simons makes a strong argument that finally Milton is inspired by this story to overcome his own contradiction. He makes it an indictment "for all kinds of social, religious and political injustice."

No wonder those who would recover gender have difficult arguments with those who argue for natural gender distinctions. When Judith stretches out the neck of Holophernes, and prays to God, ambiguity of mind confronts resolute certainty of prejud. The prejudice returns again and again, however many temporary victories are scored against it. No wonder the ancient biblical stories that began a recovery of gender in their own time inspire the long literary tradition—sampled here—that continues even to our own.

The recovery of gender necessarily entails only honest thinking about the roles of men and women in nurturing a sweet life for all living things. It can begin in bitter situations, such as Hagar adrift in the biblical wilderness, or Hagar lonely on the Canadian prairie that we have found in Rosalie Murphy Baum's study of Margaret Laurence's novel. In other words, to recover gender, the Bible, or the nineteenth-century literature of Eve Stoddard's essay, or the *Tristam Shandy* of Raymond Frontain's study, does not have to represent ideal relations between men and women. The literary work only need represent the realistic circumstances in which men and women and readers could begin questioning those relations and circumstances. In fact the Old Testament contains many such stories. Eve questions the authority of a masculine God and mate. Hagar wins a reprieve from a masculine God and angel. Rachel feigns a menstrual period to thwart the selfish designs of her father. Judith uses sweet words to beguile Holophernes, the enemy of her people. Esther uses her instinct for the dramatic to save the Jews in exile; Ruth her instinct for the romantic to save herself, her mother-in-law Naomi, and her husband Boaz from heirlessness. In these stories, and many others, the biblical narrative goes beyond type or myth to feature the subtleties in the efforts of its characters to recover a sense of gender. As the studies collected here have shown, many other works of literature in the Western tradition breathe in the same inspiration.

Notes

[1] Ernestine Friedl, *Women and Men: An Anthropologist's View* (New York: Holt, Rinehart and Winston, 1975), 2.

[2] Gerda Lerner, *The Creation of Patriarchy* (New York: Oxford UP, 1986).

[3] Lerner, *Creation of Patriarchy* , 19.

Contributors

ANN W. ASTELL, an Associate Professor of English at Purdue University, is the author of *The Song of Songs in the Middle Ages* (1990), as well as numerous articles on medieval literature.

ROSALIE MURPHY BAUM teaches American Literature at the University of South Florida. She is editor of the first edition of *Contemporary Poets of the English Language*, co-editor with Seymour Gross of the Norton Critical Edition of *The Blithedale Romance*, and author of essays on major American and Canadian writers which have appeared in various collections and such journals as *Mosaic*, *The American Review of Canadian Studies*, *North Dakota Quarterly* and *Cithara*.

JAYNE BLANKENSHIP is author of *In the Center of the Night: Journal Through a Bereavement* (1985) and was formerly director of the Rocky Mountain Women's Institute, a center for independent study at the University of Denver. She taught at the University of Rhode Island for several years and currently holds a Mellon Fellowship in the Department of English and Comparative Literature at Columbia University. Her essay for this volume received the Grandgent Prize from The Dante Society of America.

CATHARINE RANDALL COATS is an Associate Professor of French at Barnard College of Columbia University. She is the author of numerous articles on the French Renaissance, as well as of *Subverting the System: D'Aubigné and Calvinism* (1990). Her *(Em)bodying the Word: Textual Resurrections in the Martyrological Narratives of Foxe, de Bèye, Crespin and d'Aubigné* is expected from Peter Lang in 1992.

MARY G. DE JONG, Associate Professor of English and Women's Studies at the Shenango Campus of the Pennsylvania State University, has published articles on composer William Billings, novelists George Eliot and Nathaniel Hawthorne, and poet Frances Osgood. Much of the research for "God's Women" was done while she was a Fellow at the National Humanities Center in Research Triangle Park, North Carolina. In addition to guest-editing a special issue of *Women's Studies*, she is continuing research in nineteenth-century women's poetry and is writing "Heart-Songs and Hymns," a study of the cultural significance of hymns and hymn-writing in nineteenth-century America.

The author of *Elizabeth, Her Poets, and the Creation of the Courtly Manner* (1988), NONA FIENBERG received her Ph.D. from the University of California, Berkeley, in 1978. Since then she has taught Renaissance literature at The University of the South, Carleton College, Millsaps College, and Keene State College (New Hampshire), where she is an Associate Professor of English. Articles on medieval and Renaissance women have appeared in *SEL*, *Modern Philology*, and *Criticism*. She is currently at work on a book to be entitled "Writing the Self: Women's Lives in Early Modern England."

Co-editor with Jan Wojcik of *The David Myth in Western Literature* (1980) and *Poetic Prophecy in Western Literature* (1984), RAYMOND-JEAN FRONTAIN has published articles on the Bible as literature and on biblically inspired literary traditions in *Modern Philology*, *Cahiers Elisabethains*, *Bucknell Review*, *Papers on Language and Literature*, and elsewhere. A contributing editor to the Divine Poems volumes of the John Donne Variorum, he is currently at work on a study of Donne's biblical *Anniversaries*. He is an Associate Professor of English at the University of Central Arkansas.

PHEME PERKINS is currently Professor of New Testament in the Theology Department at Boston College, where she specializes in the study of Gnosticism, Johannine literature, and biblical theology. The author of numerous articles and fourteen books on the New Testament and early Christianity including *Jesus as Teacher* (1990), she has served on the editorial boards of several journals and is currently the editor of the New Testament section of the *Society of Biblical Literature Dissertation Series*. She was the first woman president of the *Catholic Biblical Association* and was the Kaneb Visiting Professor at Cornell University.

LOUISE SIMONS is an Assistant Professor of Humanities in the College of Basic Studies at Boston University. She has written on John Milton, Thomas Nashe, Emily Dickinson, and Charlotte Bronte in

Milton Quarterly, Milton Studies, SEL, American Imago, and *CEA Critic.*

EVE WALSH STODDARD received her A.B. from Mount Holyoke College and her Ph.D. from UCLA. She is an Associate Professor of English at St. Lawrence University in Canton, N.Y., where her scholarly interests are British Romanticism, and critical and feminist theory. She has published a number of articles on Wordsworth and other poets and is currently completing a book on Wordsworth and Kant.

JAN WOJCIK holds a doctorate in comparative literature from Yale University and is a Professor of Humanities at Clarkson University. He is the author of books and articles on ethics and modern technology, in addition to *The Road to Emmaus: Reading Luke's Gospel* (1989) and, with Raymond Frontain, editor of *The David Myth* and *Poetic Prophecy in Western Literature.*

Index of Proper Names